RECON 701

RECON 701

A story of Resiliency, Brotherhood, and Triumph,
as told by the troopers of G/10 CAV

COL (RET) DESMOND V. BAILEY

Deeds Publishing | Athens

Copyright © 2022 — Desmond V. Bailey

ALL RIGHTS RESERVED — No part of this book may be reproduced in any form or by any electronic or mechanical means, including information storage and retrieval systems, without permission in writing from the authors, except by a reviewer who may quote brief passages in a review.

Published by Deeds Publishing in Athens, GA
www.deedspublishing.com

Printed in The United States of America

Cover design by Mark Babcock.
Cover picture used with permission of Rick Reeves.
Picture title: Contact…Wait, Out!

ISBN 978-1-950794-84-3

Books are available in quantity for promotional or premium use. For information, email info@deedspublishing.com.

First Edition, 2022

10 9 8 7 6 5 4 3 2 1

This book is dedicated to our Warriors who gave the last full measure in defense of their country during Operation Iraqi Freedom I.

SSG Anthony Thompson
SGT James Wright
SPC Richard Arriaga

Also, in memory of General Raymond T. Odierno who motivated and inspired G Troop, 10th Cavalry during Operation Iraqi Freedom I.

Special thanks to imbed reporter Ed Timms for his colorful and detailed coverage of G Troop, 10th Cavalry Operations during the initial stages of OIF I

10th Cavalry History

KUWAIT—At a dusty and forsaken outpost, a swallow-tailed American flag with 35 gold stars flutters in the wind, an anachronism amidst high-tech weaponry shipped halfway around the globe to take on Saddam Hussein.

More than 100 years ago, a similar flag was carried by soldiers of the 10th Cavalry into battle, in campaigns obscured by time and intolerance. After the Civil War, the Army formed a handful of segregated units—among them, the 10th Cavalry. Their ranks included blacks who had fought for the Union, as well as freed slaves.

Buffalo soldiers serving in the 10th Cavalry fought the Cheyenne, the Comanche, and the Kiowa. They pursued Geronimo and Victorio, legendary Apache leaders, across the American Southwest. They chased after Pancho Villa in Mexico and charged up San Juan Hill with Teddy Roosevelt's Rough Riders.

Their exploits provided the inspiration for dozens of Hollywood westerns. But the larger-than-life troopers that charged across America's movie screens typically were all-white. And even some history books short-changed the contributions of black soldiers who fought Indians and pushed up San Juan Hill shoulder-to-shoulder with white troops during the Spanish American War.

"I don't think we've done justice to the history," said 1st Sgt. Bill Taylor, G Troop, 10th Cavalry's senior enlisted soldier. "A 10th Cavalry soldier should be able to walk a little bit prouder than even the other cavalrymen. We have a very storied, positive, successful past, but it hasn't gotten the attention that it should."

1st Sgt. Taylor's said he believes that it is important that the soldiers of G Troop be aware of the 10th Cavalry's history. He saw to it that swallow-tailed American flag, a replica of one used by 10th Cavalry during the late 1800s, came with G Troop when it recently deployed from Fort Hood to Kuwait. When he serves on a promotion board, 1st Sgt. Taylor said he typically grills soldiers about 10th Cavalry's history.

It's a history that 1st Sgt. Taylor, who grew up in the Pacific Northwest, admits he knew little about before coming into the Army. "When I was in school," he said, "it wasn't taught."

The unit has a long association with Texas. For many years, its troopers were based at Fort Concho. The 10th Cavalry also played a significant role in the construction of Fort Sill, Okla.

The first black West Point graduate, 2nd Lt. Henry O. Flipper, served with the 10th. However, he was not well-received by white officers. He ultimately was court-martialed and forced out of the military on charges that some historians say were trumped up.

"He had a rough go. He was a victim of the times," said 1st Sgt. Taylor, 40. "He was an outstanding young officer. He probably could have been the Colin Powell of his times, but it was not to be."

"Buffalo soldiers" were named by their Indian foes. According to historians, Indians thought the black soldiers fought with ferocity of a wounded buffalo and also saw a similarity in their hair and that of the buffalo's. The name was accepted by the soldiers themselves as a sign of respect and incorporated in the 10th Cavalry's regimental crest. That crest is emblazoned on earplug cases carried by many G Troop soldiers in Kuwait.

While the historical ties are maintained, the modern G Troop of 10th Cavalry, is, in many ways, different from their original counterparts. Instead of horses, the light reconnaissance unit now rides into battle in high-tech Humvees. And its ranks, more ethnically diverse, include whites, blacks, Hispanics, a Chinese-American—as well as an immigrant from Russia, another from Guyana and a third from the Philippines.

"I don't see a difference in soldiers," said 1st Sgt. Taylor. "I have outstanding African American soldiers; I have outstanding whites and Hispanics. I have the whole mix, and there's not any one group that comes out as being better than the others."

Private First Class Cyril Leboeuf, 24, of Baton Rouge, La., said he has a lot of respect for what the original Buffalo soldiers did "because they paved the way for people like me."

An uncle who served in Vietnam told Pfc. Leboeuf, "How rough it was for a black soldier to actually gain rank or have respect if you had rank." He said his grandfather, a decorated Marine who served during World War II and afterwards, felt racial tension as he rose through the ranks.

It had to change," said Pfc. Leboeuf, whose family tree includes African, French and Choctaw ancestors. "There was no way it could have stayed the same." Sometimes, he said, soldiers from different backgrounds "don't connect" but "that's different from thinking I'm better than you."

—Ed Timms
Staff Writer

There are two sets of numbers on a military vehicle—unit designation and battle number. The unit designation reflects the organization. For example, 1/G/10/4ID on the front and rear bumper identifies the vehicle as 1st Platoon, G Troop, 10th Cavalry Regiment, 4th Infantry Division.

The battle number is simply three digits. The picture above is of a G Troop, 10th Cavalry Regiment vehicle in Iraq during Operation Iraqi Freedom I (OIF I). The battle number for G Troop during 2003-2004 was 701. Thus the title of the book, RECON 701. It was the easiest way to identify G Troop, 10th Cavalry Regiment, 4th Infantry Division during OIF I.

Contents

10th Cavalry History	vii
Foreword	xiii
Preface	xv
1. The Battle of Abu Ajeel	1
2. The Brigade Reconnaissance Troop	5
3. Deployment and the Trek North	23
4. Final Destination: Tikrit	43
5. Change of Command	59
6. The Growing Darkness	83
7. The Long Night	105
8. Brothers Lost	119
9. The Mad Mortar Man and Secret Squirrels	131
10. The Unforgiving Desert	147
11. Operation Red Dawn	163
12. When teenagers and 20-somethings make history	185
13. The Mission Continues	197
14. Life After Deployment	219
15. The Secret Sauce	233
Lessons Learned (By Col(R) Desmond V. Bailey)	247
G Troop Roster for OIF I	263
About the Author	267

Foreword

My cousin, Colonel (COL) Desmond Bailey, US Army Retired, called me in the winter of 2020. There's a good decade in age between us and we have busy lives, so we rarely spoke outside of the holidays. The unexpected call came with an unexpected offer: "I want us to write a book about G Troop. After decades of trying, I never recreated such an effective, skilled, and united troop. We have to find that 'secret sauce', and we have to tell their story. They deserve to be heard and honored for what they did."

Desmond's focus on his men—his care for them and desire to recognize their achievements—drew me in. As he shared their story, what stood out to me was the age of the soldiers (usually 18-20), the troop's unbreakable bond, and the risk and terror they unflinchingly faced in the form of guerilla warfare and attacks, sometimes led by children. I thought back on my life and wondered: did I have that courage, drive, or resiliency at 18? Do I have it *now*? I had to know more.

After more than 35 hours of interviews, I learned quite a lot. The long list contains reconnaissance troop tactics; Iraq's sand flea problem; a few of G Troop's inside jokes; the secret squirrel missions with Army Special Operation Forces (ARSOF); and AK, G

Troop's camp dog that would run the property outside their base hunting the ill-intentioned (and an innocent horse). I've learned how horrific loss in war is—the chaos during and the anger and pain that lasts long after.

Yes, these soldiers helped take down Saddam Hussein and many other evil men. But those achievements were simply a result of *something*, and what matters is finding what that *something* was. There are many tangible and intangible aspects that led to the troop's success, and I'm excited that you'll be diving into them.

Huge thanks to all the guys for sharing your stories. It's impossible to convey how much it means to me, personally, and what I've learned from each of you. This is an imperfect story as only a small number (24) of the troopers contributed their stories, but I hope it does them justice.

—**Jessica Vann**

Preface

This book is for the soldiers of G Troop who served their country with valor and panache during Operation Iraqi Freedom I, 2003-2004, and were on the objective for the capture of Saddam Hussein.

I.

Saddam Hussein was not caught because an individual in a three-letter government agency figured out his location and told the military where to go.

No, it was the teamwork, grit, fighting spirit and American can-do attitude of many men and women from all services which led to the dictator's capture. Some of those soldiers were irreplaceable and critical to mission success, especially the warriors of Army Special Operations Forces (ARSOF). These elite soldiers and many others, even those at the lowest levels of the Army, succeeded in felling a dictator who had committed countless atrocities against thousands, including his own people.

The book in your hands isn't a fancy story. It is an honest perspective from those who were in the thick of it all: G Troop, 10th Cavalry, 1st Brigade Combat Team, 4th Infantry Division (G

Troop). Several of these soldiers have provided their recollections on what occurred within their small reconnaissance organization before, during, and after Operation Iraqi Freedom I (OIF I).

While this story covers Saddam Hussein's capture at the lowest tactical level, what matters most is how G Troop succeeded in this difficult and uncertain environment. The average age of these soldiers was between 18-21. They were kids in a deadly, strange, and unforgiving land. They had not trained for the type of war they faced following the initial push into Iraq; the U.S. military had not fully expected the insurgency and guerilla-type warfare that followed the fall of Baghdad in April 2003. And they certainly did not anticipate operating at such a grueling day-to-day pace that I've yet to experience since, despite multiple deployments to Iraq and other places over the past twenty years.

How did this brigade reconnaissance troop of 75 soldiers adapt so efficiently that they were conducting raids for high value targets, including Saddam himself, with ARSOF, while supporting daily and nightly operations for the brigade? How did these young men and women cope with uncertainty in a deadly, unforgiving land with resiliency and quick learning? How did their leadership leverage continual improvement and irregular operational and tactical actions to take on the unknown?

For years, I've asked myself these questions and more in the hopes of gleaning the 'secret sauce' that led to G Troop's success. If I could figure out what made them great, recreate their camaraderie and adaptability in other troops and units that I commanded, surely what came of it would benefit not only my soldiers but the Army as a whole. We must always consider how to best prepare future generations for war of any type.

Despite decades of trying, I never was able to recreate G Troop. Speaking with other officers and soldiers who were part of or witnessed the Brigade Reconnaissance Troop (BRT) in action, in my experience I was unable to recreate or influence other units I commanded to execute like them, or have their sense of brotherhood. This story is an opportunity to go back and, through the recollections of the troop's soldiers, find out just what that secret sauce is, and those lessons learned that will benefit future soldiers and officers.

II.

This is the troop's story, but some of the narrative comes from my own knowledge and experiences during that time. My contribution to the narrative serves to provide context, structure, and lessons learned from a company level commander at the time.

Before I was the G Troop Commander and the conventional force commander for the capture of Saddam Hussein, I was a member of 4ID's division staff and the 1BCT brigade chief of plans prior to deployment and during the initial stages of the push into Iraq. This position informed me in ways I didn't fully appreciate at the time, but now serves as a strong foundation for the guiding narrative of this book.

As G Troop's Commander, I was most often with the troopers, on patrols, raids and other missions. I worked directly for Colonel James B. Hickey, the 1BCT Commander. There was no battalion commander or battalion staff between us, and I frequently briefed the Division Commander, Major General Raymond T. Odierno, on our efforts across the Tigris, in the area east of Tikrit, Iraq.

Through both of my staff planning positions prior to assuming command of G Troop, I experienced the evolution of the military's grand plan from the invasion of Iraq to the Iraqi Army's capitulation to the hunt for Saddam Hussein and, ultimately, his capture.

III.

Now for the context. In early spring of 2003, we found ourselves in the middle of Mesopotamia. Our brigade crossed the berm between Kuwait and Iraq on 14 April 2003 and made the several days journey to Tikrit via Baghdad, Taji, Bayji, and Samarra. Few of us could speak the language. Only a few had served in an Arab country before. Many of us were not familiar with the culture.

In 1995, as a young lieutenant in the 82nd Airborne Division, I deployed to Egypt as part of the Multi-National Force and Observer mission to observe and report on Israeli and Egyptian military activities in and around the international border. That was a relatively calm mission full of training exercises and month-long deployments to patrol bases on the eastern side of the Sinai Peninsula. My interaction with the local populace was limited due to the isolated location of my patrol base, and it certainly was not an "active combat" zone at the time.

In my short amount of time in Tikrit, Iraq, the first several days, I felt like I was on another planet. I had no idea that we were in the middle of the Sunni Triangle, Saddam's stronghold, and that our brigade would eventually serve a key role in capturing the Iraqi dictator; and I certainly had no idea the reconnaissance troop I would command would be on the objective with ARSOF when we captured him.

When 4ID was selected to deploy, 1BCT was in the field in Fort Hood, Texas, training for a National Training Center rotation in beautiful Death Valley, California. Upon notification of deployment to Iraq, 1BCT departed the field in rapid fashion and returned to garrison. The pace of planning and preparation from notification onward was significant—six to seven days a week.

The original 4ID mission was to enter Iraq through Turkey, conduct a river crossing for multiple brigades across the Euphrates River northwest of Mosul, and then push south and east to subsequent objectives designed to isolate Baghdad and deny Saddam Hussein opportunity and routes to flee from Iraq. 1BCT was selected to be the lead brigade for 4ID.

For months we planned, and for months we waited to deploy. Our equipment was placed on ships for transport in January and February 2003. By February, the situation with Turkey was tenuous. By mid-March we were flying to Kuwait. Our northern attack and river crossing plans became obsolete when Turkey refused to allow US forces to attack into Northern Iraq from their country. The 1BCT mission was uncertain until a few days before we departed Fort Hood. 1BCT would follow 3rd Infantry Division to attack north of Baghdad and seize Tikrit.

A few days after 1BCT and elements of 4ID Headquarters arrived in Tikrit, on 1 May 2003, President Bush declared "major combat operations were over." We found ourselves from May to June wondering what the next mission would be. Terms such as "nation building" and "stability operations" were commonplace. Army Civil Affairs teams were all around and conducting "assessments" of Iraqi infrastructure and governance capability. Army PSYOP teams were "informing" the population of the situation and gathering "atmospherics"—a term used at the time to covey "local and regional feelings."

As a planner, my reference point for this period of "post- major combat operations" was Kosovo. During my education at the

Captain Career Course at Fort Benning, Georgia, several of my peers from the 82nd Airborne Division had deployed in support of the conflict in Kosovo, and we had studied their approaches and lessons learned. Cordon and Search operations, clearing villages, and countering guerilla warfare were the topics discussed, but not to the extent that any of us could be proficient in executing those operations without further extensive training. My personal focus during the career course was high intensity conflict, the X's and O's of close combat, calling for artillery, deploying infantry and tanks, air-ground integration of Army attack aviation and Air Force platforms, infantry company and platoon tactics and battle drills, fixing bayonets, and charging the objective.

So, as the 1BCT planner, it was a period of uncertainty for me. What was the mission now? What was the brigade supposed to do? How would we do it? Adding to the uncertainty were conflicting messages from senior general officers. 1BCT leadership was informed by one general officer that redeployment would occur within six months; while then LTG Scott Wallace, 5th Corps Commander, advised that we best prepare for a long deployment…the latter was correct.

By May 2003, the 3rd Infantry Division and Marines were celebrated, as they should be, for their performance in the battles leading up to the fall of Baghdad. The 101st Airborne Division was celebrated for their air-mobile operations as they settled in Mosul. The 75th Ranger Regiment was celebrated for their operations in the Western desert and the Haditha Dam. The airborne insertion of the 173rd Airborne brigade, the largest combat jump since WWII and first from the C-17 airplane, made many of us airborne infantry Soldiers envious. The war up to this point featured multiple large-scale operations that were very successful. In

May 2003 however, the situation in Iraq was calm. Sure, there were small engagements here and there, but nothing as significant as what the lead units of the invasion had faced.

So, looking back on my reference points, in my mind, it was logical to think that when President Bush said "major combat operations are over"…the "war" was over. However, as time went by, and the Iraqi insurgency began to blossom, we found ourselves in a type of war we were not prepared for. We would come to understand that our training for high-intensity conflict still served a purpose, but the situation had changed, and called for additional…and different methods to accomplish the mission. We would come to understand that we needed to hunt individuals, to collect data, analyze the data, and develop link matrices, work with local indigenous leaders such as sheiks and Imams, and other services more closely to address the evolving situation on the ground—in the land domain where humans reside, and the battle of hearts and minds (human will) exist, and wars are won.

—COL (R) Desmond V. Bailey

1. The Battle of Abu Ajeel

SEPTEMBER 2003

Abu Ajeel was a battleground, and September would prove to be one of its deadliest months. The 4th Infantry Division (4ID) headquarters faced mortar and rocket attacks from dusk to dawn, and troops patrolling the nearby town of Tikrit and surrounding villages were frequently ambushed with RPG and rifle fire.

Caught up in these attacks was G/10th Cavalry Regiment (G Troop), 1st Brigade Combat Team (1BCT). They were 1BCT's light wheeled reconnaissance troop and kept the area east of 4ID headquarters (HQ) secure. Each morning and night, they set off across a single bridge over the Tigris River to patrol the area of Abu Ajeel, a vast expanse of farmland and desert, broken only by an elaborate concrete aqueduct system and occasional groupings of mudbrick homes. They searched for weapons and ammunition caches, supported ARSOF units during raids for high value individuals (HVI), fought enemy forces, and, from observation posts set up along the wall of the palatial Tikrit palace compound, defended 4ID HQ, called Forward Operating Base (FOB) Ironhorse, from ongoing rocket and mortar attacks.

During the scorching summer months of 2003, as G Troop

fought through near ambushes and interdicted mortar attacks, the once friendly locals became withdrawn and abrupt in their dealings with the troopers. A palpable darkness settled over the area as intelligence on Saddam Hussein's whereabouts dried up, dissipating with the summer heat. By September, insurgents' efforts had grown in number and malice.

On September 18, 1BCT intelligence personnel were informed of a planned attack on U.S. forces in Tikrit. That afternoon, 1BCT commander, Colonel (COL) James B. Hickey, issued orders to defend 4ID HQ and his own brigade's FOB Raider, which was located south of the Tikrit palace complex, below FOB Ironhorse, and overlooking the Tigris River. Led by their commander, Captain (CPT) Desmond Bailey, G Troop would establish a screen line to the west of the Tigris and south of FOB Raider. A third platoon from G Troop—callsign Scorpion, made up of forward observers and artillerymen—would focus on terrain denial fires and combat patrols in Abu Ajeel, while the remainder of G Troop would support efforts from the 4ID HQ observation posts, directed by 1st Lieutenant (1LT) Eric Tapp, platoon leader for First Platoon, callsign Saber 1.

It was evening, and CPT Bailey had just established the screen line with two platoons, Saber and Black Sheep, when Executive Officer (XO), recently promoted CPT Brian Sweigart, callsign "Recon 5" broke troop radio silence.

"Recon 6, this is Recon 5. We're observing small arms fire that appears to be oriented on the troop command post—"

The transmission was interrupted by Scorpion Platoon's CPT John Williams. Adrenaline rushed his words. "Recon 6, this is

Scorpion 1. We've been ambushed. I got two injured men, three with no pulse, and one missing in action (MIA)."

"Scorpion 1, this is Recon 6," Bailey responded, desperate and angry questions racing through his mind. *How fast can I get to them? Why aren't I with them? Is our patrol base under attack? I knew this didn't sound right, why'd I let them go there?* He kept his voice steady. "Secure your wounded and move to the casualty collection point. Recon 5, situation report. Over."

"We might've observed small arms fire from the ambush, I don't think we're being attacked," Sweigart said.

"Recon 6, this is Saber 1." It was 1LT Tapp, reporting in. "There're multiple personnel converging on Scorpion at the ambush site. About sixty personnel, armed with AK47s and a few RPGs. We've got eyes-on. Do you want us to place indirect fires on the enemy?"

CPT Lance Vanzant, who commanded a company of AH-64 Longbow attack helicopters, came over the radio: "Recon 6, this is Viper 6. We're on station. What's our task and purpose?"

"Locate the two sections of Scorpion platoon and secure their movement to the casualty collection point," said Bailey. "Engage and destroy enemy personnel identified by Saber 1. Be advised, we have a friendly in the area that's MIA."

Another report came in from CPT Williams. His youngest trooper was still missing, and a second section of vehicles and troopers was stranded, surrounded by the enemy.

As they sped across the river, Bailey could see 30mm cannon fire from the attack helicopters far ahead. Bailey's driver, Specialist (SPC) Aaron Helmrich, was pushing the beaten truck as fast as it could go to reach the ambush site.

Not yet knowing this would be the longest night of the deployment for the troop, CPT Bailey wondered, *how did we get here?*

2. The Brigade Reconnaissance Troop

"While the [BRT] formation existed, nobody could ever defeat it. We were always successful."
—John Justis, Command Sergeant Major (Ret.)

Focused, agile, and comprised of skilled troopers and leadership using the latest in technology and weaponry—the Brigade Reconnaissance Troop (BRT) became an official Army unit in the late 1990s. It was a product of innovative minds and the Army's continual evolution in response to emerging threats, internal policies, and global conditions.

The mission of the BRT was to conduct reconnaissance and security operations for their brigade. Supporting tasks included zone, route, and area reconnaissance as well as screening the front or flanks of a brigade during movement or while in offensive and defensive operations.

With just 75 personnel assigned to the troop, which was equipped with hardback Guntruck Humvees, the BRT was light and fast as it scouted ahead of armor and mechanized infantry units. Its' troopers were precise and adaptive, gathering accurate information on the enemy and disseminating it to their own artillerymen and those units behind them.

From its conception in the late 1980s, the unit's full development took almost two decades yet it was dissolved in 2004 when the Army transitioned from the Army of Excellence model to the Modular Army construct. As short lived as the BRT was, its organization was extremely effective and troopers well-honed.

COL Don Campbell was already familiar with the BRT concept when he took command of 1BCT, 4ID in the summer of 2001. He'd been part of discussions between Fort Knox and Fort Benning on what the formation would look like and, from a doctrinal perspective, how the Army should employ it. Personnel and equipment for the BRT would begin arriving at Fort Hood in 1998, and by 2001 the new BRT—G Troop—would call 1BCT home. They would deploy to Iraq with 4ID in 2003 under COL Campbell's command.

"The makeup of the BRT was a major advantage," Campbell recalled. "As a small recon unit, it could get into areas where a typical armor unit with tanks or mechanized infantry personnel carriers couldn't."

The troopers of G Troop served as scouts and were organized in two platoons: First Platoon's callsign was Saber and Second Platoon's was Black Sheep. Each platoon was led by a Lieutenant (LT), serving as Platoon Leader (PL), and they were supported by a Platoon Sergeant (PSG). Both platoons had six Humvees that were divided into two-vehicle sections led by a Section Leader (SL), and in each vehicle was a crew of three scouts, including a Vehicle Commander (VC).

The troop was equipped with supporting vehicles, including the Command Humvee, light medium tactical vehicles (Humvees) and a wheeled wrecker/recovery vehicle. Every Humvee was outfitted with a Long-Range Scout Surveillance System (LRAS3), and either an MK-19 Grenade Launcher (MK-19) or .50 Caliber Browning Machine Gun (.50 Cal).

"The BRT's effectiveness was compounded by the technology they had. We were really excited about the LRAS3 and its capabilities. With the LRAS3, troopers could see far across the battlefield day or night, assist with developing situational understanding, and accurately locate enemy units, equipment, or personnel," explained Campbell.

The LRAS3, first put into operation in 2001, was truly a game changer. The system allowed troops to detect, zoom in on, and identify with extreme precision enemy locations many kilometers away. Its thermal capabilities ensured troopers had accurate views at night, and they could mount it to their vehicles or use it on a tripod during dismounted missions. By the time Operation Iraqi Freedom 1 (OIF1) began, the LRAS3 was already upgraded to include an infrared laser, which increased the range finder's accuracy and speed.

The BRT would be assigned a platoon of forward observers (FO), a team of 20 troopers from the brigade's Artillery Battalion who were trained to conduct mortar, cannon, and rocket artillery fires onto enemy formations. This additional platoon's callsign was Scorpion, and it brought six Humvees to the troop, which were mounted with either .50 Cals or M240B Machine Guns (M24). The FOs would be distributed throughout the two scout platoons, creating a "hunter-killer" combination, with the scouts locating the enemy and the FOs directing indirect, rotary, or fixed-wing fires onto them.

The command structure was standard for the Army, with a Troop Commander at the rank of Captain, a First Lieutenant that served as Executive Officer (XO), and a First Sergeant (1SG). What set the unit apart from tradition was its reporting structure.

Instead of reporting to a battalion commander, the BRT reported directly to the brigade's Colonel who served as Brigade Commander. Their reconnaissance and security missions were conducted to answer the commander's priority information requirements and provide intelligence to battalion reconnaissance platoons. This structure and purpose allowed for quicker communication with the brigade—a priceless advantage in war when seconds could mean the difference between life or death.

Given the critical and high-risk mission of the BRT, leadership selection was, to say the least, selective. The Troop Commander and PL positions required high marks and experience; those who took on these positions had to be reliable, adept, and decisive. Each Scout chosen for G Troop had proven excellence through test scores, skills, and aptitude. Hand-selected by the Field Artillery Battalion Commander, the FOs had high marks in leadership and were proficient in indirect fire support. The brigade commander was the final approving authority for all officers assigned to the troop.

Arturo Corcoles, a former SPC and Forward Observer in G Troop, explained, "We were told if you wanted to be in G Troop, you didn't have to try out, but you did have to show that you were better than everybody else. You had to earn that spot. PT score, AIT tests, proficiency in the job…that's what was considered when troopers were selected to be part of G Troop."

TRAINING UP THE BRT

During the summer of 2002, the war in Afghanistan was at a high pitch, and there was significant potential for war with Iraq. Within 4ID, the soldiers trained for war, knowing it was inevitable; the only question was who would deploy and when.

The challenge for COL Campbell and G Troop's Commander, CPT Tim Jacobson, was identifying ways to train G Troop for combat against an armored threat in open desert and urban areas. The BRT would need to be nimble, easily adapting to enemy resistance and strength. This meant quick shifts from covering the brigades' flanks to scouting ahead of the brigade and reporting back enemy location and movements. As the armored battalions would move forward to attack, the scouts would move back to protect the units' flanks once again. These movements were possible for a light wheeled troop, yet the BRT had minimal firepower and the risk of enemy contact as they scouted ahead was high. Training had to focus on defensive measures like evasion, camouflage, and hiding in plain sight, and managing this risk.

Training events attached the scouts to different battalions and gave them reconnaissance tasks that avoided outright fighting. They were to search for and identify enemy personnel and formations, reconnoiter routes for the brigade to use, and disrupt enemy attacks against the brigade using indirect fires and close air support when needed.

Engrained in the scouts' minds was to not become decisively engaged. They would shoot to break physical contact and reposition to maintain visual contact with the enemy while observing, reporting, and calling for fire.

As COL Campbell worked through situations G Troop could face, it became clear the troop had to be extremely flexible and resilient. The Colonel told CPT Jacobson, "You may have to send them out to conduct long duration surveillance missions, where your men can give us some eyes deep behind enemy lines for a few days. You may have to send them to the front of the brigade as it moves. They may become isolated and need to defend themselves. For any type of situation, I need you to develop ways to keep your guys alive."

CPT Jacobsen, who took command of G Troop in March 2002 after serving as company commander for 4ID's 1BCT, 66th Armored Regiment (1-66 AR), was a top armor Captain in the brigade. He was known for being a solid, forthright leader and straight shooter. He further focused the troop's training to fully leverage their LRAS3 capabilities. After performing long-range reconnaissance with the advanced system, G Troop would infiltrate enemy lines, establish surveillance positions, and call for indirect fires or dismount the LRAS3 system and establish observation points in restricted terrain. CPT Jacobsen also prioritized urban operations, survival training and escape and evasion exercises, which consisted of troopers reaching a specified location without being captured by enemy role players.

Training for urban operations was new for 1LT Brian Sweigart, who had joined G Troop as a Platoon Leader in 2002 for Black Sheep. His father had served in the Air Force and fought in Vietnam, and for much of his childhood, they'd moved between Hawaii and Texas, while spending some time in California and Germany. In 2000, 1LT Sweigart graduated from West Point and was soon assigned a tank PL position with 1-66 AR for 18 months, before heading to G Troop.

1LT Sweigart was well familiar with G troop's historic mission prior to 9/11: the scouts were to operate on the forward edge, identify key enemy assets, and help the Troop Commander maneuver either an infantry or tank battalion based on their recommendations. Offensive operations in urban terrain were definitely not part of the BRT's original purpose, yet he found himself training to enter and clear buildings with a three-man team.

"It was a crash course, really," said Sweigart. "We spent a little over a month training for urban raids and tactics, from tabletop drills to close quarter battles and clearing the barracks rooms."

Sergeant First Class (SFC) Rick Michaud had planned on retiring, but as he watched the Twin Towers fall in New York City on 9/11, his plans changed.

"I called up the Department of the Army and filled out all the paperwork to cancel my retirement. I had a feeling something was going to be in our future, and I couldn't see somebody coming in who didn't know the guys as well as I did, and leading them into a combat situation," Michaud said.

He was Black Sheep's PSG, and at first felt prepared for their inevitable deployment—he knew his men and he'd been to war in the middle east before. In 1991, SFC Michaud had deployed to Saudi Arabia with 3rd Battalion, 5th Cavalry out of Kirchgöns, Germany to fight in Desert Storm. Though under Cavalry colors and lineage, they were an infantry battalion equipped with M2A1 Bradley Fighting Vehicles (BFV). A sergeant on a BFV at the time, he was deployed from January until mid-June of that same year.

However, it didn't take SFC Michaud long to realize that they weren't heading into another Desert Storm scenario. Though the focus of their training remained conventional warfare, its' intensity and the added elements of long-range and urban reconnaissance pointed toward a very different battlefield.

Straight out of Basic and Advanced Individual Training (AIT), and 18 years old, SPC Igor Boyko was assigned to G Troop in January 2000. He'd joined the military after graduating high school, seeing it as an opportunity to travel and serve the country he'd moved to as a teenager. Originally from Belarus, SPC Boyko's aunt and grandparents had moved to San Francisco in the 80s, and he and his mother joined them several years later.

As a driver and then gunner with Black Sheep, SPC Boyko had access to new technology like the Force XXI Battle Command

Brigade and Below (FBCB2) communications platform installed in his Humvee.

"I always liked technology, even in high school I took some computer classes," said Boyko. "When I got to G Troop, they told me I had this new computer in the truck, which was the FBCB2. Every vehicle in a unit had a unique identifier, and the system would track friendly movements on a map. In 2000, this was pretty high-tech stuff, and a lot of the guys weren't familiar with computers and had issues with it, plus it could be buggy at times. I was able to understand how it worked and assisted others if needed, otherwise we'd have to have a civilian contractor come out to fix the problem."

Training missions could last from a few hours to several days and included driving the vehicle to a hiding spot, dismounting, and carrying equipment—such as the .50 Cal and LRAS3—to a designated observation post.

"I enjoyed being a gunner, and I was pretty good at it. You are sitting higher in the vehicle with a .50 Cal and the LRAS. You had to be on alert all the time, sometimes stopping and scanning the area with the thermals or helping the driver by watching out for things in the road, like homemade bombs. I felt comfortable in that position, and I had a good crew," recalled Boyko.

SPC Boyko also gave the troopers a refresher course on vehicle identification. At the time, Iraq relied heavily on Russian equipment from the 60s and 70s, and it was imperative the troopers be able to recognize the silhouette of a vehicle whether during the day or through thermals at night.

"Our job was to find the bad guys and gather as much information as we could to estimate their fighting force," explained Boyko. "I pointed out features of vehicles, like the differences between a T-60 and T-72 tank. We needed to know the different models and their weapon systems and other specs."

Though training on gathering intel was limited, SPC Corcoles took a suggested online course on interviewing individuals. Not everyone took the course, but it ended up serving him well once they deployed to Iraq and began speaking with the locals to gather information.

"We didn't receive formal training because the way wars were fought up to that point was force on force, symmetrical warfare. While we were deployed on that first tour, the war shifted. There was no defining line of enemy forces, they were all around us. We were in the middle of a hornet's nest, unsure of who the enemy was. We had to figure it out on our own," said Corcoles.

SPC Corcoles joined G Troop at the start of 2000, and he was quickly introduced to SPC Boyko because they both came from California.

"I remember thinking, 'oh, sweet' when I was told another guy was from California. So, I go up to him, and all I hear is this really thick Russian accent. I figured he'd just gotten to the U.S.," Corcoles said. "Boyko was a good leader. Even when he was promoted to sergeant, he was still the same guy, genuine and compassionate, only difference was he started giving us tasks."

SPC Corcoles was assigned to Scorpion platoon as a gunner, but occasionally would serve as VC or driver. In a small unit like G Troop, it was critical that every trooper knew the duties of his crew and could assist them if necessary. Most of the troopers had gone through Emergency Medical Training school and were certified combat lifesavers. In war, they would serve as their own medics.

As his platoon completed training for entering buildings, clearing rooms, and dealing with homemade bombs, which would eventually be called IEDs, Corcoles recognized that G Troop was preparing for something quite different from other units.

SPC John Almen had joined the Infantry eight days after graduating high school in 1986. After two years, he left the service but then joined the National Guard 10 years later. Knowing war was inevitable after 9/11, he rejoined the Army as a scout and, in May 2002, was assigned to G Troop as a Black Sheep gunner.

That summer, SPC Almen experienced just how fast and lethal G Troop could be, thanks to their constant training, small size, and light vehicles. During a training exercise at Fort Carson, Colorado, they took part in mock war exercises against another 4ID brigade. The exercise included Observer/Controller (OC) personnel who acted as both coach and referee in the field, evaluating and instructing the troopers while simultaneously serving as OC/Fire Markers. After the scouts observed key positions of the much larger opposing brigade, they would call for fire over the radio, sending the OCs to the designated location to mark an artillery strike point on the ground and assess hypothetical casualties.

"Instead of moving around in noisy equipment like Bradleys and tanks, we were jumping in and out of Humvees to observe a location—we were much stealthier and had fewer assets moving around," Almen explained. "Pretty soon, the OC/Fire Markers stopped applying our fire missions because they were tired of moving to all our target locations. Our platoons had notionally destroyed a great number of the opposing brigade's personnel and equipment within 30 minutes. We were just that good."

"Now in garrison, we had all kinds of problems with guys getting in trouble and lack of discipline," Almen added. "But you put us in the field, and the unit executed the mission better than any combat unit I was ever in. We had a mission, and we trained for that mission constantly."

FIRST IMPRESSIONS FOR THE FRESH RECRUITS

Cole Lay grew up in Oklahoma on 92 acres of land that had belonged to his family for half a century. After graduating high school in 2001, he began working for his father's security company. On September 11, everything changed. By September 18, Lay was enlisted.

The teenager arrived at Fort Hood as Blacksheep's newest Private First Class (PFC), fresh out of Basic and Advanced Individual Training. Sitting on a bus with new troopers being taken to their unit's barracks, Lay recalled feeling a bit uneasy. The reliable "hit the ground running with a drill sergeant standing over you" structure was gone, and there was no telling what would come next.

"The driver stopped outside a building and warned us that if anyone asked us to hang out in that building, to tell them no — they were all crazy there. He then turned to me and told me that building was my stop," Lay said. "At that point, I really wondered what I'd gotten myself into."

Instead of the zoo he expected, a single person was waiting for PFC Lay. 1LT Tyler Schaefer, the troop's XO, had remained behind when G Troop left for a training exercise that morning. After a day assisting 1LT Schaefer, 1SG William Taylor returned to the barracks on a supply run and took PFC Lay back out to the field with him.

"They handed me my gear, and it was immediately boots on the ground. SGT Southwood took me right under his wing," Lay said. "He welcomed me to the group, told me what we were going to do that day and how we were going to do it. No one treated me like the new guy. I didn't once feel like an outsider. The hesitancy I'd been feeling was out of the equation at that point. I remember being excited again and thinking, 'I can do this.'"

PFC Lay's platoon took a Blackhawk into the field, landed,

and headed back to observation posts for overnight operations. During the march, they stopped to watch crossroads and call back any vehicle or troop movements to 1LT Sweigart. Assigned first watch, PFC Lay stayed on the radio calling in movements. He was too excited to sleep, and so continued throughout the night, relatively confident he was only butchering some of the call signs.

When the troop returned the next day, the teenager was exhausted but proud. "After confirming with SGT Southwood that I'd been on the radio all night, 1LT Sweigart turned to me and said, 'So that's why we got proximity of, but never an actual spot report.' I thought I was doing everything amazingly well, but I didn't know what anything was. Sweigart kind of laughed in a good-natured way, but at that moment I realized I still had a thing or two to learn," said Lay.

Brandon Ellis wanted to join the military for as long as he could remember. He grew up playing Army, and when his older brother left to join the infantry, his determination only grew. Immediately after graduating high school, Ellis enlisted. Though he'd struggled in school, he excelled in Basic and AIT training—the information and required skills simply resonated with him. PFC Ellis joined Black Sheep as a driver on February 1, 2003—just a few weeks before the unit would deploy.

When he reached Fort Hood, PFC Ellis spent three days in-processing before finally being taken to 1BCT where he was told to wait for someone from his troop. From 9:00 a.m. to 12:00 p.m., he watched other soldiers leave with their units. Eventually, the private was the last one left.

"I finally got up and found someone, gave them my rank and name, and asked if anyone was coming to get me. Their response wasn't very positive. Apparently, G Troop was known for being full of troublemakers," said Ellis.

A few hours later, PFC Ellis was finally taken to G Troop's barracks where the approximately 5'3"-tall Staff Sergeant (SSG) Michael Crosby greeted him with a command to drop and do pushups: "You know why you're doing pushups?"

"No, Sergeant," Ellis answered.

"Because you're taller than me."

SSG Crosby's response was nothing new; the drill sergeants in Basic had done similar things many times, and it was clear to the Private that the command was made in good spirits. This was very much representative of the unit, he soon learned. Upon first hearing of the troop, one might focus on the trouble they got into back at the barracks, but what might slip past is the fact that when they were out in the field, they did their job and did it extremely well.

WORK HARD, PLAY HARD: CREATING A COHESIVE UNIT

Two defining aspects of G Troop that have stuck with its troopers almost two decades later were their unspoken understanding of where the line was drawn and the natural camaraderie that connected them as friends and eventually as brothers.

Lay explained, "We could goof around, we could have fun. The SGTs and troopers would all smoke and joke, but when the business started, that all went away. We lived life hard and fast—but we were just a bunch of 18, 19, 20-year-old kids. Above us, the non-commissioned officers (NCOs) kept it from being too much, and it never got too crazy. Looking back, I know that doesn't work everywhere, but with G Troop it did."

"I'm not sure when we got the reputation of troublemaker. We were considered a really good unit, but I guess we did like to party. Train hard, play hard," said Boyko.

Of course, in Killeen, Texas there isn't much partying to be done. Corcoles recalled one club they could walk to and three country themed clubs within driving distance. Most nights, the troopers would stay in the barracks, playing spades or dominos, holding video game competitions, or barbecuing. No matter how long any of them had been in the troop, close bonds, which weren't relegated to platoons, formed quickly.

"It's been difficult to recreate that bond in other units," said Corcoles. "I think G Troop was different because we were all new and spent so much time together. Most of us had never seen combat and very few of us were married or had kids. After we finished our tasks for the day, we'd keep working with the equipment to get more proficient using it, we'd go through books and quiz each other. We'd go to the movies and the gym together. If we were out and someone got into a little tussle or something, we'd run to our brother's help."

A few weeks after his 22nd birthday, SPC Daniel Saffeels was transferred from 1-66 AR to G Troop. It was mid-summer in 2002, and he would be a team leader for Saber. SPC Saffeels had grown up in Iowa with his parents, brother, and sister, and had joined the military primarily to leave the Midwest behind.

"G Troop was a different type of family, we did everything together," said Saffeels, recalling how he would sneak up to Waco with Private 2nd Class (PV2) Aaron Helmrich—an Iowa local as well—to hang out with college girls. Sometimes the troopers would throw darts at a map of Texas and head out for the weekend based on where the darts landed. Not every dart landed near a large or lively city, but they were usually up to figuring things out once they got to the chosen location. Even in the smallest of towns in Texas, there was always a fireworks stand...

The growing bonds and sense of loyalty within the troop wasn't relegated to just the specialists and privates. The NCOs knew how to be tough and strict, yet fair and caring. This balance and an effort to be a leader, mentor, or confidant blurred hierarchical lines at times but boosted morale and helped the troopers grow as men and troopers.

"One of my closest friends and my mentor is Marcus Solis. He was a sergeant, got to G Troop in '02," said Corcoles. "He picked on me so much. He told me later that he picked on me because I had potential, and he was gonna beat it out of me if he had to. He did break my nose at one point, but I'll admit it was my fault. I didn't think he cared about what I had to say or who I was. Eventually, he put himself on the line for me, and I finally accepted the fact that he wasn't going to give up on me and did care. I was all ears after that."

SGT Solis' care for the troopers and leadership style stuck with Corcoles and inspired him as he took on leadership positions during his career.

"He taught me that a real leader cares about the success of his people below him, and the people below him should know what that leader has accomplished. He said that throughout my career I would have some bad leaders, a lot of okay ones, and a handful of really good ones. Every single one of them would have something to teach me. Whether it was a positive or negative experience, even the bad leaders would have something they were good at," said Corcoles.

SGT Solis also ensured the troopers discussed issues they had with one another, instead of letting aggravation and resentment build up—distance and anger were detrimental to a troop, especially when at war. The SGT would lay a tarp down and tell the men that if they had any issues with someone, they were to discuss it there. If they still wanted to fight after talking, the sergeant would let them, stating he didn't care who won or lost, but after the fight, they were to consider the problem solved. The troopers soon learned that at any point they could go up to anyone in G Troop and talk about issues instead of dismissing them or waiting until they became much bigger problems.

Though 2002 brought in new troopers and commanders, the camaraderie and sense of care in G Troop didn't change. Black Sheep's platoon sergeant, Michaud, was a father figure for some of the young men.

"Michaud would make sure that no one was sitting in the barracks alone during the holidays," said Boyko. "He would invite us to his house for dinner. I talked to guys in different units to see if their PSG invited them over for Thanksgiving dinner, and they all said no. It was unheard of because there's a clear line. But it showed he cared about the troopers and wanted to make sure everyone was taken care of. We noticed that, and it made us want to do our best."

SFC Rick Michaud and several troopers at his home during Thanksgiving slicing the turkey with a saber

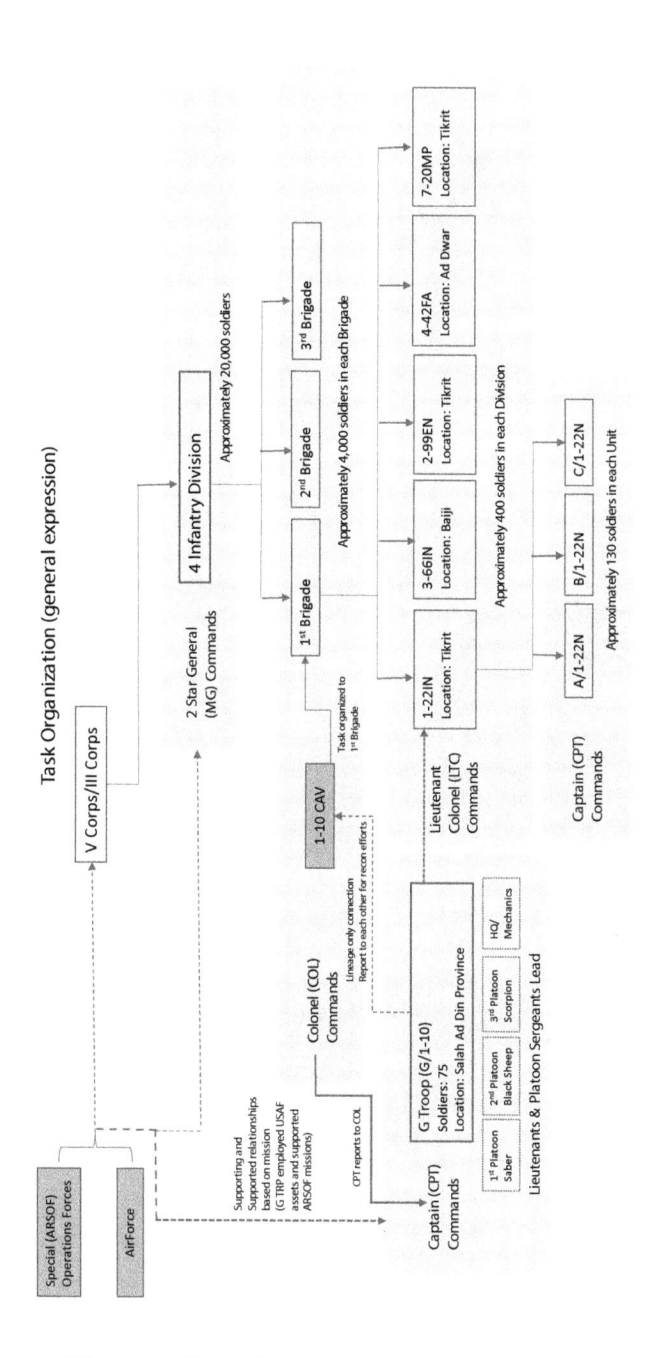

Figure 1 — General expression of the brigade task organization

3. Deployment and the Trek North

OCTOBER 2002 – APRIL 2003

"Sorry baby, I can't stay. I gotta be at war in the morning."
—G Troop Scout

In the fall of 2002, the 1BCT staff, battalion commanders, and their staffs, and subordinate commanders at all levels deployed briefly to Fort Irwin, California, the Army's National Training Center (NTC) for desert warfare. In addition to planning and training for mock war exercises, members of its staff took leadership training at the NTC. A discernable, yet suppressed energy ran through CPT Dez Bailey's team. War was certainly on the horizon. Each morning, they would read the "Early Bird News" that came out in secure transmissions from the Pentagon and try to figure out which Army units would deploy first—and when it would be 4ID.

Dez Bailey grew up on war stories. His grandfather, Frederick Vann, had served in World War II, enlisting at the age of 16, fighting in the China-Burma-India theater with the Gurkas along the Burma/Ledo Road against the Japanese. His five great uncles had also served in the Army and Navy during the war, and his closest uncle Pursur Vann, was at Peral Harbor during the attack. Each of them had returned home to their mother alive and well, a welcoming and news-worthy miracle.

Bailey's first job began at the age of 14, which was cutting grass. In high school, he worked in construction with his father, Charles Bailey, while also serving as captain of his high school football team as a senior—working hard came naturally to Dez, and he found pride and joy in it. His father's favorite phrase was "hit it like you live!" A phrase associated with getting work done on the construction sites.

Paying for college wasn't easy, so Dez joined the U.S. Marines Reserve and served as a Squad Rifleman. After three years, he enrolled in the ROTC program at Troy State University in Troy, Alabama. During his final two years in college, Dez led the university's ROTC, and his senior class was the first Army ROTC class to graduate from Troy. After graduation, he was commissioned an infantry officer and attended both Airborne and Ranger school, and was eventually assigned to 1st Battalion, 325th Airborne Infantry Regiment, 2nd Brigade, 82d Airborne Division where he served as a PL, company XO, and battalion logistics officer. Following this assignment, Bailey took command of B Company, 1-19th Infantry Regiment, an Infantry Basic Training unit at Fort Benning, Georgia. He was promoted to CPT in 2001, and upon completion of command, he attended the Infantry Captain's Career Course (ICC). After graduating ICC in 2001, he was assigned to the 4ID G-3/5 Plans and Exercises section. By 2002, he was assigned to 1BCT and after a confident request, was given a position as the brigade's Chief of Plans.

By November 2002, the brigade was a few days into a field training exercise in the Fort Hood Training Area. CPT Bailey was asleep in the plans tent, having spent the past 18 hours leading his team in planning exercises. Late into the night, Major (MAJ) Mike Silverman, the 1BCT Operations Officer, woke him and said, "Pack up the tent, we're going to war."

It was just past sunrise when SGT Southwood, PFC Lay, and SPC Kamdon Shaw received an abrupt and unexpected End of Exercise communication. They were in the field, hiding in the attic of a building across from the opposing force's command post. During the night they'd snuck in and had been relaying information to their unit, which was scattered across several outposts. SGT Southwood had taken an active role in getting PFC Lay up to speed and was teaching the private details to include as he radioed information to 1BCT operations staff.

"What's going on," Lay asked. Something was up—when you go into the field, you never go back to the rear early.

"Not sure, but let's head back," said Southwood.

Soldiers on the opposing team stepped out from their posts the moment the three men exited the building. "Who are you," someone called out. "When'd you get in there?"

"Sorry guys," Lay responded with a confident grin. "We're leaving now, but thanks for having us."

As they left the camp, Southwood said, "I bet it's deployment orders."

HURRY UP AND WAIT

The days were long for the brigade planners as they worked with their operations officer and commander alongside 4ID's Commanding General, Major General (MG) Ray Odierno and his division staff.

"For brigade planners, this time period was pretty tough," Bailey recalled. "We had to mentally prepare ourselves for deployment and work with General Odierno and his staff to determine how we were going to fight the Iraqi Army."

The brigade staff's weekends were now workdays and days could go 20 hours long. Updated briefs from 4ID headquarters appeared constantly, and CPT Bailey's team spent hours reviewing them, studying imagery of Iraq, and reading intel assessments to devise plans for assigned missions, which included carefully organizing the sequence of unit deployment to ensure the right mix of combat power for each mission. The plans had to be finalized as soon as possible.

Each brigade in 4ID focused on a particular aspect of the division's initial mission, which was to enter Iraq from the north and fight Iraqi army units from Mosul in the north to Kirkuk, Baiji and Tikrit further south.

The days were long for G Troop, too. The equipment and vehicles going with them had to be repaired, cleaned, packed, and transferred to a boat that would cross the Mediterranean to reach Turkey, their launch point into Iraq.

Most time consuming was determining the load plans that mapped out how each Humvee would be organized. This process was akin to Tetris, as the scouts had to pack rucksacks, NBC masks, personal items, uniforms, food, and much, much more. Crews puzzled out different plans and the best one was finalized and replicated throughout the troop. This set structure ensured that no matter which truck a trooper was in, everything would be in the same place and accessible.

SPC Jeremy Lapp, a 24-year-old from Illinois who'd been assigned to G Troop in December 2001 as a mechanic, had been spending evenings and weekends with the other troopers—but now he spent every day in the brigade's motor pool with the rest of his team, led by SGT Brian Egli.

"Once we found out we were deploying, everything was focused on getting those trucks ready to go," said Lapp. "Even up until early morning the day the trucks were shipping out, we were replacing an engine on one of them."

Meanwhile, NCOs, like PSG Michaud, made sure everyone's affairs were in order; bills had to keep getting paid while some services, like cell phones, could be suspended. As he mentally prepared for deployment, PSG Michaud at least felt secure in the leaders he was with—SSG Tommy Darden, SSG Braxton Swilley, and 1LT Sweigart.

"They were all the people I'd want to be in a war with. But, despite the troop's leadership and having the experience of Desert Storm, I wasn't confident or excited about the deployment. There was fear of the unknown, anxiety around that. But I tried to settle my mind thinking this time would be similar to the last," said Michaud.

Within two and a half weeks, the BRT was ready for deployment.

The waiting began.

For close to two months, there were political debates between the U.S. and Turkey—the country no longer wanted the U.S. to use their ports. By early March, it was clear that 4ID would have to enter Iraq from the south through Kuwait. News came down from the Department of Defense that the unit deploying from Fort Hood, Texas would be 4ID, and the first brigade to deploy, would be 1BCT, led by COL Campbell.

The division's equipment, which was on transport ships heading to Turkey, would have to shift course, potentially jeopardizing the carefully arranged order the planners had constructed to ensure each specifically timed mission had the equipment and support it needed CPT Bailey and his team would have to update plans alongside the 4ID HQ staff, including how best to approach and position subordinate battalions in Samarra, Kirkuk, and Tikrit.

"Nothing feels more like a kick in the stomach than shredding the orders you spent four months developing," said Bailey. "I think the base order for the attack from the North was three, 3-inch binders. It was extensive."

Now that order was worthless. The brigade planners were starting from scratch with a very short timeline. As they planned their new approach, CPT Bailey's team received word that the transport ships, now heading down the Suez Canal, were out of sequence. It would take considerable effort to determine which ships would arrive at the port in Kuwait first.

Despite having a path forward, as news channels aired the 3rd Infantry Division (3ID), 101st Airborne Division (101st Airborne) and U.S. Marines launching into Iraq, CPT Bailey felt the war would be over before they'd arrive.

"The waiting was the worst part. You've already decided that you're going to go. You just want to get it going, get it started," said Helmrich, who joined the Army in response to 9/11. He'd set out for basic training after completing his first year of college. In October 2003, at the age of 19, he joined G Troop. Five months later, the PFC was waiting impatiently to be deployed.

With bags packed and their remaining belongings locked in storage, most of the scouts felt the same. They were eager to take on what they'd trained so hard for.

"I remember watching the news with the guys," said Boyko, "bombs were going off on the screen, the war had started. We knew we'd be there soon, and that was exciting. I felt we were well trained and prepared, but knowing this was the real deal, that had me nervous."

At first, weekends waiting at Fort Hood were quiet, without the typical joking around and drinking, as they waited for the inevitable orders to deploy. Weeks passed with no word, however, and living out of packed bags became more and more frustrating. Fed up with wasting weekends that could be their last in the U.S., Scorpion platoon headed out.

Corcoles recalled, "Our whole platoon was at a nearby bar, and someone got *the* phone call and yelled out, 'We gotta go!' Everyone was asking what he meant, was he being serious. I remember hearing behind me the funniest thing. One of the guys was telling a girl he'd met that he had to leave. He told her, 'Sorry, baby, I can't stay. I gotta be at war in the morning.'"

At 3:00 a.m., Black Sheep received the call to quickly gather their belongings and load the plane that would take them to Kuwait.

"Getting that call was an eye opener. It was real now, it was happening, and I was eager to go. I'd played army growing up, I'd been waiting for this moment for a very long time," said Ellis.

On March 27, 2003, the 4ID colors were cased in a ceremony on Cameron Field, the infantry division's parade ground at Fort Hood. Over the following days, the division, including the 75 troopers of G Troop—a few hungover from their recent outing—set off on an 18-hour flight to war.

SPC Saffeels remembers writing in his Bible and then looking out the window to watch the sun set over the Atlantic Ocean far beneath them. "My family didn't travel, so it was the first time I'd even seen the ocean. I didn't even know you could fly for so long," he shared.

After a brief stop to refuel in Milan, Italy, PFC Lay put his

Walkman's headphones on. "At some point, we were over Egypt, and I was listening to some tunes and having a thoughtful moment. This was it—I was heading to Iraq. I had confidence in our purpose and my unit. There was a good crowd around me, especially Darden, Marroquin, Southwood, and Swilley. Our NCOs looked out for everyone," said Lay.

The PFC was neither worried or doubtful, he'd felt those emotions after being cut off from his training unit and sent to Fort Hood. "I wasn't fearless, I'm sure there was anxiety in there," Lay explained, "but I was 19, and at that age you have a shroud of invincibility. You don't think too deeply about consequences. That would come in the six months to follow."

As they neared Kuwait, the stewardess sitting near PFC Ellis and SGT Chris Sharpless, pulled out her gas mask. "The last time we landed, we got gassed," she'd told them. The jolt of adrenaline that carried the troopers five rows back to quickly grab their gear wouldn't be the last.

PREPARING FOR THE TREK NORTH

G Troop landed in Kuwait in the middle of the day. Before exiting the plane, the civilian crew told them that if rocket sirens went off, not to turn around because they'd already have the doors shut.

"When the door opened, it felt like we were leaving the climate-controlled plane to step out onto the surface of the sun," said Lay. SGT Jose Marroquin, a 25-year-old Texan assigned to Black Sheep, immediately commented on the heat after stepping onto the tarmac. Expecting the significant shift in temperature, he'd been hydrating during the flight, but even being from Texas he noted Iraq heat was different.

The troopers loaded up on two busses that would take them

to the port where their gear and vehicles would be ready for off-loading. At a U.S. military checkpoint, they were stopped, and the checkpoint soldiers checked both drivers' credentials. Neither had clearance to go any further.

"Our driver was taken off the bus, and we sat there unsure what to do. Well, we commandeered it," said Ellis. "Darden and Saffeels ended up driving the buses, but we didn't have a clue where we were going. We drove around and finally made it to the designated area—but none of our equipment was there. We ended up sitting at the docks for a couple of days waiting on the boat to come in."

The sound of incoming rocket sirens at Camp New York was more common than not, and soldiers kept their chemical masks near at hand. Sandstorms swept in, the dirt and dust so thick at times they couldn't see their own hands held out in front of them.

Ed Timms, a reporter with the Dallas Morning News who was embedded with G Troop, already had an apt quote for his next article; SPC Almen had told him that Kuwait would make for a great beach, if only they could find the water. Though there was water to drink, there weren't many showers available, and troopers were washing their uniforms in buckets of sudsy water using washboards reminiscent of the 1800s.

Getting supplies would be a common problem for the first half of the deployment, and issues were already starting to show. "There weren't enough ammo rounds, so I had magazines that were nothing but tracers," said Lapp. "I had no body army, no vest. Mechanics wouldn't get body armor for a while, and some of the scouts didn't have it either."

Not knowing how long they would have to go without being resupplied, the scouts coordinated, cleaned, organized, and triple checked their weapons, ammunition, chemical masks, suits, and detectors, plus food and water.

In preparation for their trek north, the troopers blacked out the Humvee lights, double checked weapons systems, and replaced broken parts. One Humvee was already broken beyond repair with the state of a few others was questionable, and jokes started circulating:

"How do you know your truck's out of oil?"

"How?"

"It's not leaking."

Life at Camp New York was simply camping in the desert among a dried-up sea of tents. Even 4ID HQ was a row of dull brown tents with plywood floors like any other, and for the third time that day, MAJ Silverman, the operations officer for 1BCT, found himself leaving HQ and heading to the planners' tent.

The planners huddled around a table, discussing and refining deployment orders to get the troops to 4ID's final destination: Tikrit. Ships arriving out of order had necessitated changes. While G Troop would still spearhead the move north with 10th Cavalry Squadron (1-10 DIV CAV) close behind dealing with remaining enemy forces, 1-22 Infantry Battalion (1-22 IN BN) was still waiting for their ships. 1-8 Infantry Battalion (1-8 IN BN), a mechanized unit from 3rd Brigade, would go in their stead to dispatch enemy formations and secure advantageous terrain.

"It's depressing going up there, Dez," Silverman said, motioning vaguely to where 4ID HQ set.

"Why's that, sir?"

"Because the 3ID and 101st are reporting battle damage assessments. They're taking down the enemy, and all we're doing is talking about how many dang vehicles and personnel we have on the ground."

MAJ Silverman knew he wasn't alone in his frustrations. Morale was high and hundreds of soldiers were ready to put what they'd trained so hard for into action.

"Yes sir, that does suck," CPT Bailey agreed.

"The Iraqis are fighting back, so expect resistance as we travel north. And we've still got to beat the Marines to Tikrit — the boss wants us to get there first."

ACROSS THE BERM

On April 14 at 2:00 a.m., elements of 4ID entered Iraq with G Troop leading the way. Their goal was Tikrit, and to get there they would travel through Baghdad, Taji, Balad and Samarra while taking on tactical missions. 3ID and the U.S. Marines had made up the first wave of forces. Elements of the 82nd Airborne Division were called forward to secure the supply routes, and it was G Troop's job to make sure that no enemies escaped or came back — they were to continue pushing the enemy into a corner and clear out key areas ahead of their division.

Scouting a few kilometers ahead of the small BRT was a section of two vehicles led by SSG Tommy Darden.

"I had my wingman, SGT Southwood in the other truck. It was just six of us, in light skinned Humvees, crossing the berm into Iraq, four kilometers from the rest of the troop. It makes you apprehensive," said Darden.

SSG Darden was southern born and bred, a 31-year-old from Knoxville, Tennessee with three sons and a wife back home. On September 11, 2001, he'd been with a group of 200 soldiers at a Special Forces assessment selection when a TV was wheeled into their room. At first, they thought it was part of the selection course, but then the news was turned on and the chaplains came in. Over half of the soldiers quit selection that day and went back to their units, including SSG Darden. At the time, he was a platoon SGT with 1st Brigade S3 shop, but after serving for a year, he was given the option to choose a new unit. He chose G Troop.

Now the troop's Senior Scout, he would guide the troop safely through Baghdad, into Taji Airfield—where no dismounted soldiers had yet to go—then Balad and Samarra, where the Marines may or may not be waiting.

"It was my first time going to war. I didn't know what to expect. I had good guys in my section, though. My gunner was Boyko—I love him to this day. My driver," said Darden, taking a brief pause, "well, when he was assigned to my truck, he didn't have a driver's license, he'd never driven."

PVT Brian Mosier, Darden's driver, was 23 years old and had grown up in Staten Island, New York. Through the first month of training, Mosier had a "rough go of it," according to Darden. But both the Senior Scout and SPC Boyko got him trained up fast.

"We were a good crew," says Boyko. "Mosier was the East Coast guy, Darden had the southern accent going, and I'm Russian. We used to joke and talk a lot of smack to each other."

For 36 hours they drove non-stop, listening to reports from 101st and 82nd Airborne that warned of mortar attacks. The highway and its signage were covered in dust and poorly maintained. Water bottles filled with urine flew out Humvee windows. Small towns rose along the flat skyline, and then an hour would go by with nothing to see but desert. From time to time, they'd pass through a village of 10 or 12 huts built with compacted mud and brick.

Finally, the troopers stopped to refuel at a U.S. military checkpoint, which reminded SPC Almen of roadside rest stops his parents would pull into for a picnic under a metal umbrella shade.

They drove on, through the night, with Humvee lights blacked out and the stars bright above them. If they did pass by villages or towns, there was no electricity to light the vast darkness.

"It felt like we traveled back in time, just very, very primitive. The people were so poor, but they seemed friendly. They would wave at us, give us a thumbs up," said Boyko.

Finally, the troop stopped to secure a spot the second night. The scouts grabbed a few minutes or an hour of sleep where they could, but it was always the light sleep of someone on guard, the unknown nagging at the back of their minds.

"The troop circled their trucks around the mechanics and CPT Jacobson and his crew. I remember getting up on top of my truck, it was a Humvee with a big box on top and was about seven feet tall. I laid down but couldn't sleep. Being out in the middle of nowhere scared the crap out of me. I don't think anybody got much sleep on the trip up," said Lapp.

"Having your body on high alert for so long is exhausting," said Helmrich. "There's a reason why a lot of us used nicotine by the end of the war."

The temporary but acute sleep deprivation had many of the soldiers dozing off at the wheel. Trucks jerked and swerved. In an exhausted momentary daze, Saffeels clipped an abandoned Toyota on the side of the road. From the gunner's seat of another vehicle, Corcoles watched a Humvee in front of him swerve, barely missing a semi-truck and its empty flatbed. Rucksacks carrying their personal items were tied to the doors of all the Humvees, and one caught on the flatbed, ripping open. A puff of socks, underwear, and shirts flew up, scattering across the highway.

Somewhere in that progression of sleepless days, they began seeing populated areas. These small cities had mostly evaded earlier fighting, and their streets were filled with liberated civilians. People held brightly colored flags and poles tied with strips of white, red, and green cloth as they marched along the streets, cheering at the passing Humvees. Children wove quickly through the crowds, laughing and waving at the soldiers.

Lay had expected war zones; the lively colors and cheerful welcome alongside destitution were surreal. He'd seen World War II photos and heard stories from his grandfather, one of the last pilots to fly the cargo route from India to China, of liberated towns full of cheering people.

"You may think you have an idea of what poverty looks like, but it isn't close to what you see in a third world country," Lay said. "They lived in mud huts with no windows, and some didn't even have doors. The people were clean, their clothes were clean. It seemed to me, and this really was just my own impression, that they had gotten up, put on their best garb, and came out to watch us ride through and show their support."

"The Air Force had come through, but we were the first ones of the brigade to be on these roads, and we didn't know what to expect. The first day we didn't experience much or come across any threats. But, in the days to come, we would begin scouting out roads, seeing enemy tanks, and performing raids," said Ellis.

As they neared Baghdad, the burned-out tanks, blown up cars, and other remains of battle grew. Some were the results of recent attacks by the Air Force while other pieces of equipment and vehicles were from past wars, several years old and rusted over.

SSG Darden's lead section would stop at Iraqi vehicles and T55 or T54 tanks, shooting at them with the trucks' .50 cals or dropping a live grenade down the barrel of a tank to ensure they wouldn't be used again. Sometimes the tanks were occupied by Iraqi soldiers and the troopers would call in tanks or Apache or Kiowa helicopters for support.

"We destroyed weapon and ammunition caches, and then pushed on, updating command along the way and hoping the Air Force had done their job in and around Baghdad. We were destroying stuff, yeah, but at the same time it was amazing to think that at any moment it could destroy you. We never knew," said Darden.

THROUGH THE GATES OF BAGHDAD

It was afternoon when G troop passed beneath the capital city's arched gates. Though it was several days since the U.S. and its allies had launched a massive aerial assault intended to kill Saddam Hussein and instill "shock and awe" among Iraq's leaders, columns of smoke rose from neighborhoods still fighting fires. The smell of burning rubber and oil and the chemical tang of gunpowder overwhelmed the city. Dust and debris lingered in the air over heaps of stained rubble and burned-out vehicles.

Very few civilians walked the streets. Sometimes shadowed faces could be seen from windows. Occasionally groups of waving children would appear standing in front of buildings that looked like they'd been used for target practice.

Sporadic gunfire could be heard close by, sharp and abrupt—3ID remained engaged with the enemy. In the distance, the tops of Scud missiles attached to their launchers were visible between buildings. Nervous energy thrummed through the soldiers. They weren't sure what they should be looking for, but they *were* ready for *something*.

"It was scary," Ellis said. "Everyone in Baghdad was a potential threat because that's where Saddam was when the war began. Baghdad was his town. And then we received a strange report about their zoo being bombed, and animals were loose. My thoughts shifted from dealing with human enemies to getting mauled by a tiger. What do you even do about zoo animals in the middle of a war?"

When Lay's platoon reached a bridge that connected the southern and northern ends of Baghdad, they passed over it quickly. "We weren't sitting there having photo ops," he said, "we were extremely exposed, we were easy targets. Despite that, it's still a moment captured in my mind, a shot in time where I looked out and saw the southern end of Baghdad in pieces."

G Troop passed through the northern elements of 3ID and established a blocking position for 1-10 CAV and 1-8 IN. The units' AH-64s were destroying enemy vehicles, and G Troop was to detain military personnel trying to escape and stop any evacuating civilians to disarm them.

Meanwhile, SPC Corcoles's platoon was fully stopped on the bridge, hanging out with two artillery units from 3ID. Extremely exposed or not, SFC Joe Flores' Humvee had a flat tire, so their crew had stayed behind to help change it while the rest of the convoy continued north.

"This is something not many people talk about—the logistical part of everything," said Corcoles. "G Troop had tons of food and water, but we barely had enough ammunition. And while we were sitting there with the 3ID guys, we found out they had tons of ammunition, but barely any food and water. So, we ended up bartering. I got .50 cal ammo and cigarettes, they got water and food. It was a logistical hiccup, but since our troop was in the front of the line, we needed that ammo."

G Troop settled in north Baghdad overnight, setting up a 360-degree perimeter with their trucks. They would pull security for the brigade's command group, which included COL Campbell and CPT Bailey.

Thought it was an opportunity for the chief brigade planner to rest, he had too much on his mind. The day before, MG Odierno's helicopter had landed close to the Command Group's location, and the general had summoned COL Campbell. When the colonel returned, he'd suggested that they may not be going to Tikrit after all.

"All I can say," said CPT Bailey, "is that if we had executed the 'be prepared plan', that MG Odierno had delivered that day, it would have been a significant event for the U.S." At the time, however, it was just one more rock for Bailey to add to his rucksack and another mission to plan for and coordinate.

Throughout the night, occasional small arms fire would break through the popping of helicopter blades and screaming jets that crisscrossed ceaselessly overhead.

CLEARING OUT TAJI AIRFIELD

On April 16, 2003, G Troop, 1-10 CAV, and 1-8 IN were assigned to clear multiple buildings and ammunition storage facilities on the outskirts of Baghdad, including the Taji and Balad Airfields. This would be the first combat operation for 4ID since they'd left Vietnam in December of 1970. G Troop's mission would be entering nearby aqueducts and sneaking through the northern enemy line to set up observation posts just outside Taji Airfield, which was situated about 30 kilometers north of Baghdad. From there, they would call in air support or artillery strikes as needed to dismantle the base and detain any remnants of the Iraqi military that had fled Baghdad during 3ID's invasion.

PFC Lay's crew was settled into their observation post. SPC Shaw and PFC Lay were pulling security with M-19 and rifle, respectively, while SGT Southwood stuck to the radio, keeping track of any movement south. Though the Air Force had bombed all the hangars, no troops had set foot in or around the airfield. It was time for more targeted attention. A tank from 1-8 IN shot at a bunker with stored ammunitions. Explosions pulsed upward and out.

"Is it coming this way?" Lay asked, watching a Scud missile with boosters only partially ignited, loop lazily away from the bunker and into the air.

"Just stay put," Southwood said. The missile finally fully ignited, shooting off to their side and exploding.

PFC Lay shifted uneasily, concerned that the scattering munitions may not all head the same, safer route as the Scud missile.

Nearby, mushroom clouds of smoke rose over a chain of explosions.

Maintaining situational awareness was challenging for the brigade tactical command group. Throughout the day, COL Campbell continually asked where the BRT was located. They had to keep the scout unit out of any unmanageable engagement. Digital messaging was still in its infancy, and it took a long time for messages to go through. Even with digital systems in the vehicles, the signal was intermittent and radio communications unreliable. Though exceedingly beneficial, FBCB2 communications platforms installed in each Humvee suffered the same intermittent outages; tracking friendly and hostile forces on an active battlefield remained challenging.

There was no sure-fire perspective, only COL Campbell's repeated question, "Where's the troop," met with spotty radio communications.

That evening, as the explosions dissipated and smoke thinned out, G Troop entered what was left of Taji Airfield. They parked their

Humvees in a defensive perimeter. Throughout the night, one member of each vehicle crew would provide local security while others finished clearing out the base and looking for intel or sleeping.

Already, SPC Corcoles, SGT Solis, and other FOs from Scorpion platoon had caught a group of civilians sneaking out. Of course, their presence on the airfield made little sense, and they were temporarily detained in a makeshift cell as the troopers continued their search.

In the abandoned barracks, Corcoles kicked at a pile of uniforms stacked against a wall covered by a mural of Saddam. "What in the heck is this?"

SGT Solis picked up a jacket and rummaged through the pockets, pulling out an ID. "It's military issued," he said, handing it to SPC Corcoles. "These uniforms are the Republican Guard's."

The Iraqi Republican Guard had existed as part of the military since 1964 and were elite troops that reported directly to Saddam Hussein. By 2003, it included three units: the 1st Republican Guard Corps, the 2nd Republican Guard Corps, and the As Saiqq Special Forces Division. It appeared they'd uncovered remnants of the 2nd Republican Guard's 1st Hammurabi Armored Division.

They gathered several more IDs, wallets, and military documents from the abandoned uniforms and then headed to the detainees. One of the Iraqi men could speak some Spanish, which both men were well-versed in.

"We aren't soldiers," an Iraqi said in Spanish. Others agreed in broken English, explaining they were trying to find useful equipment to sell.

SGT Solis shifted through the pile of military cards, looking at photos and then at the men. "Hold up," he finally said, grabbing an ID and holding it closer to one of the detainees. "Dude, this is you! This guy is full of crap—this is him!"

Quite quickly, ID after ID was matched.

For the remainder of the night, G Troop guarded the prisoners and combed through the buildings that still stood. There were maps on the walls, hung next to worn posters in Arabic detailing American jets, tanks, and similar equipment. Though there were safes, they had been cleared out, leaving little for the scouts to sort through.

After clearing the Taji and Balad airfields, 1BCT continued north along Highway 1, toward Samarra. Located east of the Tigris and 125 kilometers north of Baghdad, Samarra was a key city in the Saladin Governorate with a population just under 350,000. The U.S. Marines had already occupied the city, recently relieving the U.S. Marine Reconnaissance Battalion, which had then set out for Tikrit. 4ID had hoped to beat the Marines to Tikrit, but the missions at Taji and Balad had slowed their rate of march. They had come far, however, and would go much further into unknown territory.

4. Final Destination: Tikrit

APRIL – JUNE 2003

"We secured the palace in Tikrit and maintained security while controlling air assets and artillery, bouncing from patrols to raids to destroying weapon caches. We'd hunt down targets and chase them in our Humvees through fields with a helicopter spotlight on them. It was a lot—but we were used to it."

—SPC Arturo Corcoles

After conducting a relief in place with the U.S. Marines on April 18, 2003, 4ID was assigned responsibility for Salah Ad Din Province. The province covered over 24,750 square kilometers (approximately 9,550 square miles), including Abu Ajeel and the city of Tikrit, which was Saddam's hometown and a power base of his regime. Marine forces had occupied the city, but it would remain Saddam's final stronghold and one of the most dangerous and intense insurgent battlegrounds during the war.

In the west, Salah Ad Din Province is defined by Lake Tharthar, an artificial reservoir built in 1956 to collect floodwaters from the Tigris. To the east lays a mountainous terrain named the Jabal Hamrin Ridge (Jabal Hammer). To its south lays Ad Dawr, and slicing down the center of the province is the Tigris River.

4ID's primary mission was to disarm the Mujahadeen-e-Khalg—an exiled Iranian resistance group located in the province—suppress anti-American demonstrations that were springing up throughout Salah Ad Din and defeat remaining Iraqi resistance forces.

1BCT was to oversee the central, capital city of Tikrit, Ad Dawr to the south, and Baiji to the north. Additionally, governance tasks required the brigade commander COL Campbell to meet with local leaders and re-establish rule of law; this included escorting Civil Affairs teams and PSYOP teams as they broadcast pro-Iraq and pro-coalition messages and assisted with infrastructure assessments.

1-22 IN was assigned Tikrit proper, while 299 Engineer Battalion (299 EN) was responsible for the area west of Tikrit to the Tharthar Reservoir. 3-66 Armor Battalion (3-66 AR) was assigned responsibility for Baiji, and 4-42 Field Artillery Battalion (4-42 FA) would manage Ad Dawr. Each of these units had anywhere from 400 to 600 soldiers. Meanwhile, G Troop, with only 75 troopers was to perform operations across Abu Ajeel, a 75 by 80-kilometer area (approximately 30 square miles) that included the region east of Tikrit to the Jabal Hammer, north to Baiji and as far south as Ad Dawr.

SECURING TIKRIT

The troop reached their final destination on April 18, having traveled 842 kilometers (523 miles) and completing numerous missions in just three days. Tikrit was made up of vast shades of brown with mud and brick buildings, dusty trees, and faded asphalt. Here and there, pops of color would appear: a beat up white and orange taxi, a man in a pale brown hajib wearing a red headdress, a barefoot boy in a yellow t-shirt, or columns outside a business with peeling blue paint.

The city was built up along the Tigris River valley. Palm orchards and farms radiated eastward, fed by mazes of above ground aqueducts. The swampy green of the river dulled the more fertile landscape.

SFC Michaud saw Saddam everywhere—faded murals on exterior walls depicted a younger version of the war criminal and newer, brightly painted works showed him smiling in military uniform or dressed in a suit and tie. Posters of his image hung from every light pole in the city. In the months to come, soldiers would be ordered to remove the posters and eventually insurgents would plant homemade bombs behind them.

"You could tell he was loved," said Michaud. "Not only was Tikrit his hometown, but many members of Saddam's government were from the area, either his own family members or close allies. There was poverty, but Tikrit was well maintained, very nice compared to other cities."

Nevertheless, compared to the expansive Tikrit Presidential Palace compound that lined several kilometers of land along the western side of the Tigris, Tikrit resembled a battered and destitute city. Hidden behind tall concrete walls with a singular bridge for access, it was Saddam's very own Versailles. The wealth of Iraq was practically compressed into such palaces that were built across the country for his family, government officials, and supporters of the Bathist party.

Marine forces had temporarily moved in, but it was G Troop that would ensure the palace complex was secure and transitioned to a base for 4ID's headquarters. It took about a month to get the compound ready. During that time, there was little trouble beyond civilians sneaking in with crowbars and hammers to steal slabs of marble or even finer adornments like gold toilets.

Some of the buildings were destroyed from earlier bombardments by the Air Force, yet many remained untouched with diamond chandeliers, colorful tile floors, thick rugs, and golden statues set in marble walls collecting dust.

The scouts set up in a small, though no less elegant, space with a pool and waterfall.

"The swimming pool was nice and shaded," said Boyko. "A bomb had gone off nearby and blown up a lot of glass, which was at the bottom of the pool. Every time we swam, we wore our boots to avoid getting cut."

Some of them slept on cots in the building while others set up tents outside. SPC Almen chose his sleeping bag on the hood of his Humvee and tried to get some sleep whenever he could, though there was very little sleep past early morning once the temperature rose above 95 degrees Fahrenheit. Working under G Troop's XO, 1SG Taylor, SPC Almen stuck around the compound, but the majority of G Troop spent their days and nights running patrols in their area of operations (AO).

"At the beginning, it felt like we were tourists in a combat zone. Daily operations were makeshift until 4ID was firmly established there. Sometimes it felt like we were just creating missions to figure out what we were even going to do, how we were going to work the AO," said Saffeels.

Despite the ambiguity, there was little downtime, and the troopers would go days without much sleep, fitting an hour or two in where they could.

"We were running recon missions non-stop, clearing roads, clearing buildings—just making sure everything was ready for the rest of the brigade to move in. It was exhausting but honoring to be one of the first ones to move into these areas and help the brigade," says Ellis.

They were given a set of playing cards; each card had the face and name of Saddam's closest allies, ranked by their importance. The soldiers memorized them, and always stayed alert to find them as they patrolled Tikrit and the surrounding areas.

"It felt like we were doing police work, driving in neighborhoods talking to people, sometimes through interpreters," said Boyko. "We got to know the playing cards and faces really well and kept an eye out for them while we patrolled."

G Troop had pushed north so quickly, their supply lines hadn't caught up. Showers weren't available for several weeks and MREs were scarce. They grabbed supplies, food, and drinks in the city when they could.

"I think our favorite thing to do was to go to town and get sodas and this rotisserie chicken. They would cook vegetables under the chicken, so all the grease would drip onto them, and then wrap all that up in fresh flatbread. It was so good," said Ellis.

By May, 4ID headquarters had arrived—and G Troop was told to leave the compound.

"They didn't like the picture of scouts sleeping in their Humvees or in makeshift tents just waiting for our next mission," said Saffeels. "Without showers or supplies, it felt like we were Mad Max-ing it sometimes, so actually moving to the Frat House was good for us, it gave us a sense of normalcy."

The Frat House, or FOB Buffalo, was a two-story home that had belonged to one of Hussein's family members. Located about a kilometer south from the main palace complex, it was surrounded by orange groves and abutted the Tigris River, with only one way in or out. To one side, a home that an extended family member had resided in was leveled from the Air Force's attacks in March. Behind them lay 1-22 IN's AO, and from the rooftop, the scouts could see farmland and aqueducts spreading out from across the river. Cattails lined the Tigris, and on the opposite banks, reeds bent over where civilians came through to drop their boats in and fish.

"If the fishermen didn't have a battery to shock the fish, they'd throw dynamite. Though once they'd gotten shot at a few times, they stopped using explosives," said Saffeels.

Sometimes Iraqi bodies would float down the river, swollen and water-logged. The troopers would wade into the murky waters to pull them out.

FOB Buffalo was a relatively secure base, but nightfall brought danger. The windows were busted out, and any light within the building became a clear target for gunners or mortar shots. The soldiers began using red lens flashlights and soon blocked off all the windows in one of the larger rooms with wood and sandbags. This space would serve as their troop command center.

OPERATIONS IN TIKRIT

CPT Bailey and his team of five other planners developed brigade-level plans for defeating enemy forces. They were also tasked with tracking zone reconnaissance efforts across the province, like how many weapons and munitions caches were destroyed.

"When it was time to work, we would row hard," said Bailey. "But we definitely cut up and had some fun times—especially on the *veranda*."

The rooftop veranda—voiced with aristocratic flair—was where the planners would gather for breakfast or dinner to eat MREs and look out over the Tigris, nearby orchards, palm groves, and farmland. The view was a welcome relief from the rocky, weed-ridden flats that surrounded Highway 1 as they traveled up from Baghdad. From this vantage point, CPT Bailey often found himself watching G Troop head across the damaged bridge to conduct combat patrols.

"Sometimes I'd be asked what I was thinking about, and I'd say that I wished I was down there with the brigade recon troop, whipping around in a Humvee, trying to find the bad guys," recalled Bailey. "Not that I minded building PowerPoint brief after PowerPoint brief with a few rounds of Age of Empires in between. I really just wanted to get into the fight."

From April through June, many of the troop's patrols were simply interacting with civilians. They would visit shops in Tikrit, play volleyball or soccer with children, or even get haircuts at a barbershop.

"I ain't gonna lie," shared Corcoles, "it surprised me how talented these guys are with haircuts. They were the best haircuts I've ever gotten overseas. They liked us a lot because we'd pay them in cash, and the U.S. dollar was worth a lot there. For the most part, everybody was nice. We weren't out there being jerks to everyone, and they knew we were looking for specific people."

The civilians were helpful, and some began reporting information to the soldiers. But there were those who would help the enemy as well for a few hundred dollars. It was hard to know whom to trust.

"We'd be driving down a road, tired after hours of patrolling, and suddenly a machine gun would fire at us. We'd push through, then turn around and battle back. But it would just be one or two guys in civilian clothes, and as soon as we turned around, they'd drop their weapons and run," said Ellis.

With adrenaline pumping and hearts racing, the scouts—now wide awake—would chase down the militants. Sometimes AH-64 attack helicopters would track the runners overhead, and the scouts would quickly catch their attackers. At other times, the enemy numbered more than a few, and the scouts' only option was to hunker down, hit the gas, and hope they weren't hit.

Even the locals were unsure who was friend or foe. Ellis recalls being on a dismounted mission in a village and suddenly hearing gunfire. An older man had heard them and was shooting his AK-47 in the air to scare away what he thought were thieves.

"Iraqis were allowed to have an AK-47 to protect themselves," Ellis explained. "And this man had no way of knowing who was coming toward his property. We were all trying to protect ourselves, and not everyone we came across was going to be a combatant. It was a constant challenge of figuring out who was and who wasn't."

The man's concern over thieves was warranted, too. They would steal grain from farmers, as well as brass casings from ammunition—if not the ammunition itself—which they would melt down and sell. The scouts would come upon caches that held thousands of rounds, and standing among the mounds of ammunition, Iraqi civilians would be breaking them apart, dumping out the gunpowder and stashing away the brass casings.

G Troop found weapons and stacks of high caliber ammunition hidden everywhere. While investigating a farm as part of an area recon, a trooper could kick a pile of grain sacks and hear the metallic sound of AK-47 magazines. Walking through a palm grove and looking up, they might see guns hanging from the trees. Driving through a valley, they found several SA-7 Surface to Air Missiles, and their 25-year-old, resident engineer 1LT Tyson Mangum was tasked with blowing them up. Intel would come in on a specific family or house, and the scouts would perform nighttime raids that uncovered stashes of weapons, leading to arrests.

On one such late night raid, it took SPC Almen five solid kicks before the steel frame door gave way. Glass shattered somewhere inside the poorly lit home as a shaking figure came forward with his hands up, speaking Arabic.

"Get this guy outside," Almen said, and two of his crew stepped forward to detain the man.

The Iraqi suddenly new a little English. "No guns," he said.

SPC Almen stepped into the house with SFC Michaud. It didn't really matter what the man said, the intel had come in and they would ensure there were no guns or bombs. Upstairs, a baby began to cry over the sound of hushed, female voices.

The women were a risk as well, and sometimes that made this type of raid harder than it should be. No one wanted to frighten children or women, and the women had no power or control over what their husbands, fathers, and brothers chose to do. But G Troop already had learned not to assume innocence, no matter age or gender. A woman could be carrying a homemade bomb under her robe. Troopers shepherded two women, one holding a toddler, outside. The older one — most likely the man's mother — wailed with tears streaming down her face.

Before heading back in, Almen asked the man: "Where're the guns? You have guns?"

"No, no guns. No guns."

Back inside, SFC Michaud had climbed to the second floor. "Check this out," he called down. SPC Almen took the stairs two at a time. To his sergeant's right, an open space was filled with dozens of rolled up rugs. Michaud carefully unrolled one and, at its center, was a loaded AK-47.

It was 2100 hours, and PFC Lay was performing dismount work in an urban area, south of Tikrit proper. Enemy activity had increased in the area, with multiple small arms and mortar attacks. Overhead, an AH-64 kept track of his platoon and any unusual movements nearby.

"Black Sheep 4, this is Viper. We got a bunch of military-age males going into a single building," the Apache radioed down.

"Roger, Viper, take us there," responded Michaud.

They followed the pilot's directions, heading down a few streets.

"Black Sheep 4, I see your IR beacons, that's it, the door on your left."

"Alright, on three," said Michaud, "kick down the door and push in."

PFC Lay tightened his grip on the M16, the weight of his gear, the sound of a car horn, and the breathing of his team members now very distant. The door was his focus, what was behind it mattered most. They all knew what to do, and they knew the trooper beside them well enough to move as a singular formation once that door came down.

The door flew open, and they rushed into the building, spreading out to cover the space. For a moment, the flashing TVs in the dark room was almost blinding. He caught oddly familiar sounds—cheering in a stadium, the generic male voice of an announcer.

"…And a great save, he tipped the ball away well."

A woman's voice, "He sure did, Phil."

A dozen teenage boys were staring at them, video game controllers falling out of hands as the FIFA tournament noisily continued on their PlayStations.

"America!" One of the boys finally shouted, and a few others followed suit, grinning.

A scout finally spoke up, "So, we gotta clear this, right?"

"Thinking back on that PlayStation party," said Lay, "it was such a surreal moment. We all had a big laugh, but we never really knew what we were going to run into. Even though it was a war zone, there were still going to be kids hanging out with friends or someone having a cup of tea with their family at home. We were in the combat mindset and Iraqi civilians, though not at all oblivious to what was going on, were just trying to live their lives."

According to 1LT Sweigart, "The locals were friendly, and at first it was pretty great getting out and conducting patrols. We'd meet the locals and try to help them get back up on their feet a little bit. This lasted for about two months. Then things started to change, they started to get dark."

For the scouts like PFC Ellis, nothing changed about their operations, but unease and tension soon became palpable. "We were running daily missions, finding ammunition caches, destroying rockets, going through houses to make sure nobody had weapons to use against us. After a while, though, we noticed a change in the number of pop-up ambushes and how civilians acted toward us."

Having information—and telling the U.S. military—was dangerous. A woman who'd been giving G Troop solid intel since they'd arrived disappeared even as they put together plans to relocate her to a safe place in southern Iraq. The once friendly barber in Tikrit stiffly told SPC Corcoles and his crew to get out of the shop. Other shop owners started telling them that they were no longer welcome.

"It happened in a few places, and a few different times," noted Corcoles. "At first, we'd leave thinking the guy was just being a jerk, but it soon clicked that it was something more significant. Resistance forces were coming in, trying to control the towns. They were threatening people."

Some days, shops would be completely closed. And that was when they knew to be on alert. According to Helmrich, "That was one of the more obvious signs that we needed to heighten security.

Someone was either going to attack us there and then or they were preparing to."

The scouts had to figure out who was there, how they were threatening the locals, and what they were planning.

"By June, we knew the enemy was preparing to fight," said Bailey. "Attacks were increasing, especially mortar attacks against 4ID HQ. We figured that many of the Iraqi soldiers who had wilted away during the coalition's push into Iraq had regrouped and were preparing to conduct major attacks."

Salah Ad Din Province

Recon 701

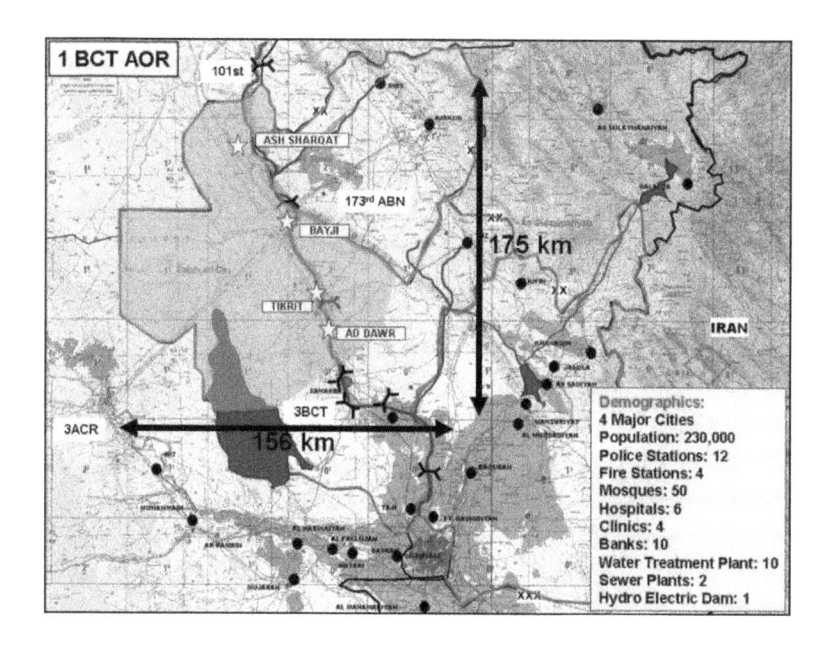

Map of Salah ah Din Province

Murals of Saddam Hussein found in and around Tikrit

Desmond Bailey

Murals of Saddam Hussein found in and around Tikrit

Buildings located in the Tikrit Presidential Palace compound

G Troop's temporary Patrol Base inside the Tikrit palace complex.

Location of FOB Raider (1BCT) and FOB Buffalo (G Troop's Frat House).

Desmond Bailey

A view of the Tigris River from the veranda.

5. Change of Command

MAY – JULY 2003

"I'll take my chances with G Troop."

—Captain Desmond Bailey

On May 1, 2003, President George W. Bush declared major combat operations in Iraq over and the war a success. As 4ID forces consolidated in Salah Ad Din Province, rumors about the future of the conflict spread. National news reported units from 3ID preparing to return home. Senior military leaders stated that transition of the country to Iraqi control would occur in six months. Local security patrols and stability and transition operations began as active resistance diminished.

Major command changes came to 1BCT: COL James "Jim" Hickey would replace COL Don Campbell as brigade commander (COL Campbell moved to 4ID HQ to become Chief of Staff for MG Ray Odierno). G Troop would also receive a new troop commander. The new troop commander had been through the brigade's train-up and deployment, carefully following the ever-changing environment, crafting plans and mission sets for multiple units, and receiving intelligence. Hickey, a recent graduate of the War College, was pre-positioned in V Corps headquarters (the parent unit of 4ID) waiting to take brigade command. The incoming, new leadership could see the big picture coalescing, and it didn't point toward an end of combat operations.

Initially Bailey thought the war had passed him by. He'd crossed over the berm from Kuwait into Iraq and reached Tikrit without entering the fray. 3ID was being praised, rightfully, for their success in Baghdad, and all he had done was watch them from the backseat of the 1BCT Operation Officer's Humvee. His disappointment only grew when a four-star General told the brigade staff that they'd be out of Iraq in six months.

The plans staff no longer viewed the situation as a war, instead they had entered a transition period that involved civil affairs and PSYOP amidst plans to return home.

"I remember the Brigade Headquarters Company First Sergeant coming into the plans tent and asking for the Infantrymen to raise our hands. A few of us did, and he handed us a paper to sign so we could receive a Combat Infantryman's Badge. I laughed and asked if he was joking. I didn't want it. As far as I was concerned, I wasn't in combat until I'd fired my weapon at the enemy," said Bailey.

Despite the President announcing that major combat operations were over, COL Campbell found the morning meetings with MG Odierno becoming more interesting. Instead of discussing the amount of combat power needed, conversations had shifted to the evolving type of combat they faced and who was in charge across the provinces. There was concern that Iraqi soldiers would reorganize.

COL Campbell and MAJ Silverman had attended Lieutenant General (LTG) Scott Wallace's (V Corps Commander) visit with Battalion Commander Pepper Jackson who commanded 3-66 AR.

Wallace had asked them, "Gentlemen, do you think you're leaving soon?"

They believed they'd be leaving before Christmas, possibly as early as the Fall. LTG Wallace told them to plan for a year instead.

"When we returned to Tikrit that evening, Silverman told me Wallace's statement had killed his mojo, and asked if we truly were going to spend a year here," said Campbell. "I told him yes, and we'd better buckle up."

For the next few days, COL Campbell and MAJ Silverman studied intelligence reports. The focus for 1BCT was changing. The brigade plans staff would begin incorporating transition tasks while still directing battalion scout platoons and G Troop to conduct zone reconnaissance throughout Salah Ad Din Province. Along with continuing to look for weapons, ammunition, and any resistance, battalions were directed to improve base defenses and meet with local leaders to re-establish order.

A straight, 227-kilometer drive north on Highway 1 took MAJ Silverman and CPT Bailey to Mosul. It was a hot, dry drive of about two and a half hours. On the way there, CPT Bailey had caught a glimpse of G Troop in their Humvees, conducting zone reconnaissance. While in Mosul, MAJ Silverman was to check on a tank company from 3-66 Armor that was assigned to the 101st Airborne Division.

The second largest city after Baghdad, Mosul had grown along the banks of the Tigris and was home to over 1.5 million Iraqis. If the Turkish parliament had allowed U.S. troops to enter Iraq from Turkey, attacking Iraqi formations in and around Mosul would have been the first objective of Golf Troop and the 4th Infantry Division. Instead, in March the U.S. had strategically bombed and then airdropped Special Forces units and the 173rd Airborne nearby in Irbil. By April 11, Mosul had fallen, abandoned by Saddam's Army 5th Corps.

After meeting with the tank company, MAJ Silverman and CPT Bailey departed the FOB and stopped on the outskirts of Mosul to purchase a few Cornish hens and RC Colas. It was their first non-military ration meal since they'd left Kuwait and was the most delicious thing Bailey had eaten since arriving in Iraq.

Like their hot meal, the brief trip itself was a welcome relief. Mosul in May was an unexpected green, and as they'd left 101st ABN DIV FOB, children had gathered around, handing them flowers. The heat was less intense, with the high that day in the upper 80s. Short grass, thinned out by the sand beneath it, blanketed the rolling hills outside the city. Tall wildflowers with purple orbs and thistle-like leaves skirted the dirt roads.

"Command changes are coming down the pipe," said Silverman. "I'm sure you heard COL Campbell's heading to 4ID HQ to be Chief of Staff…and I'm going over to 2nd Brigade. There'll be more changes in the battalion. You ready for command?"

CPT Bailey grinned. "I'm looking forward to it. I've had enough fun being a brigade planner."

Smirking, Silverman asked, "So, what company are you interested in?"

Infantry stuck with infantry, and Bailey knew Silverman assumed he'd say 1-22 IN. But he'd spent too many mornings and evenings on the veranda watching G Troop, he'd heard enough stories about what their raids had uncovered, and after learning what LTG Wallace had implied earlier that month, CPT Bailey had a sneaking suspicion those stories were only the start.

Bailey paused before answering. A few yards from them, a young woman bent over a metal tub, bathing her arms and hands in preparation for prayer.

"Since you're asking," he finally said, "It's the BRT...G Troop."

MAJ Silverman's eyes widened. He paused a moment before responding. "You might be a good fit for that troop, but that command usually goes to an Armor officer, and I think Raider 6 has already selected a guy for that command."

"Well, I hope I'll be a good fit, because that's the company I want."

"I don't get it," Silverman said, shaking his head. "You're an Infantry officer, take command of an Infantry company. It's best for your career."

Bailey immediately replied, "I'm ready to get into the fight. Most of the Infantry company formations are conducting fixed site security or patrolling the same areas every day, inside the towns and cities. But I see G Troop out on recon missions all over the place. Hell, I've developed most of the missions for them as the brigade planner...That's where I want to be."

"Take a seat," COL Campbell gestured to the chair in front of his desk.

It was late May, and the colonel had requested CPT Bailey's presence at FOB Raider, 1BCT's headquarters. After taking a quick splash bath and changing into a fresh uniform, Bailey had reported to the brigade commander in his quarters.

"I understand you think you're good enough to take command of the BRT."

"I'm not sure if I'm good enough, sir, but it *is* what I want to do."

COL Campbell leaned back, a side-faced grin on his face. "I'll give you the command. But you have to understand one thing: it's typically an Armor officer command, and you're an Infantry officer. The Infantry branch may frown on your decision, and not commanding an Infantry formation could have implications on your progression in the Army. I can't guarantee you'll get a second command after the BRT. Are you okay with that?"

"Yes, sir, I am. I'm here right now. Heck, I might not live through this deployment. I'll take my chances with G Troop."

For about a week, MAJ Silverman helped CPT Bailey prepare for his upcoming command. He had the captain develop a command philosophy and identify his immediate focus for G Troop. During those discussions, they would talk about challenges the troop currently faced, and what the summer months might bring.

CPT Bailey spent more and more time at FOB Buffalo, G Troop's patrol base, to get up to speed. The troop commander, CPT Jacobson, worked closely with him, showing CPT Bailey their equipment, reviewing the task organization, and discussing how the troop generally operated. The missions G Troop had conducted since crossing the berm and what they'd experienced gave him a stronger understanding of how the troop performed missions. As Chief Brigade Planner, he'd developed tasks for the BRT, but hadn't fully understood how they were executed until now. This information also gave him insight into the quality of the unit's platoon leaders, sergeants, and section leaders.

"I knew what I was taking command of at that point, and was happy about it," shared Bailey. "The only concerns I had was how well the troop fought dismounted and conducted Battle Drill 6, which is entering and clearing a room. From what I'd heard, we'd be entering a period of increased raids and dismounted infiltrations, and we'd be expected to support Special Operations Forces."

As CPT Bailey expected, with the incoming brigade commander's focus and evolution of the war, his troop was about to become very busy and very aggressive.

"Meeting G Troop's leaders before assuming command was especially important to me," says Bailey. "I've tried to recall my first impressions of them all, but it was such a rapid process, with so much to think about. When I reflect on G Troop as a unit, they've coalesced into a singular team of troopers working in sync. What does stand out in my memory are their personalities because they played into how well everyone worked together."

1SG Taylor was about six feet and 200 pounds; he'd named his crew's truck Old Bill and always wore cavalry boots. When CPT Bailey came on board, 1SG Taylor sat down with him to talk about the troop's purpose and shared a copy of the Scout Leaders Reconnaissance Handbook, which CPT Bailey would discuss with him as he finished each section.

"1SG Taylor was a true cavalryman, tactically and technically proficient, very familiar with reconnaissance missions," said Bailey.

When he met the Black Sheep platoon leader, 1LT Brian Sweigart, CPT Bailey decided maybe he was too short and skinny to be a scout. Here was another over six-foot-tall man, this one even more imposing than 1SG Taylor. 1LT Sweigart was competent, driven, and had a solid grasp of the troop's mission. Bailey knew from the outset he was someone to discuss ideas with and listen to when he had a recommendation.

When introduced to SPC Joshua Szott, who was a fire support soldier at the time, Bailey knew that if he needed to form a brute force squad, the troop had the sizeable personnel.

SPC Szott was relatively new to G Troop himself. He'd joined the Army in 2000, the day he turned 17. A Forward Observer assigned to 3-66 AR, SPC Szott had traveled from Kuwait up to Baiji, spent a few months supporting ARSOF missions and then had been assigned to G Troop in May as a team sergeant for Scorpion platoon.

1LT Tyson Mangum was a reserved, professional, and reliable lieutenant. With any task and purpose in hand, he made things happen and kept a positive attitude.

LT John McClusky was Bailey's fire support officer and exceptionally well-versed in his field. He took initiative in meeting the local leaders and developing contacts in a thoughtful way.

The BRT's Executive Officer (XO) at the time was LT Tyler Schaffer, a fiery and smooth-talking trooper who was the primary information collection officer for the troop headquarters, tracking all activities and findings from their operations.

"My confidence was boosted for several reasons when I met Staff Sergeant Tom Darden. He was from Tennessee and had a thick southern accent, he was a former Infantry mortarman, and he and I were about the same size. I figured if he can make it in this outfit, so can I," recalled Bailey.

G Troop had a single female trooper, 25-year-old Nicole Ann Foisset, a sergeant and New York city native. She was one of eight support personnel serving in the 4th Forward Support Battalion and was assigned to G Troop as lead mechanic. When it came to maintenance on the Humvees, there was no one better qualified. She'd decided to join the Army during her third year at the University of Massachusetts. Knowing it would give her an opportunity to travel and pay for her education—she planned on earning a master's degree—she joined the Army.

"I first met Foisset when she was laying under a Humvee, holding the transmission in place with one hand and the impact drill in her other, to mount the transmission back in," Bailey said. "She's very talented and used her skills to not only keep our trucks running, but to help out the Iraqi people. Several times she accompanied combat patrols across the river to fix irrigation pumps for the farmers."

All the SSGs, including Joey Womack, Marroquin, and Swilley, were competent NCOs, and Bailey was confident in their skills. SFCs Michaud and Flores were proficient, knowledgeable, and engaging — overall, a team of solid senior NCOs for the troop.

There was no doubt that some of the best officers the Army had were under CPT Bailey's command, and he knew that their skills and attitudes would reflect in the troopers under them.

After graduating from the Virginia Military Institute in 1982, Hickey joined the Army and was assigned to 3rd Squadron, 7th Cavalry and then L Troop, 3rd Squadron, 11th Armored Cavalry Regiment, both in Germany. In 1999, he commanded 2nd Squadron, 3rd Armored Cavalry Regiment through training and operational deployments in Bosnia-Herzegovina. He was a Russian linguist and had graduated from the Defense Language Institute in Monterey, California, and the U.S. Army's Russian Institute in Garmisch, Germany. He held a Master of International Public Policy from Johns Hopkins and had attended Georgetown University as a U.S. Army Senior Service College Fellow.

"Nothing flustered Colonel Hickey, and he was exceptionally intelligent. In any situation, he would come up with a battle plan quickly. He was aggressive against the enemy and expected high performance from his troopers," said Saffeels, who would join Hickey's security detail later that summer.

The troopers knew Hickey was a calvary squadron commander and had worked at the National Training Center in California. A quick internet search brought up a paper he'd written for NTC observations titled *Closing with the Enemy*, which detailed how a company team should fight. This paper would eventually become one of Bailey's touchstone documents that would guide his tactical studies and how, as a future battalion commander, he would train and employ his soldiers in mechanized formations.

"Colonel Hickey preached what he'd written in *Closing with the Enemy*. He ensured all his commanders knew it by heart. It was a useful reference because it was tactically sound and allowed me to understand how he thought and how to communicate with him," said Bailey.

Shortly before CPT Bailey took command, he and Jacobson received word from Brigade HQ that Hickey wanted to go on patrol with G Troop ahead of his assuming command. They quickly developed a plan focused on entertaining—and not pissing off—the colonel. Jacobson, being most familiar with the area, would take the lead, guiding Hickey through their AO while providing an area assessment.

Though tactically sound, the plan assumed COL Hickey required an orientation of G Troop's operations. "We found out pretty fast that the colonel was already oriented," said Bailey. "He was in rapid fire mode, wanting to know every single detail. For any area of interest on the map, he wanted to know what had happened there, who's watching the location and for how long, and what the troop was doing to find and kill the enemy there."

On June 12, 2003, CPT Dez Bailey formally took command of Golf Troop, 10th Cavalry Squadron, 1st Brigade Combat Team, 4th Infantry Division.

Two weeks into CPT Bailey's command, COL Hickey took command. G Troop's first mission with the new commander was a large-scale cordon and search in a section of Ad Dawr, a city directly south of Tikrit controlled by 4-42 FA. Prior to the combined arms rehearsal at 4-42 FA's headquarters, CPT Bailey had 1LT Sweigart's and 1LT McClusky's platoons conduct a recon of the areas they would be searching.

1LT Sweigart returned with pictures taken on his personal camera. Though most were crooked and a few blurry, the lieutenant explained that he'd set the camera close to himself and taken the pictures as they drove through Ad Dawr. Though it meant awkwardly aiming the camera, he'd ensured the locals didn't notice what he was doing.

The pre-mission reconnaissance approach that NCOs Darden and Swilley used took them out of their Humvees. With candy they'd received in care packages, they stood in front of their target buildings, talking to, and taking photos with the kids who inevitably gathered. Behind the groups, in each photo, were the doors and fences they'd need to breach. The scouts were creative, crafty, and discreet in their approach, using their own resources to inconspicuously accomplish their reconnaissance mission.

The information gathered by both 1LT Sweigart's and 1LT McClusky's platoons further informed the troop's plan of attack, which Bailey treated as a raid. Bailey included his leaders in developing the plan to ensure their crucial insights on things like entry and exit points, number of vehicles needed to secure certain objectives, and names of the locals they'd met were incorporated. During the rehearsal they'd make sure the plan aligned seamlessly with those of 4-42 FA.

By July, CPT Bailey was planning and observing the platoons' daily operations and ensuring they accomplished missions directed by 1BCT, which included expanding the brigade's AO and completing zone reconnaissance. To track their progress, he created a map that divided G Troop's AO into zones. Each day the troop conducted reconnaissance in a zone and provided the brigade with a report.

This was a more organized approach, but they needed to know more. Without a larger perspective that could move fluidly from detail to detail, they couldn't effectively shift from reactive to proactive operations. And they needed to, now. Reports coming in warned of a brewing insurgency.

CPT Bailey sat down with 1LT Schaffer, placing an area map in front of them. "You guys have talked about all the munitions and enemy equipment you've found and destroyed. Where exactly did you find it?"

"We've found a lot of stuff since we were assigned the east side of the river," Schaffer said.

"Where, exactly? Attacks on our forces are being planned *now*. Let's figure out where those guys are active."

"Sure." Schaffer pulled out a green notebook and handed it to the captain. "Everything we've ever found or done is recorded in here."

CPT Bailey flipped through pages of pencil-drawn, 10-digit grids and lists of caches written down with detailed information on amounts and types of munitions, weapons, and equipment. "There's only one problem with this," he said, setting the notebook down. "It doesn't mean crap to me like this. It needs to be on a map. Get me a computer."

Over the course of a week, CPT Bailey added the patrol routes and key locations into the MCS Light computer, using different colors and shapes to signify enemy activity or types of equipment and weapons found. By incorporating overlays, he could show everything the troop had discovered at once or drill down to specific types of caches. They could now identify patterns in enemy activity and how that correlated with hidden munitions and weapons. This allowed the troop to direct their reconnaissance and surveillance efforts in certain areas to see if the enemy reseeded caches.

When he took command of 1BCT, COL Hickey's strategy was to concentrate the battalions in the cities of Salah Ad Din Province. There, they would either capture, kill, or force the enemy into the less populated desert. G Troop would hunt the fleeing enemy while maintaining a counter-mortar/rocket mission to protect 4ID HQ.

The pace of missions increased as the brigade struggled to gain intel on Saddam. The locals in Tikrit and Abu Ajeel became more distant. June and July remained quiet, yet a foreboding sense grew. LTG Wallace's warning that they wouldn't redeploy home anytime soon made more sense to CPT Bailey as he studied the troop operations map and enemy activity. Each day, he updated it with data from the troop's briefs and sent them to COL Hickey. It was clear Hickey also understood the rising risk, though putting a finger on the pulse of it was proving tricky.

Every day and night, the troopers were either patrolling, performing dismount operations, interdicting mortar attacks on 4ID HQ, or taking a break for refit. They started supporting Army Special Operations Forces (ARSOF) missions more often. Those troopers given time off were likely to be called in for a mission with ARSOF—finding time to rest was challenging. The troop practically lived out of their vehicles now, and many of the trucks needed repairs. All of them were in desperate need of new tires, but supplies were still low and vehicle parts a rare find.

"Getting parts for the trucks was my team's biggest challenge," said Lapp. "We didn't have anything. There was nothing for us to do but fix what we could, but these guys were blowing tires left and right. We ended up taking the tires off the mechanics' trailer so the trucks could run. We eventually ran out," said Lapp.

Fortunately, the mechanics had a singularly skilled leader for the first half of deployment: SGT Brian Egli.

"He was a backyard mechanic genius and had a mind for engineering," shared Lapp. "On the way up to Tikrit, a truck lost a belt and we had nothing to replace it with. SGT Egli tied together some 550 cord and weaseled it in there in a way that got the truck working. He was very clever, and I learned so much from him."

As mission sets increased, CPT Bailey began organizing his troop differently, assigning troopers based on which personalities and skillsets best fit mission requirements instead of sticking with standard platoon and crew assignments.

"He knew our troop was different when he started seeing how we worked," said Sharpless. "Everyone from different platoons mingled together. We were a tight knit group of guys. He knew we were unique."

To the Army, this choice technically meant Bailey was putting together unqualified crews. To be qualified, each crew that went out had to have the same driver, vehicle commander, and gunner every time.

"I didn't care about platoon organization or the more industrialized approach to everything. I knew what we could do—I was a product of that. I wanted to know what we can do *now* and how we can do it *better*," Bailey explains. "By focusing on which troopers were most qualified for a mission or task, we had a higher chance of success. Troop unity was strengthened, too. They became even more interdependent and adaptable."

This method gave troopers opportunities they wouldn't ordinarily have, including troop mechanic and SPC Lapp.

"I'd made up my mind that I wasn't going to sit back and watch the war go by. I volunteered to join up with the Scouts whenever I could. I did it all—foot patrols, ground vehicle patrols, firing mortars. What I did didn't matter to me, just as long as I got to go. These guys were my friends, and I didn't want them out there by themselves all the time," said Lapp.

CPT Bailey quickly made an impression on the mechanic, who recognized the change in leadership style early on. "I work at Toyota now, and we have a phrase called "Genchi Genbutsu," which means "go and see for yourself." CPT Bailey personified this idea; he'd go out to see things firsthand. I can guarantee you the Scouts loved him so much for that—he went out there and got in it with us," said Lapp.

TROOP CHANGES

With the command change came shifts in G Troop's assigned personnel as the troopers continued the Army's traditional development route or came to the end of their military service. Throughout the summer and early September, the scouts and forward observers were reassigned to other units, those whose enlistment had ended returned home, and new troopers arrived to replace them. Several of the troopers earned promotions during this period, including 1LTs Schaeffer and Sweigart to Captain in the early fall. SPC Corcoles returned to 4-42 FA while SPC Justin Fugate came over from the same unit to join Scorpion platoon, along with SGT Anthony Thompson. Thompson was fresh from deployment in Germany with only a month's break back home in Texas. PVT Joseph Sparks, who had deployed with 1BCT HQ was assigned to Black Sheep as a driver.

SPC Thomas Ribus, SGT Jason Beberniss, SPC Almen, and Saffeels, who was now a SGT, transferred to COL Hickey's security force and remained with the colonel for the rest of the deployment. Boyko and SGT Robert Cornwall would also join COL Hickey's convoy as a gunner, but only for a month before heading back to the U.S. with SGT Hector Medina in early September. Each of the men were carefully chosen by CPT Jacobson based on their demeanor and land navigation and shooting skills.

"I was upset at first, because I didn't want to leave G Troop," said Saffeels. "It ended up being a beneficial experience, though. I saw a different side of combat; how other units work, and how things operate from a larger perspective."

SGT Saffeels commanded the lead truck in the colonel's small convoy. SPC Almen was his gunner and both SPC Ribus and SGT Beberniss served as the driver. SGT Saffeels spent much of his time with Command Sergeant Major (CSM) Lawrence Wilson and Major Brian Reed, 1BCT's new Operations Officer, ensuring all the drivers and gunners were ready and mission capable.

"Colonel Hickey was very hands on. He never wanted to sit back and watch things happen," shared Saffeels. "He would talk to the troops, get a feel for how things were operating, and where he could help. He'd talk to leadership in the Iraqi Army, interact with the populace."

Summer, winter, day and night, COL Hickey's convoy of three trucks was out on the road. They would go on patrols and raids with G Troop, head up to Baiji where 3-66 AR guarded an oil refinery and pipelines, and drive through the deadly RPG Alley to visit 1-22 IN. The colonel would meet with ARSOF or Iraqi Army leadership, and then patrol through Tikrit or Ad Dawr. Sometimes they found themselves in the middle of riots, fires burning in the road, and stacked tires forcing them to detour. Unseen assailants would fire weapons from within the crowds, and once the rioters were dispersed by 1-22 IN, there would be abandoned bodies of civilians gunned down or trampled by their own people.

During one of COL Hickey's visits with a tribal leader, SPC Almen recalls the troopers being invited into the Sheik's home to eat. While the tribal leader's men watched over the trucks and equipment, the troopers ate chicken and vegetables wrapped in large rounds of flat bread.

"You've had a cup of espresso before, but not in 125-degree heat and not as strong as this tea," said Almen, describing a time Hickey met with a tribal leader, who sent them a tray of local tea. "I had to put a glove on to pick up this small, clear cup. I could see a quarter inch of sugar at the bottom, and I stirred it up. It was like drinking a cup of tar. I swear I got third degree burns on my lip and tongue. But you had to drink it because they were being polite, and we wanted to be considerate as well."

"The tea there is amazing," said Joseph Sparks. "A Sheik had it served to us in little teacups lined up on a massive platter. It was so hot; it burned my taste buds. Not all the guys would drink it, and there were six glasses left, so I drank all of them. It's a good bit of go juice."

Sparks had wanted to be in the military for much of his life. Both his grandfathers had served in World War II, one as an ambulance driver in the Army and the other as a Marine who'd landed on the beach at Iwo Jima to wrest the island from the Japanese Imperial Army. From northern Alabama, he grew up in a close-knit family with parents who spent their careers serving the country and their community; Sparks' father worked for the Department of Defense and his mother was an elementary school teacher and then school counselor.

When he joined G Troop at the age of 22, PFC Sparks was assigned to Black Sheep platoon and would be a dismount and driver. However, until he got his feet wet, he'd be what they jokingly called a JAFO—just another freaking observer. Though he'd missed the initial push into Tikrit and earlier combat operations, it wasn't long before his feet were soaked. They were in the thick of it, and operations were at a high tempo.

"One of my favorite things was kicking in doors, and I was good at it, too," said Sparks, recalling a mission where they were to search the abandoned home of a Hussein family member to ensure it was truly deserted. Once in the house, Sparks was called over to a locked door.

"I kicked it with everything I had. Nothing—absolutely nothing. I kicked it again, and again. Took about five times before I realized they had me on the wrong side. By then, everyone was laughing. I handed my rifle to SSG Swilley, got down in a football stance four yards away, and took off. I hit the door, heard a crack as I bounced back a little. I got back down and did it again. Next thing I know, half of my body is in the other room, splintered wood everywhere. I called back to everybody: It's clear!"

Further into the summer, the troopers were much thinner. Ears protruded, eyes had sunk in, and noses were sharper. SFC Michaud and SGT Marroquin had a mission planned for Black Sheep that would take them dismounted through the Tigris riverbed, where grasses and cattails grew five feet tall.

"We had to wear camo face paint, and all the guys were in the communal bathroom applying it, like they're getting ready to go out on a hot date," said Sparks. "I've already got mine on, green, brown, and black all over my face, my head's shaved, my nose and ears are protruding because I'd lost a lot of weight. I jam my head into the room, just to take a quick look, and someone says they've seen me in a movie recently—wasn't I one of those Orcs or Uruk-hai in Lord of the Rings?"

No one was too good to get ripped on, Sparks shared. Once they were out in the grasses, the shorter SGT Marroquin was able to walk comfortably, remaining hidden, while the other troopers had to crouch awkwardly through the area.

"We told him he was a jerk, and laughed and joked with him," said Sparks. "It was all good natured, just how brothers have been as far back as antiquity. We mess with each other, bicker, because we cared about everyone else much more than ourselves."

Within fifteen minutes of joining G Troop, PFC Fugate was heading out on a mission.

"The moment I met SGT Flores, he told me to grab my things and throw them in the truck—we had a mission to go on," says Fugate.

Born and raised in Tucson, AZ, PFC Fugate joined the army right out of high school, concerned that he'd otherwise be heading in the wrong direction. He deployed with 1-22 IN at the same time as G Troop. Within two months, he shifted to 4-42 FA, and by early summer was the newest gunner for G Troop's Scorpion platoon, assigned to Team 2 with SGT Caleb Branch and their truck's driver, PFC Robert Andrade.

"Andrade was a good leader and motivator, though he was cussing me out all the time, like when I was packing the truck up before heading out on a long mission. He'd take it all out and show me how to pack it up so that everything could fit. He was cocky, but sometimes in the military that's good, as long as it isn't over the top," said Fugate. "We could all be obnoxious sometimes, but it came with the territory because we covered a battalion-sized area with 75 people, which is absurd."

Along with patrols, raids, and other missions, Scorpion platoon performed harassment and interdiction (H&I) fires from 4ID HQ, which involved firing artillery at known and potential enemy locations at random, ongoing intervals. Sometimes the gate guards would give Fugate and his team a hard time.

"Once I told them that they could either let us through or we'd radio Captain Bailey and let him know they weren't letting us in to protect Ray Ray's life. One of the guards was surprised and asked me who Ray Ray was. I told him it was Major General Odierno, the guy who lived there. They let us in immediately that time," recalled Fugate.

Once every five to six days, a scout wouldn't have to go on dismount patrol, which would give them free time to shower, do laundry, write letters, listen to music, or watch movies on a portable DVD player. Showering was best done at 3:00 a.m. if one wanted to avoid scalding hot water fed from a metal tank on the FOB roof that cooked in 100° F heat all day. Washing clothes wasn't a time sensitive process, but it could be time consuming. Their 10-gallon washing machine could only handle two uniforms at a time, and the troop burned out at least two of them during their deployment. Often the troopers would huddle around a small DVD player that included a screen—they'd bought it in Tikrit and asked their families to send them movies.

"There'd be eight of us, almost in each other's laps, trying to watch *The Lord of the Rings* or some other show," recalled Sparks. "When I had the time, I'd also write a letter home or listen to Labeouf's CDs on my Discman. He had a massive CD book filled with old time radio shows. They were the coolest thing."

"When I wasn't busy fixing trucks or scavenging for parts off other trucks, there was always guard duty. If I didn't have that, I was hanging out with the guys who weren't on mission, playing cards or PlayStation," said Lapp.

This type of downtime was few and far between, and it always came after the troopers ensured their weapons and equipment were prepped for the next day.

"We weren't by the book, because there was a lot of cutting up, but we always got our tasks and work done first. Everyone in G Troop was really sharp," says Sparks.

After a thoughtful pause, he adds, "There were smart people, people with varying degrees of experience. Some of the guys had been in the army for a decade, had fought in Desert Storm. But, for the most part, we were just willing kids thrown into the fire. I'm 39 now and, looking back, I wonder what it must have been like for our NCOs, like Darden and Swilley. They were just 27 and 28 years old and were responsible for the health, safety, and life of guys who were eight or 10 years younger."

Captain Bailey at the 1BCT Tactical Command Post between Taji and Balad Airbases during the initial attack into Iraq by 4ID in April 2003.

A picture of Mosul's main entrance, taken from Major Silverman's vehicle.

From left to right, MAJs Steve Pittman and Mike Silverman south of Mosul Iraq

Recon 701

From left to right, MAJ Brian Reed, CSM Lawrence Wilson, and CPT Desmond Bailey

CPT Tim Jacobson on patrol, Tikrit, Iraq

Desmond Bailey

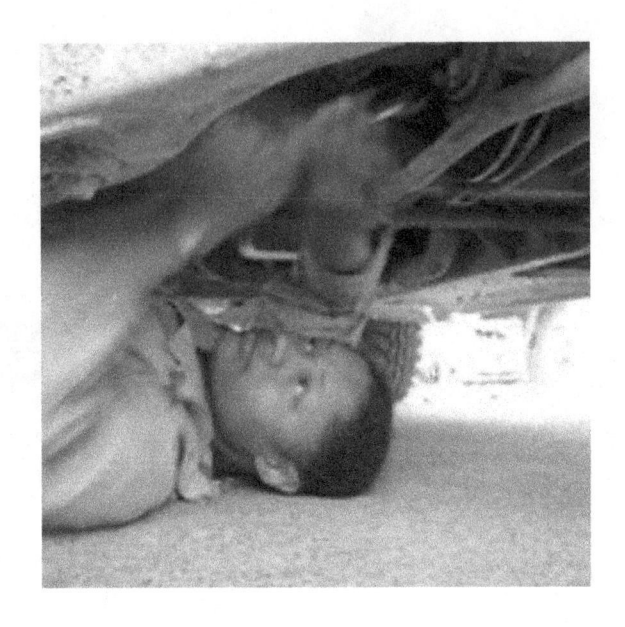

SGT Nicole Ann Foisset working on a Humvee.

6. The Growing Darkness

JULY – SEPTEMBER 2003

"Raider Main, this is Recon 6. Contact… wait… out!"
— Captain Desmond Bailey

When you press the enemy, they have a choice: press back or run. From July through October 2003, the insurgents chose both. Hickey's aggressive plan to hunt down Saddam's remaining military and paramilitary forces and push them out of the urban centers was met with resistance. However, the battalions in Tikrit, Baiji, and Ad Dawr gave them little choice but to retreat to the hinterlands and open desert.

The insurgents increased rocket and mortar attacks, and ambushes became more common. The methods of attack expanded as they pulled together what resources they could, even going so far as to pay civilians to attack American soldiers.

In Tikrit, the soldiers of 1-22 IN were attacked with Pepsi bombs and cinder block bombs. 3-66 AR soldiers in Baiji came across more and more landmines. G Troop spent more time out in the hinterlands and farmlands to find out who was behind the escalating mortar attacks on 4ID HQ. The BRT's operations tempo would only increase.

The first attack with a Pepsi bomb occurred in Tikrit as soldiers from 1-22 IN conducted a patrol. A soda can filled with gunpowder and coated in metal nuts and bolts was dropped from the upper story of a building. It was resourceful to an extent, but rudimentary. CPT Bailey figured there was little to worry about; if all the enemy had left was gunpowder and soda cans, they were done for.

Days later a more concerning attack occurred, this time with a roadside cinder block bomb full of gunpowder, ball bearings, and nails. 1-22 IN's company commander CPT Brad Boyd was wounded from the explosion. Shortly after, a 299 EN vehicle ran over a landmine the enemy placed at the entry road of their FOB. Like the other units in 1BCT, G Troop faced more risk from quick ambushes with small arms fire, IEDs, mortar fire, or the more dangerous RPG attacks.

The enemy didn't have the same capabilities as the U.S., but they were crafty.

"The unskilled or dumb enemy fighters die off first—they make a bomb wrong, blow themselves up, or we capture or kill them. The herd thinned out, and all that was left by mid-summer were the smart ones," said Sparks.

Insurgents would hide along the main highways, tucked beneath aqueducts, hidden behind houses, or parked in a wadi, waiting for the soldiers to pass them. One morning, ahead of sunrise, PFC Lay was pulling front left security in the gunner's seat of his truck. Muzzle flashes lit the dimness, and he rotated the turret to return fire. As they sped past the alley where the enemy hid, his turret froze, refusing to move any further.

"Back at the motor pool, I start doing maintenance on the truck," recalled Lay, "and I find an AK round stuck between the turret's ball bearings. That's what stopped me from turning the turret. If it hadn't, maybe it would've gotten caught in my armor, who knows…it's just one of those close calls."

These attacks of opportunity were common and had no rhyme or reason to them. At any moment, the hidden enemy could see their trucks or hear them talking; they would attack and then run. Responding to random, unorganized acts of violence with a coordinated response was challenging.

"You'd have to almost put out a massive net of troops, which we didn't have, in order to have people close enough to respond to any given thing. We caught what we could, we missed others, and we hoped we'd be in the right spot at the right time to make an efficient response," says Lay. "And we always wondered—was that Farmer Joe who shot at us or a 17-year-old kid trying to prove to their elders they had the right stuff to be part of the resistance?"

G Troop's constant searches and raids helped curb potential attacks. Any guns and ammunition beyond the allowed AK-47 and two magazines were confiscated. Bags of wire were taken as well if the individual didn't own equipment like a tractor, a car, or electronics.

"We didn't give them much time or ability to put certain things together. Every day we went into homes, sometimes hard, most of the time soft. Eventually IEDs were coming in from out of sector, and a few times we caught them trying to get rockets in. But we kept the pressure on them, kept them wondering where we would strike next," said Sparks.

G TROOP'S FIRST MAJOR AMBUSH

That night they would head out on another mission, which could lead to Saddam's capture. It was Operation Sherman which involved units from ARSOF, 3-66AR in Baiji, 1-22IN and G Troop. Their task was to isolate a home surrounded by mud huts on a small island in the Tigris. Timing meant everything as the intelligence suggested Saddam would only be at the location for a short period of time. After discussing the plan with COL Hickey over an early dinner, CPT Bailey returned to FOB Buffalo and met with his XO, LT Schaffer, 1SG Taylor, and LT McClusky and discussed the final details of the large-scale raid.

They were finalizing details of the raid when several nearby explosions muted their discussion. SFC Washburn's voice came over the troop radio, "RPG! RPG!"

SGT Christopher Beran followed up, "We've made contact. Enemy has RPGs. Saber 4 is hit!"

The continued explosion of RPGs and accompanying small arms fire, including SPC Lebeouf's MK19, flooded the communication. Four trucks from Saber platoon were on mounted patrol across the Tigris, and the Blue Force Tracker Unit showed the two under attack halted just prior to the major traffic circle on Tikrit's main road.

CPT Bailey exchanged glances with LT Schaffer, and LT McClusky's expression said enough: *What're you gonna do now, Commander?*

This was it, his first contact with the enemy as troop commander. He took a deep breath. "Get our crew," he said to 1SG Taylor, "we gotta go!"

PFC Ellis was on dismount mission with Black Sheep platoon when they received word that Saber was under fire.

"Get ready with the med kit for any wounded," SGT Marroquin instructed him from the front seat.

He could practically hear his heart thumping over the sound

of the engine. PFC Ellis, like all the scouts in G Troop, had been trained in the basics of first aid — he hoped it was enough.

The brief ambush was long over by the time they arrived. The traffic circle — dubbed the traffic circle just a few hundred meters east of the ambush point — was a high traffic area, surrounded by small businesses and close to the bridge that connected the palatial compound to Tikrit and surrounding farmland. Despite how busy it was, there was limited lighting at night. They drove through it constantly; it wasn't a surprise, really, that they'd been attacked. What *was* unexpected was how.

An RPG had been fired at the first of two patrolling Humvees. It had slammed into the truck's right passenger side, while AK-47 rounds passed over the gunner's head and blasted into the ground.

Moments after they pulled up, SFC Washburn was pushed up into the seat beside PFC Ellis. The sergeant seemed to be the only injured scout. Both SPCs Lebeouf and Wooley, who were in the truck with SFC Washburn, had come out unscathed. After a quick assessment, PFC Ellis confirmed that SFC Washburn, though very shaken, wasn't seriously injured. Shrapnel had sliced across his arm, and the worst damage was to his eardrum, which was most likely blown out.

They'd faced pop-up ambushes here and there. Contact with the enemy was nothing new. But one of their own was injured from an RPG, and their Humvee was stuck in the middle of the road, useless. This was a significant and dangerous situation.

By the time CPT Bailey arrived with his element, the remainder of Saber Platoon and a few troop mechanics were coordinating evacuation and removal of the vehicle. Black Sheep had secured the site and was providing first aid. A few of the platoons' sections had set up a cordon search and were questioning the civilians who'd been nearby. Already a few Iraqi police officers were speaking with the soldiers.

COL Hickey and MAJ Silverman arrived with their crews soon after.

"We're five minutes late for movement on tonight's raid. What's the plan," Hickey asked CPT Bailey.

"Get after it, Dez," Silverman said.

Nodding, CPT Bailey radioed his platoon leaders, instructing them to link up at the traffic circle, just a few hundred meters east of the ambush point. Because of G Troop's quick response and C/I-22 IN's medical support, the ambush wouldn't have a significant impact on 1BCT's mission.

The troop had something; CPT Bailey realized. They'd responded well enough during the ambush by returning fire while simultaneously getting the troopers in the damaged Humvee out of the danger zone. Afterward, they'd executed the right tasks without receiving specific orders. There was more to G Troop than he'd expected — and there needed to be, because now the stakes were higher and survival required they adapt and evolve.

When the remainder of the troop arrived, CPT Bailey jumped into his Humvee and grabbed the hand mic. "Alright, let's execute the mission. We're 15 minutes behind schedule."

Though their response was quick and injuries minimal, as G Troop debriefed the ambush the following morning, more came to light.

"A palm-sized piece of metal from the RPG shot through the passenger side and the chamber that held up the differential, shaving the tops of one-inch bolts clean off. I ended up pulling it out of the tire on the driver's side. That's the type of force that missile had. Washburn was lucky," said Lapp.

Members of SSG Washburn's section could only recall seeing three combatants who had attacked from behind an above ground aqueduct. They had one RPG and two AK-47s against six scouts with .50 CALs and MK19s.

CPT Bailey told them, "We had the combat power to take them down. Kill or capture the enemy."

Later, CPT Bailey met with the platoon leaders and sergeants for a refresh on standard operating procedures. Referencing his worn Ranger Handbook, CPT Bailey reviewed actions on contact for near ambush, reiterating that they should be fought through. The troop needed an aggressive mindset to deal with the escalating attacks, yet this was vastly different than what they'd trained for.

"The mentality of scouts is to not become decisively engaged. We don't have half the firepower of an infantry platoon, and on top of that our platoons were broken up across a large area and positioned in observation posts or two vehicle patrols. Our job was to locate the enemy or gather intel. We were to break physical contact and maintain visual contact, not continue the fight," said Lay.

It was necessary that the scouts begin fighting back with more force. While some of the vehicle commanders had already done so, CPT Bailey immediately commanded the remainder of the troop to remove the doors to their Humvees. Because they weren't armored, the fiberglass doors offered no protection from enemy fire. With the doors gone, the troopers could quickly dismount, overwhelming the enemy with superior fire power and more elements (themselves) to focus on than just two vehicles.

"Until you're attacked by the enemy, and he takes a bite out of you, you don't know what his capabilities are. After that ambush, we knew they had RPGs and that we'd have to adjust our tactics," said Helmrich.

Every day and night, the troopers were either patrolling, performing dismounted operations, or interdicting mortar attacks on 4ID HQ. They started supporting ARSOF missions more often. The few troopers given recovery time were likely to be called in for a mission with ARSOF—finding time to rest was challenging. The troop practically lived out of their vehicles now, and many of the trucks needed repairs. All of them were in desperate need of new tires, but supplies were still low and vehicle parts a rare find.

Lay recalled, "The number of missions we were pulling in different directions quickly grew, and so did the pressure. We knew we had to get things right because we were basically creating the standard operating procedure for the units that would follow. We couldn't mess up because this wasn't just about 'getting it done,' we had to get it done the right and best way. That onus of responsibility weighed on all of us.

"Of course, we did make mistakes, I would be stunned if we hadn't because there was no rulebook for this type of war. It wore on us. There were some fistfights, and for no reason. No one could tell you why before or after, and there was no lasting damage to relationships. It was just tense, and there had to be outlets." Lay recalls.

AN ENTERPRISING FIRST SERGEANT

1SG John Justis deployed to Iraq with 3-66 AR, and by July, his unit was just north of Baiji, occupying a three-story building that would serve as the battalion's forward most position.

"We were in a real hostile town, full of insurgents," described 1SG Justis. "We got the base running but were constantly fighting and getting blown up on the roads by IEDs."

1SG Justis was leading counter-IED patrols while balancing

the endless duties of a First Sergeant, like tracking equipment maintenance, managing chow runs, and providing water to the company. It was on a counter-IED patrol that one of his troop's tanks ran over a triple stack of M21 mines. The shaken crew survived the explosion, but the tank's hull was split. Word quickly spread that the American M1 tank could be destroyed.

Word also reached COL Hickey, and when he came to investigate, it was 1SG Justis who briefed him on the details and plan of action. The colonel was adamant the company fix the tank and get it back into action, otherwise the enemy would sense a weakness and continue similar attacks. Without question, 1SG Justis took on the seemingly impossible task while continuing to fight against the enemy. The following week, COL Hickey returned to Baiji to personally inform him that he was reassigned to G Troop.

1SG Justis had plenty of reconnaissance experience, beginning in 1986 with the Light Horse Recon formation at Hohenfels, Germany. As a former Observer/Controller at the National Training Center, Justis had spoken about BRT-style concepts for years, and he was excited about the opportunity.

On his arrival at FOB Buffalo, 1SG Justis hit the ground running. "I met with the outgoing First Sergeant, William Taylor, for one day and then began my 30-60-90-day assessment to evaluate what's going on before making any changes. It was clear early on that the sooner some changes were made, the better off we'd be," Justis said.

His personal motto, "Make Shit Happen," had gotten him through the worst of the fighting in Baiji and always gave him the energy to do whatever was needed for his troopers. Something at the BRT was broken, and it was up to him to "Make Shit Happen" and fix it. Though it would be some time before he met CPT Bailey or the majority of G Troop, since they were always out, 1SG

Justis already had a mission in mind: he needed to understand the BRT, how it worked, where it didn't work, who the key scouts were, and what the troop needed.

"The first thing that caught my attention was a pile of beat up and broken Humvees with bald tires," shared 1SG Justis. "The scouts were driving hundreds of miles every day trying to find Saddam, main resistance leaders, and foreign fighters. They were setting up traffic control points, some of which led to vehicle chases on and off road. How were they doing any of that with their vehicles in such terrible shape?"

He visited the troop's maintenance area to speak with SGT Foisset about the state of the Humvees. From the lead mechanic, he learned one of the downsides of the BRT's organization: since they reported directly to 1BCT and acted as a separate group, G Troop wasn't being sourced for any parts. The organization had worked well at the National Training Center in the 1990s, but in the middle of Iraq during armed conflict, it wasn't working at all.

After several days of watching and listening, 1SG Justis caught on to the troopers' schedules. They would typically go 20 hours on patrol or missions, come back to sleep for two hours, and then go back out for an even longer period. 1SG Taylor had run chow, but there were many other ways the BRT needed to be supported. There were no morale boosting things to do, nothing for the troopers to come back to that could help them switch off for a few hours.

"After going 24 hours moving, shooting, and communicating, it's important to turn all that off so when you do go to sleep, it's more restorative. Otherwise, you'll become a ghost, exhausted and not thinking. Eventually, mistakes will be made," said Justis.

1SG Justis brought in a basketball and hoop, but the first day it was installed, two troopers injured their ankles playing. It was taken down the next day and quickly replaced with a TV and satellite dish.

"It was overwhelming trying to find out what everybody was and wasn't doing. I ran around by myself trying to find out where they were at night, joining patrols where I could. When I did formally meet him, I wanted to tell CPT Bailey what was needed. I knew that he was basically doing the same thing I was — going on missions, identifying what the guys were doing right or wrong after he issued an order. I knew we were both frustrated by the pace of operations and having to reel people in who'd been running wide open for months," said 1SG Justis.

Eventually, he was on full power mode to "Make Shit Happen." The troop needed ammo and equipment — 1SG Justis found a way to get it. They needed a refrigerator and replacement for the beat-up washing machine — he had it taken care of. He found the food coming in from the D-Main Dining Facility (DFAC) lacking and went to DFAC himself to ensure his troops got the best food the Army had to offer.

"The most positive change our troop had was 1SG Justis. He was a big part of our morale and tightness," said Lapp. "He was always involved with us, and if we needed something he made sure we got it. He knew the weight he had, and he threw it around when he needed to. You knew he was in charge, but he was a nice guy…even when he was an asshole."

The battle of the broken Humvees was ongoing a few weeks into his new assignment. Half of the BRT's trucks couldn't be driven, and all their tires had next to no tread. It was time to bridge the organizational gap.

1SG Justis visited FOB Speicher, an air installation close to Tikrit and 11km west of the Tigris. The FOB was mostly open space formed by a perimeter wall with tents and a few hangars and ammo bunkers within. He searched out the Supply Warrant Officer working in the brigade support area.

"I'm with G Troop, from 1st Brigade," he told her. "We're in bad need of some parts for our trucks."

"You guys don't really have a parent unit, so nobody's resourcing parts for you."

"I got that." He handed her a list of parts. "But we need this stuff urgently. What about those tires over there? It's a huge pile."

The officer agreed, "They're all new, but they're assigned to somebody else."

"So…I can't have any?"

She shook her head.

"Really? Okay. Keep that thought." 1SG Justis left FOB Speicher, a plan forming in his mind. There was no way a HQ needed all those tires. Their people worked nine to five jobs, they weren't out in the desert every day running patrols and fighting for their lives.

Later that night, 1SG Justis grabbed a few of the troopers and rolled back over to the brigade support area where they discreetly procured the tires. With everyone at the BSA off at 5:00 p.m., the guys had time to switch out the tires on their trucks then and there. They left a pile of very worn tires behind.

Frequently the enemy shot mortars across the river, hitting the stone walls and sandbags that filled FOB Buffalo's broken windows. It was common sense that every trooper had to be prepared for security threats at all times. This night was clearly not going to be one of those times, 1SG Justis realized as shirtless men wearing flip flops and sporadic pieces of body armor rushed past him to huddle around CPT Bailey, who stood in full gear.

My god, we're in Apocalypse Now, Justis thought.

The alarm had woken him, and without hesitation he'd jumped out of bed, threw on his gear, and grabbed his rifle. Once on the roof, it was clear the alarm was only a drill, but there was no relief to be had.

"I'm sure you thought you were ready," Bailey said, frustration sharpening his tone. "Response time? *Pretty* good. But what about the security plan?"

Silence.

Their commander continued, "Who's awake? Who isn't?"

Silence.

"What attire are we sleeping in so we don't show up to a fight looking like a toga party?" He pointed to several pairs of bare feet. "How are you going to maneuver on an enemy outside the wire like that?"

The pace of operations was hard to sustain, but there was no avoiding it. G Troop was exhausted, yet they were resilient—it was up to leadership to get them re-focused and refined.

HONING THE TROOP

"I think most of the troopers believed they weren't being taken care of because they were misfits or 'Goof Troop.' Once I fixed the DFAC situation and got them set up with things like the fridge and new tires, they realized that they were better than that. Now they had an aggressive commander and mission and a First Sergeant who took care of his troops," said Justis.

CPT Bailey and 1SG Justis did get their first—and many more—opportunities to sit down and talk shop. Their approach to improving the troop aligned once they figured out how the other operated.

"Justis was the kind of First Sergeant who wouldn't let you screw up, and I appreciated his willingness to provide opinions. He'd hound me about getting rest, allowing my crew to rest, and providing the platoons with refit time," recalled Bailey. "That had always been the challenge because we had to manage so much as a small unit."

The troop continued improving standard operating procedures for responding to enemy contact, deploying checkpoints, conducting raids, and supporting ARSOF. CPT Bailey assigned SSG Darden, a former infantryman and mortarman, as well as other former infantry soldiers from the troop to conduct refresher training to the platoons on how to enter and clear a building properly. Starting with the basics sketched out in the sand, the scouts refined entering and clearing a room (Battle Drill 6).

At the same time, 1SG Justis worked with the NCOs to clarify their roles and purpose as scouts: gathering and reporting information and assisting the senior NCOs as they developed their battlefield support plan.

"I refined our battlefield support plan because it was missing key aspects like floating target reference points, ambulatory evacuation points, and helicopter landing zones for emergency evacuations. Up until then, they'd been running around thinking they could make it up as they go or the commander would designate those areas as they planned for each mission," said 1SG Justis.

Once he was done, the battlefield was to G Troop's advantage, instead of something they determined for every patrol.

"1SG Justis joined the BRT at the right time. He knew where to focus, and his efforts to pass on his experience to our NCOs gave me time to develop the platoon leaders and gain a better understanding of our area of operations," said Bailey.

CPT Bailey assigned each platoon leader a functional area to build a staff organization within his troop (today, this is called a company operations and intelligence support team, or COIST, but back in 2003, CPT Bailey gave it the elaborate title of "troop staff").

1LT Jose Valero, a platoon leader for Black Sheep, was his intel officer who gathered the data from every patrol. 1LT John Williams, the new troop fire support officer, served as the key leader engagement officer because his platoon, the Scorpions, had a knack for finding Sheiks and connecting with the locals. Saber platoon's newest leader, 1LT Tapp, who was previously an infantry platoon leader in A/1-22 IN, became CPT Bailey's human pattern analysis officer and observed patterns of life in the villages, movement of traffic, and enemy attacks. Following LT Schaffer's departure from the unit, the Black Sheep platoon leader, LT Sweigart, assumed the position of Troop XO and soon after was promoted to Captain. (Both 1LTs Valero and Williams were also promoted to Captains around the same time as Sweigart). CPT Sweigart's main duty was to consolidate and build the AO Assessment using the data gathered from the three platoon leaders. This internal organization made the troop extremely effective in terms of understanding the AO, where the enemy could be, and where to focus their counter mortar operations each night to reduce attacks on 4ID HQ.

There are consequences for being an effective and flexible unit. For CPT Bailey, "The brigade took notice of our performance, and that meant an increased workload. But that worked just fine for us. We could capitalize on all the information gained from sister battalions and our own troop. I could see the pieces of the Salah Ad Din puzzle coming together."

COL Hickey wanted to maintain pressure on the enemy, and the one force he could control without disrupting battalion formations was G Troop. If the colonel needed information about an area not controlled by a battalion, he sent G Troop. If ARSOF requested support for a raid, he assigned them G Troop. The troopers continued conducting mounted and dismounted patrols and fighting through ambushes on the eastern side of the Tigris. They were running at a breakneck pace and putting more and more pressure on the enemy.

The enemy pressed back.

THE ENEMY SETS A TRAP

The war had no front line—the enemy wouldn't stand in front of Coalition Forces and fight, they remained hidden and illusive. Deep into the summer, several mortar attacks against 4ID HQ were successful. They originated from the east side of the Tigris, G Troop's area of operations.

To contend with the growing threats, COL Hickey authorized terrain denial fires, employment of mortars, attack aviation, Paladin artillery, and AC-130 gunship assets to identify and fire into "known points of origin" to deny the enemy access to those areas from which they launched attacks. Authority to control these assets and fires east of Tikrit was provided to the G Troop commander and facilitated by the Scorpion platoon—the artillery troopers of G Troop.

Integrating and synchronizing the daily and nightly terrain denial fires increased the complexity of the troop's mission. Not only were they responsible for conducting continuous reconnaissance patrols, interdiction patrols, and supporting ARSOF at a moment's notice, but now they also had to integrate and synchronize a significant range of assets that would employ munitions and could create an extreme amount of collateral damage.

"You want as many assets as you can get, but with more assets comes more responsibility and more requirements," explained Bailey. "When we received the counter-mortar terrain denial fires mission, I called a meeting with the platoon leaders and platoon sergeants. Scorpion's Platoon Leader, CPT Williams, had recently replaced McClusky who'd been promoted to Captain and moved to the Brigade Fires section. They were both critical to aligning these assets. I needed Scorpion platoon to help develop the fires plan and manage the routine terrain denial fires. This meant coordinating with 1-22 IN mortars, 4-42 FA fires, and a few air platforms that would support our mission. Since McClusky was now at Brigade, he helped us get the mission going."

For any of their missions, success required a holistic approach that incorporated strategies and concerns from all leadership in the troop. CPT Bailey remained focused on synchronizing indirect fires and reconnaissance patrols, the troop XO, CPT Sweigart, aimed to keep FOB Buffalo secure and integrate all the information collected by the platoons during their patrols, and 1SG Justis focused on morale, resupply, and rest to ensure the troopers could sustain the high operational tempo.

By distilling their concerns, they soon arrived at a course of action: daily patrol schedules and observation posts requirements on 4ID HQs' perimeter walls, FOB Buffalo security, and rest cycles that platoons rotated through. Using the zones he'd created earlier; CPT Bailey would roll dice each day to determine which zones the platoons would patrol or observe and which would receive terrain denial fires or aviation attacks. The dice kept the troop from forming a pattern, but intelligence from brigade, or observed enemy activity, could always trump the dice roll.

"We made sure the plan was flexible because partnering with ARSOF or a brigade level mission would upset the sequence. Breaking the overall mission down in this way and providing a relatively reliable routine that incorporated time off raised morale, which the troop needed," said Bailey.

The counter-mortar mission required G Troop to place observation posts on 4ID HQs' perimeter walls, where they had a commanding view of their AO. Using the LRAS3, the observers facilitated the fire missions by directing fires against those attempting mortar attacks. Once the targets for a mission were identified, the observers ensured the target area was clear. No one wanted to hurt civilians or needlessly destroy infrastructure. CPT Sweigart would oversee fire plans with Scorpion platoon and ensure each platoon had the bullets and maintenance support needed to maintain the schedule.

Now they had options when the troopers made contact with the enemy. CPT Bailey could send a patrol or attack aviation to the area of activity, or he could let the observation posts conduct a fire mission.

The plan worked, but the enemy fought back; neither the ambushes nor mortar attacks slowed. When they heard a mortar firing, CPT Bailey's section and the platoon on patrol would move to the sound of the guns in an attempt to close with and destroy the enemy. There was some success with this approach, despite the size of the AO. However, by late August, the insurgents recognized the response and set traps.

One evening in early September, an 82mm mortar, protected within a walled courtyard about three kilometers from the palace complex, began firing rapidly at 4ID's HQ. CPT Bailey and a section of Scorpion Platoon rushed toward their origin.

The enemy was ready.

RPGs flew in front of the Humvees, and for the first time since arriving in Iraq, CPT Bailey saw the green tracers of Soviet-era ammunition streak through the BRT's formation. Just as they were trained to do, PFC Helmrich slammed on the brakes and the gunner, CPL Monroe fired back with his .50 CAL. Scorpion

Platoon followed course, responding with a combination of .50 CAL, 240B and M29 fire.

Stopped within a raging wall of green, explosive light, CPT Bailey realized they were being fired on from both sides of the road.

"Keep friggin' moving," he yelled over the explosions and crack of small arms fire. "We're in the kill zone! Move forward!"

PFC Helmrich slammed on the gas, pushing through the ambush, and stopping 70 meters forward. CPT Bailey's crew and Scorpion platoon dismounted, firing into a darkness lit only with orange and green lines of fire.

Gripping the hand mic, CPT Bailey said, "Raider Main, this is Recon 6. Contact...wait...out!"

When the bursts of rounds ceased, the enemy dead or running, CPT Bailey returned to the truck and gave orders to search the surrounding area for wounded enemy. The area where the insurgents had staged the ambush was on fire and abandoned munitions were exploding. Regular 6 — LTC Steven Russell, commander of 1-22 IN — with his own patrol had seen the wall of fire from across the Tigris and rushed over to provide support. Before heading out, LTC Russell reminded CPT Bailey his mechanized company was at the ready whenever needed.

A security team was left at the site and 1-22 IN provided a platoon to assist in searching for the enemy while the remainder of G Troop continued their nightly missions. Throughout the night a fire burned across the ambush site, interrupted only by exploding munitions. With daybreak, all that could be found were blood trails and abandoned sandals, no enemy KIA. *No one should've survived the wall of fire we laid down*, Bailey thought.

After investigating the ambush, they learned the enemy had used both the aqueducts walled courtyard — that belonged to a small family who had no prior knowledge of the attack — for cover. The aqueducts, littered in hundreds of .50 CAL and 240B round impacts, had clearly been a smart choice as the structures meandered alongside the road, sometimes a few feet above ground and other times only a few inches. The unseen attackers had hidden behind the aqueducts where they dipped closer to the ground, fitting their rifles in the few inches of space. Others had crawled beneath them, using the three-foot wide concrete span to provide overhead cover.

It was clear that someone in the insurgency knew how to observe the troop's actions and reactions, set up an ambush, and lure them into a trap. CPT Bailey was thankful none of the troopers were injured. The enemy had selected the perfect area for an ambush and the aqueducts and walled court yards of surrounding homes had proved useful for their purpose.

Unbeknownst to the troop, MG Odierno was sitting on the front porch of his quarters at 4ID HQ and witnessed this ambush. The following day he came to the troop FOB, handed out a few coins to the troopers, and watched SpongeBob SquarePants cartoons with Scorpion platoon.

"Being an artilleryman, he seemed to enjoy hanging out with them that day. We all thought his visit was special, and we appreciated the attention. I think it made us work harder at our tasks," Bailey recalled. "We were fortunate to have the leaders we had. From division commander to brigade commander, they were aggressive, supportive, and friggin' smart. By September, several junior leaders had emerged within the troop. 1SG Justis was handling his support requirements, the platoon leaders and platoon sergeants understood the daily patrol schedule and were executing with minimal guidance, and I could finally absorb what *had* happened, what *was* happening, and think about the next mission."

G Troop had found their stride.

Recon 701

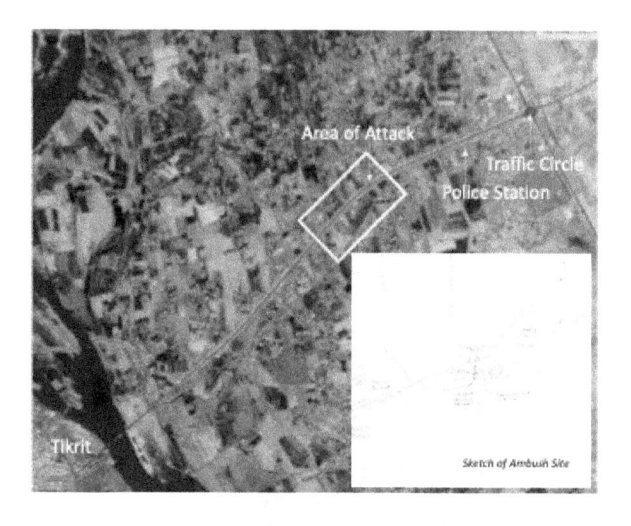

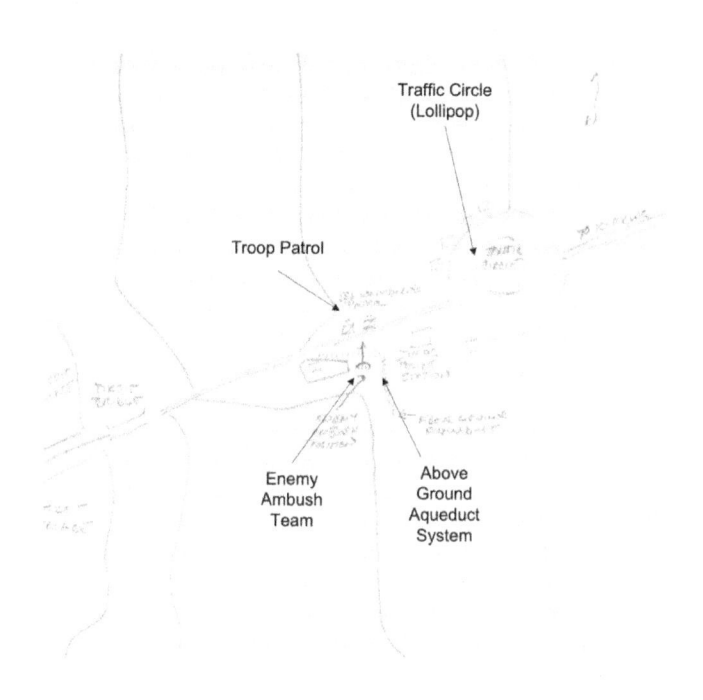

CPT Bailey's after action report sketch of the site of G Troop's first significant ambush in which an RPG was launched at Saber Platoon, just past "the Lollipop"—a traffic circle on this road into Tikrit.

*From left to right, MSG Rick Michaud, MG
Raymond Odierno, and 1SG John Justis*

7. The Long Night

SEPTEMBER 2003

"They're gone, but not forgotten. The memories of our brothers never leave us."

— Specialist John Almen

In September, enemy activity throughout Salah Ad Din Province hit an all-time high. COL Hickey's plan to keep the pressure on was working, and the enemy fought back in earnest. Mortar attacks and ambushes became an almost daily occurrence. The terrain denial fires plan was in full swing, and intel uncovered by 1BCT led to regular raids that unearthed elements of the insurgency.

G Troop was so involved in these efforts that attack aviation elements would fly to the eastern side of Tikrit and ask if the troop required support. The U.S. Air Force's fixed wing aircraft and AC-130 gunships contacted the brigade often, asking if "Recon" needed assistance. Even at brigade HQ, staff members joked with CPT Bailey, calling him Contact 6 instead of his actual call sign, Recon 6.

Their success was just as noticeable to the enemy. If G Troop could be stopped, 1BCT's plan to hunt down insurgents in the hinterlands would face a major setback.

On September 18, COL Hickey received intelligence that an attack was planned on an American base in Tikrit. Believing the target was 1BCT's FOB Raider, COL Hickey instructed CPT Bailey to take two platoons west of the Tigris and south of FOB Raider to conduct a screen line. As a screening force, platoons Saber and Black Sheep would report enemy activity and impede or destroy as necessary. Scorpion platoon would continue their regular patrols within Abu Ajeel and head out to a small village just north of Ad Dawr.

Prior to departure, CPT Bailey approved a previously off-limits zone for Scorpion to drive through. The zone had a levee road that was inaccessible for some time because of an aqueduct cutting through it. The night before, CPT Bailey and 1SG Justis had taken their patrols down the road and confirmed it was now passable.

This particular stretch of road had an L-shaped bend a few meters north of a rock quarry, which could provide enemy forces with plenty of hiding locations and direct fire cover. CPT Bailey believed that, from several points within that zone, the enemy would place mortar fire on FOB Raider, 4ID HQ, and possibly FOB Buffalo. Four Humvees from Scorpion, under the command of CPT Williams, would interdict any attacks as they patrolled the new zone as well as the area across the river from FOB Raider. The small remainder of G Troop troopers were stationed on the walls encircling 4ID HQ and FOB Buffalo. From HQ's observation posts, 1LT Tapp, who recently joined the troop, would coordinate terrain denial fires on the eastern side of the Tigris, watch for enemy activity, and provide support to Scorpion platoon.

Within Scorpion platoon, SPC Szott had the night off, but with so much going on lately, they'd been mixing crews so more vehicles could go on patrol. They were all a little overworked, but the night could get interesting given the intel warning, so they manned an additional vehicle.

He was the last one out to the vehicles, and SPC James Wright was already up in the gun turret of the lead Humvee. The 27-year-old was previously a Marine who'd decided to leave behind civilian life once again after 9/11. He'd told SPC Szott once that it was his duty to take care of his country and his family, including his wife, who'd also served in the Marine Corps and re-enlisted alongside him. She was back at Fort Hood, a nuclear, chemical, and biological weapons expert with 1st Cavalry Division while SPC Wright was the driver for SGT Ray's vehicle.

"Hey, listen, man," Wright said, "Let me take the gun tonight."

"Works for me," Szott said, jumping into the driver's seat beside SGT Ray.

As the crew was preparing to depart FOB Buffalo, SFC Flores decided to join the patrol this evening, anticipating that contact with the enemy was likely, he wanted to be with his platoon, so he took a position in the rear passenger seat of SGT Ray's vehicle.

Taking up position as lead vehicle, SPC Szott and the three vehicles behind him set off across the Tigris and headed south. For several weeks there'd been significant harassment fire and mortar rounds aimed at 4ID HQ. Finally, from their observation posts, G Troop determined where the enemy was firing from.

Just ahead of the targeted area, SPC Szott took a hard left. It felt like the right thing to do, a strange impulse. "What're you doing," Ray asked from the passenger's seat. "You're going the wrong way."

"Yeah, but we can go this way," Szott replied, thinking back to when he'd been on overwatch and seen the mortar fire flashing on the ground.

"Back it up and go the way we know."

"Alright, but I think the enemy's this way, closer to the river." Szott backed up the Humvee and turned onto their regular route.

Suddenly, while traveling along a very narrow canal road, green tracers lit through clouds of dust and dirt 2-3 meters from the lead vehicle driver's door. RPGs exploded brilliantly in the dark. Small arms fire came from either side, crisscrossing the road; the patrol was caught in an "L" shaped ambush.

SPC Wright screamed "contact!" as he returned fire with his M240B. With muzzle flashes just two meters away, SPC Szott attempted to exit the driver's seat, returning fire with his rifle, but was met with an RPG denotation at his feet pushing him back into the seat of the vehicle. Dozens of rounds hit the truck.

"To be that close to a bullet was something you never forget. First you feel the heat, then the pressure of the air next to your cheek then you hear it a second later." Szott recalls.

"The gunfire was close and overwhelming, but we continued to return fire; we were in a fight for our lives."

Prior to the attack, Scorpion's four crews had split into two sections to cover more ground. SGT Caleb Branch, SPC Fugate's vehicle commander, had just finished up their typical round of questioning with a civilian—had they seen any orange and black taxis driving around?—and they were back to patrolling.

At one of the village's few crossroads, SPC Fugate called down to PFC Robert Andrade, "We always go right, let's go left."

PFC Andrade turned left and the Humvee behind them followed. A few meters away, SPC Fugate saw the two Humvees commanded by SGTs Ray and Thompson turning right. From the gunner's seat, SPC Fugate flipped off SPC Wright who was gunner for the SGT Ray's truck. SPC Wright acknowledged with the same friendly gesture as his truck began turning left, stalled for a moment, backed up and then continued straight down their regular route, a lightless road lined by ditches. Where the levee road had once ended, they would now continue, driving between open land and a rock quarry where they'd concluded insurgents were shooting mortars from.

The sharp, cannon-like whoosh of multiple RPGs firing rang through the streets, followed with immediate explosions and small arms fire.

"Contact," Fugate yelled. "Turn around, turn around!"

SPC Andrade whipped the Humvee around, pressed hard on the gas. The truck turned wide, lurched forward. Green tracers lit the area ahead of them. SPC Fugate could only see one Humvee, stopped, and was surrounded in a wall of small arms fire. Where was SGT Thompson's truck? Hadn't they been directly behind the lead Humvee?

SPC Branch and Andrade jumped out of the truck, checking out the front of the vehicle. SPC Andrade cursed. "What is it?"

Branch called up, "We're stuck!"

SPC Fugate motioned for the other Humvee to go around them. They stopped briefly beside SGT Branch, then sped off toward the firefight. If the truck was stuck, there was no point in SGT Branch and SPC Andrade sticking around when they could be supporting their guys.

"Go on," Fugate said, "I'll secure the truck and radio SGT Ray." No comms had come through yet, and the silence was unnerving.

Multiple reports were coming in from those on guard at FOB Buffalo. They were under attack, and it was small arms fire from across the river. Another report claimed that something—most likely a mortar round—had flown over the gate into FOB Buffalo.

CPT Sweigart rushed up to the palace roof alongside SSG Womack. Green tracers dotted with larger explosions glared outward from the distant village Scorpion was patrolling. The distant, thunderous explosions in between briefer, steadier cracks meant RPGs. That report hadn't been made over the radio—yet. CPT Sweigart needed to get Scorpion support however possible, and fast. But first, FOB Buffalo had to be secured.

It was easier said than done amidst the confusion. With the majority of more experienced troops on patrol or conducting the screen line, G Troop's base only had a few troopers pulling guard.

"Get some wired comms up here," CPT Sweigart ordered. They needed to communicate with everyone throughout the FOB to check reports and clear fires. He then radioed CPT Bailey: "Recon 6 this is Recon 5, we're observing small arms fire that appears oriented on the command post—" recalls Bailey.

CPT Williams, who was with his platoon on the east side of the Tigris disrupted the transmission, his voice sounding almost frantic. "Recon 6, this is Scorpion 1. We've been ambushed. I got three men with no pulse and one MIA."

As CPT Sweigart continued listening to reports coming in, it became clear that if someone *had* shot a mortar or two over the gate, it had been a quick diversionary tactic. No enemies were mounting an attack below the FOB walls, and it seemed that the fire they'd received was splash from the ambush on Scorpion.

CPT Bailey came over the radio, "Recon 5, situation report. Over."

"We might've observed small arms fire from the ambush," Sweigart replied. "I don't think we're being attacked."

Nearby, MSG Michaud was directing gunners to keep shooting flares over the Scorpion patrol so they could have better visibility. The remaining gunners on the troop command post roof were returning fire. Amidst the chaos, CPT Sweigart tried to determine if the troop command post was under attack and if the troopers firing from his location might place fires on the Scorpion platoon in the ambush area.

"I didn't think they could even see what they were shooting at, which could become problematic quickly—if they overshot, they would most likely hit their own men," Sweigart recalls.

He mapped out where the enemy and Scorpion platoon were, and had the troopers slow down and check their fire to avoid firing upon their own men.

Another communication from CPT Bailey, "Do you need support from one of my platoons?"

"Negative," Sweigart replied.

PFC Lay was on roof guard at FOB Buffalo, along with a mix of other troopers, including SGTs Sharpless, Michaud, Swilley, and PFC Ellis. He'd spent the evening walking back and forth between the hand crank radio that would buzz the command center below, and the mounted 240 machine gun that faced in towards the trees close to the FOB, away from the river.

The customary darkness was interrupted with the white flashes of mortar rounds landing along the cliffside and inside the road that ran into their base. Most likely another mortar man launching the 60-millimeter rounds from the back of his truck. PFC Lay immediately cranked the radio and just as he began to report the attack, the mortar rounds hit inland with an echoing thud, missing the base. The roof guards at their .50 CALs and 240 machine guns fired into the wood line.

Further up the eastern side of the river, where Scorpion was patrolling, dim flashes burst, followed by muted explosions and rapid pops. Was it another ambush or had Scorpion found the group who'd been firing mortars at Raider? *Either way, the prob-*

lem is... Sergeant Ray hasn't radioed, Lay thought. *Crap.* SGT Ray was leading the patrol, and if they were in contact, he should have communicated by now.

Flares shot up in the air, lighting up the river and trees. Green and red tracers erupted from Scorpion's patrol area. Seconds, minutes had gone by and still no communication from Sergeant Ray. Their FOB was still being fired upon, and troopers yelled at one another over their own rapid fire.

PFC Lay jerked as someone grabbed his arm.

"Private." Swilley stood beside him, calm among the confusion.

"Sir," Lay said, the blood pounding in his ears easing off. If you didn't know what to do or were wondering what the hell you were even doing there, SGT Swilley always appeared just in time to re-focus you in that chaotic moment.

The sergeant let go of his arm and pointed south, away from the lights and sounds of battle. "I need you to illuminate that building. We're taking fire from it."

As his vision adjusted, PFC Lay could make out a three-story house. "Got it, sir."

Aiming above the house, he shot a white star-cluster.

Aim's a little off, he thought as the shell burst through a window on the top floor, filling a room instantaneously with thick smoke and white light. Flames erupted from within.

His aim was *absolutely* off. But the building was now illuminated, and FOB Buffalo would no longer take fire from it.

"...Alright," Swilley said. "Target suppressed. We're moving out, get in your truck."

The fire fight continued to rage on with more RPGs detonating and rounds impacting and penetrating the driver's side of the vehicle.

"Our crew served weapon stopped suddenly and I could feel

SPC Wright fall against my shoulders. Worse yet I could feel a warm liquid covering my back. Wright was saying something, but it was just background noise to all of the explosions and gunfire. We needed to get off the X (an expression used to describe an objective, or in this case, the kill zone)." Szott explains.

With his legs still numb from the explosion, relief swept over him as he could feel his toes pressing against the gas pedal. They exited the kill-zone as fast as possible.

Szott continues, "SGT Ray was back in the passenger seat, trying to operate the radio. With one hand on the wheel, I used my other hand to try and assist SGT Ray with repairing our radio that had also been shot."

SGT Ray's hand was badly injured, and he couldn't use his fingers.

"Thompson drove off the road, into a ditch," Ray said shaking his hand at SPC Szott.

"His left hand looked like he was holding a broken bag of hot-dogs as he began to struggle with the radio…"

"You good," Szott asked, taking the radio from him.

"Yeah," Ray said, lifting his head up. He cleared his throat and yelled my gun is jammed; where is Wright? SFC Flores responds.

"Wright is down, he isn't breathing." Replied SFC Flores.

Suddenly, SPC Fugate came over the platoon radio. His vehicle was stuck in a ditch within a small village to the north of the main ambush area. Now they were in contact, but SGT Branch and PFC Andrade exited the vehicle and returned fire with support from LT William's crew. LT Williams, with SGT Dale Sylvester (Sly) and his crew, PFC Jason Carr and SPC Shane Valley, immediately turned their vehicle towards the ambush site and drove south cross-country to assist their sister section.

Back in the main ambush area, SPC Szott coordinated with Viper, who had two AH-64s on station. He provided Viper 6, the Company Commander for the aviation unit, with the location of SPC Fugate's crew and then coordinated support for his crew as they broke contact and departed the ambush area.

"Viper 6 was more than happy to lay down some 30-mm love." Says Szott.

From the passenger seat of SGT Ray's vehicle, SFC Flores took the repaired radio and began to call in the Nine-line so medical support would be ready to receive his injured troopers.

Still driving the Humvee, SPC Szott reached down to feel a large piece of hot shrapnel still inside his right thigh. He quickly pulled it out, but the heat was so intense that he quickly let loose of it. Remembering the pain in his left thigh, he quickly felt his leg and found a large hole on the side. Somewhat panic stricken, he felt the other side of his leg and found a much larger exit hole.

"I've been shot." Szott reconciles to himself.

"SGT Flo," he said, "You only called in two injuries, I'm hit in the legs."

"What…wait what?!" Flores' voice was tinged with panic.

"I got shot in the leg!"

"We have to go back and get them!"

SGT Ray jumped up on the gun, loaded and racked the 240B while SPC Szott quickly reloaded his M4.

"I could feel pure fear running through me and I remember saying to myself, "this is it, this is where you die." Recalls Szott.

In a single exhale he could feel all the fear leaving his body, peace and acceptance to the same. With the fear leaving his body he could only feel renewed strength and anger as he slammed the pedal to the floor. The team of 4 had 3 badly injured, this was the

Army's definition of "combat ineffective" and going back to the kill-zone was to welcome death, but they were not going to leave anyone behind.

The enemy fire was overwhelming. They were heavily armed and dug-in. They were upwards of 20 enemy concentrating all of their fires on the lead vehicle in hopes to create a 2.5-ton road block with the vehicle.

Despite the enemy focusing their volume of fire directly at the lead vehicle, SGT Ray, SPC Szott, and SFC Flores came roaring back into the kill zone with guns blazing. In the face of their daring counter-attack, the ambushers froze and then fled desperately into the darkness of the desert. The final, kamikaze assault the crew made to save their comrades was the right one.

SGT Sylvester's section arrived at the ambush as SGT Ray and Szott approached Thompson's vehicle. PFC Carr recalls seeing the bodies of SGT Thompson and Arriaga lying in the road – they apparently fell out after being hit. Both Sly and Ray's crews continued to return fire, as they approached Thompson's vehicle, but the attackers were fleeing the scene and only offered sporadic bursts of small arms fire as they disappeared into the darkness.

When they reached SGT Thompson's smoking Humvee, SGT Sly and Carr jumped out to check on the soldiers. SPC Szott parked his vehicle in position to shield medical evacuation efforts. SPC Szott noticed an un-detonated RPG round in the Humvee – still smoking. SFC Flores and SPC Szott exited their vehicle and ran to the injured soldiers on the ground. SPC Szott turned his friend Arrioga over, his face and glasses were covered in a coat of dirt, and he was unresponsive. SGT Sly reports that SGT Thompson isn't breathing. Assessing the situation, CPT Williams contacts CPT Bailey and reports, "Recon 6, Scorpion 1, I have two soldiers who are breathing and have no pulse, and one missing…"

"He isn't breathing." Szott shouts.

SGT Sly and Carr picked up Arriaga and placed him in the backseat of their truck and Thompson on the front of their hood – no time to wait for a standard casualty evacuation vehicle, they had to use the vehicles they had. SPC Szott's leg is starting to cramp from his wound, but he and SGT Ray assisted their sister crew with loading the casualties in the vehicle. But they weren't done yet; SPC Cross, SGT Thompson's gunner was missing. Both crews began looking for Cross, calling out his name and running through the smoke and darkness to find him. After several minutes, they decided to evacuate the casualties. CPT Williams informed CPT Bailey that Cross was still missing, and both crews departed the ambush site and drove directly to the casualty collection point. CPT Bailey and the other two platoons, Blacksheep and Saber, were beginning to establish a perimeter around the ambush site with an emphasis on finding Cross.

SPC Christopher Cross—was one of their newest and youngest troopers. He'd dismounted and raced out of the kill zone on foot once he saw his truck was on fire. With his SGT and driver unresponsive, and SGT Ray's vehicle exiting the kill zone, he was alone and surrounded by the enemy. Taking flight he ran to several civilian vehicles, looking for one with keys in the ignition. After a few moments, he heard the rumbling exhaust note of a Humvee. It was SSG Marroquin's crew establishing a perimeter around the ambush site. As he ran to the vehicle he shouted "RECON!...RECON!".

From start to finish, the initial ambush was under five minutes. For G Troop, however, it would signify the longest night of the deployment—and for many of the troopers, the longest night of their lives.

For their actions SGT Ray and SPC Szott were awarded the Silver Star.

Recon 701

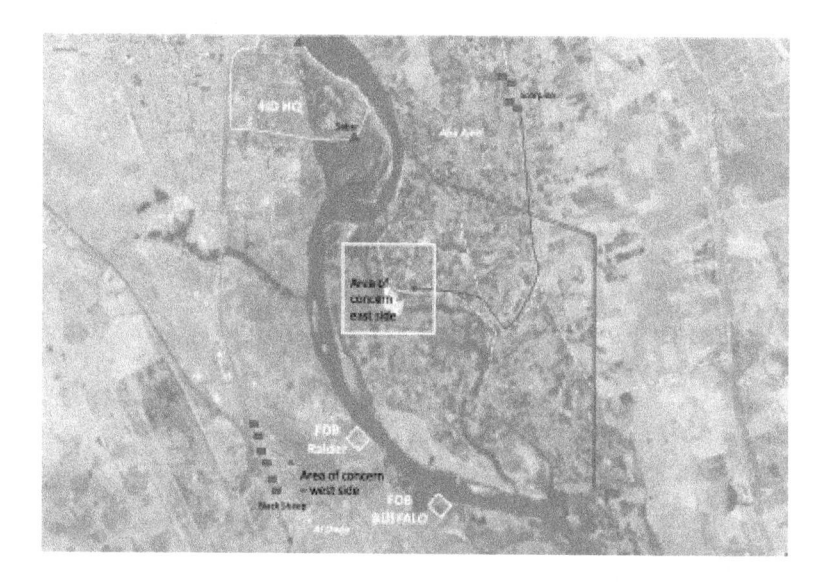

On September 18, 2003, G Troop responded to a potential attack by conducting a screen line—led by CPT Bailey—on the west side of the Tigris, near FOB Raider and stationing troopers at 4ID HQ and FOB Buffalo. Scorpion platoon would patrol an area of interest in Abu Ajeel.

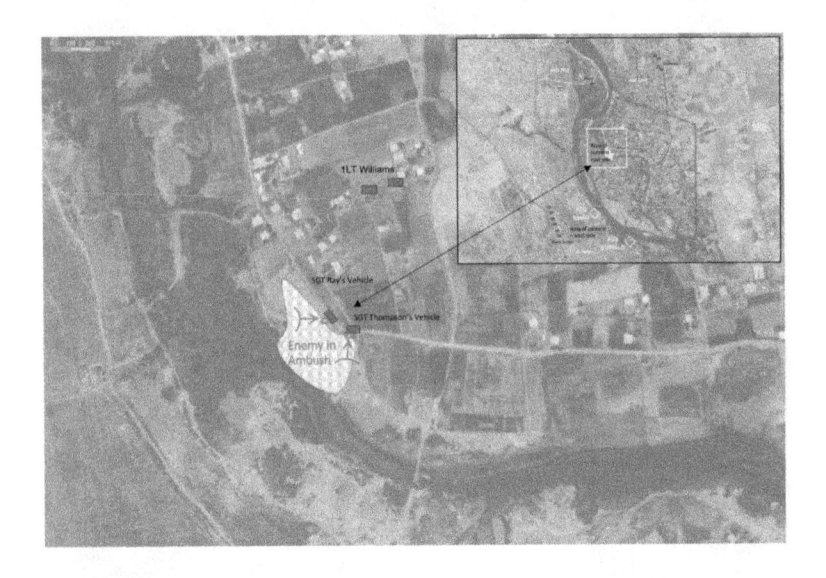

SGT Ray and SGT Thompson's vehicles were caught in an L-shaped ambush. This type of ambush is typically set up at a bend in a road and triggered when the opponent is well into the kill zone. Cross fire from the short and long 'legs'—which form an L shape—of the ambushers prevents attempts at getting out of the kill zone.

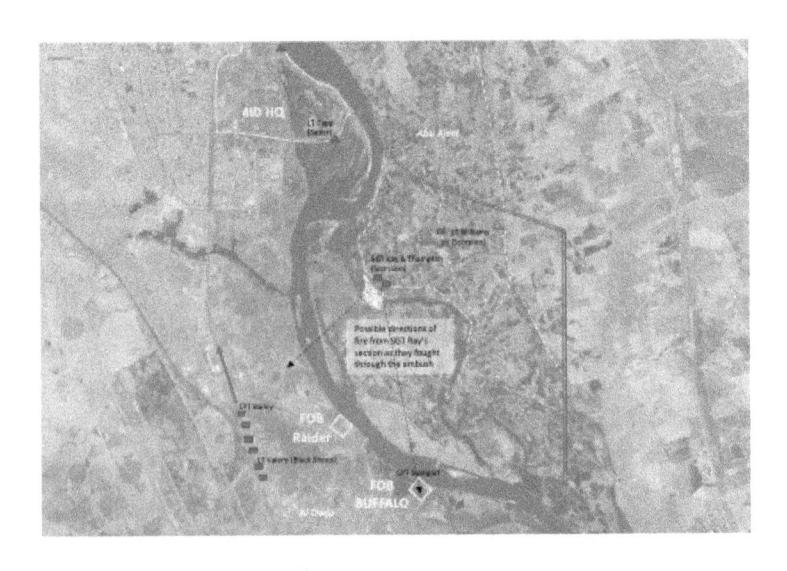

Possible Directions of Fire from SGT Ray's section as they fought

8. Brothers Lost

SEPTEMBER 2003

"We expected to hear them on the radio, sit down next to us at the chow hall, or jump in our truck."

—Aaron Helmrich, Specialist

"Sitrep?" Justis asked the sergeant.

SFC Flores gave him a breakdown of the ambush and told 1SG Justis that he was bringing in Wright, Arriaga, Thompson, Ray, and Szott.

It was everything he'd never wanted to happen, and it'd only taken a few, interminable minutes.

"Take the floating bridge," Justis said, "the other bridge is too risky for this."

He immediately contacted CSM Pete Martinez, the 1-22 IN Command Sergeant Major whom Justis had worked with back at 3-66 AR. "Pete, I got KIAs coming across the bridge, and I need support on the other side."

"What do you mean you got KIAs?"

Justis shared what he could. "I'm rolling right now to get them to you and get 'em evac'd."

"We'll take care of them, Justis," Martinez said, his brief shock replaced with a sober, reverent tone.

By the time CPT Bailey arrived with his crews from Saber and Black Sheep, 1SG Justis, SFC Flores, and CPT Williams were working with 1-22 IN to get the evacuation vehicle loaded. SFC Flores had driven in with SGT Thompson on the hood of the Humvee and SPCs Arriaga and Wright in the back.

CPT Bailey was oddly quiet as he helped carry SPC Wright's body to the back of the vehicle. His features churned from anger to exhaustion, hatred to grief.

From the HQ observation posts, 1LT Tapp reported upwards of 60 enemy personnel in the vicinity of the ambush, armed with rifles and RPGs. He gave their locations to Viper 6 over the radio, and moments later 1SG Justis heard an AH-64 open fire with its 30mm cannon.

"Cross is still out there in the chaos," Bailey finally said.

Justis placed his hand on the commander's shoulder. "I got the men. You go kill the enemy."

Bailey grabbed his radio, ordering Saber and Black Sheep to cordon off the area, recover their men, and move inward. They'd search every house and detain every man between the ages of 18 and 38 until the enemy was found. He followed up with Viper 6 and then departed with a vehicle crew from Saber, heading south to execute the fight from higher ground.

When SPC Szott and SGT Ray arrived at FOB Iron Horse, medics rushed toward them asking for the walking wounded as others ran forward with gurneys. With no energy or desire to speak, SPC Szott waved his hand and walked into the aid station. His leg now starting to hurt and function poorly, he walked steadily into the aid station. The medics, once they realized their walking wounded had walked by them, rushed forward, grabbing him in a panic.

SPC Szott slowly raised his hand again but this time to create distance. "Back off! Get your hands off me!"

"I need to get your gear off," the medic replied desperately, taking a startled step backward.

"I'll take my own gear off, here hold this…" Szott held his rifle tight with adrenaline still pumping, he didn't want to let it go. He took off his Kevlar helmet and body armor with one hand. Finally, very purposefully loosening his grip, SPC Szott handed over his weapon. Szott was placed on a medical gurney next to SPC Arriga and SPC Wright as they attempted to revive them. As they treated his wounds, he stared into his friend's eyes, wishing he could do something, anything.

I should have known, Bailey thought, clenching his fists. *They weren't going after the largest force; they were going after the smallest unit.*

When COL Hickey had first given him the orders, he'd voiced concern. They weren't completely positive who the attack was aimed towards, and sending such a large part of G Troop's force to a single location could put the remaining troopers at greater risk.

He hadn't fought hard enough. He should have said no or sent another section with Scorpion platoon. He shouldn't have opened the levee road for patrols—a road that had been off limits for patrols for some time due to a small canal cut through it. Bailey and 1SG Justis had just days before the incident patrolled the area and noticed the canal cut had been filled in, so Bailey opened the road for patrols just hours before the Scorpion patrol departed for the mission.

Bailey also thought that even if they were good at seeing indicators of enemy movement, he shouldn't have kept 1LT Tapp and the remainder of his platoon on the 4ID wall, he should have put them out with Scorpion to give them more combat power. He could have asked 1-22 IN to man the observation posts that night and sent out even more of G Troop to back up Scorpion. There were so many choices he could have made that might have prevented the losses.

While CPT Bailey watched the cordon swiftly come together, SSG Marroquin with Black Sheep reported that they'd found SPC Cross.

SPC Cross is safe, CPT Bailey inwardly repeated. The relief he felt was significant, but it paled to the rage that tightened his throat and chest—the thoughts racing through his mind were of avenging his wounded and fallen comrades.

It wasn't long before COL Hickey arrived with his crew. "We're here to support you," he said just before sending SGT Saffeels' crew to join the cordon. As the gun truck drove off, he said, "You got three KIA, and two WIA."

"Our MIA's been found. Unharmed," Bailey replied.

"Good. I've tasked 1-22 IN to send a company across the river and assist. It will take some time before they're here. What's your plan?"

Beneath the light of flares, insurgents ran from Viper's 30-mm cannon fire without thought, throwing their weapons into cisterns, hoping to disappear into the desert or blend in with the civilians.

The cordon tightened around the village as COL Hickey repeated that 1-22 IN was deploying a mechanized company to assist. This time he told CPT Bailey that he was to coordinate with CPT Brad Boyd, C/1-22 IN's company commander. G Troop would keep the area isolated while CPT Boyd's company cleared it. Every car that came in would be checked, every person questioned, every military age male detained.

Through night vision goggles, Bailey watched rounds from an AH-64 Apache explode in a fine line behind an attacker. The man barely made it across a road and into a house.

"Light 'em up," Bailey said over the radio.

The helicopter shot a few rounds into the building, and a swarm of children ran out.

"Cease fire! Cease fire! Troops, close in on the house and detain the individual."

Hickey gave a slight nod. "Stay focused and don't jump to conclusions."

"Yes, sir."

1SG Justis joined CPT Bailey soon after, informing him that some sections of the Scorpion platoon were still clearing houses near the ambush site.

Justis advised, "I suggest the rest of the Scorpion platoon be removed from the battlefield."

"Yes, good call," Bailey said.

At the end of the long night, they'd detained around 40 military-age men. One had admitted to taking part in the ambush and agreed to point out others involved. The infantry soldiers lined them up, while the detainee, sitting in the back of a Humvee, identified seven individuals who were part of the ambush. These individuals were immediately handed over to the 4ID military police.

Leaders of the resistance had provided these young men with RPGs, rifles, and very little training. They'd paid them to attack the American soldiers who would come by. The men had hidden in the rock quarry, aqueducts, and ditches, waiting as instructed. Their marksmanship was poor and several times they'd forgotten to pull the safety pins out of the RPG before launching. The attack could have been far worse.

SPC Almen, SGT Saffeels, and SPC Ribus had observed the ambush from FOB Raider, left immediately with COL Hickey, and arrived after it was over. They hadn't known much to start, only that there'd been an attack and they were to help cordon off the area.

When they'd set off to join G Troop's cordon, it was clear that the colonel was going to let CPT Bailey handle whatever he needed to take care of, and all three men agreed that it was the right choice. Their captain was a strong leader, and no matter how hard it was, he wasn't about to let emotions take over.

Once the firefight had ended and the enemy detained, COL Hickey tasked the troop to overwatch the ambush site for the remainder of the night. When the sun came up, other members of the troop arrived to remove the disabled Humvees and recover any equipment that might have been left at the ambush site.

SPC Almen walked over to one of the trucks. It looked like Swiss cheese with all the bullet holes. SPC Wright's Kevlar helmet lay on the ground, upside down and bloody.

Three of his own gone. It was too much. He walked away.

Once the site was cleaned, he, SGT Saffeels, and SPC Ribus would head out once again with the colonel. The mission would continue whether they were dead or alive, and he couldn't let the loss of his brothers affect his focus. If he did, the chances were high that he'd be the next one dead.

He missed them; he would always miss them. But he had to concentrate on the mission because there were two men—who were very much alive—in the truck with him, and he intended for them to stay alive.

SPC Szott would later learn that when the casualty report was called in, he and SGT Ray had been reported KIA. Because of this, the medical evacuation aircraft were called off and the two were taken by ground evacuation about 80 kilometers south to Air Base Anaconda, just outside of Balad.

"For much of the following day, most of G troop had been told I was dead. Everyone was so shocked to see him at the hospital recovering from four hours of surgery," recalls Szott.

Once at the air base's Combat Surgical Hospital, SPC Szott argued with the nurse trying to take down his mother's name and phone number.

"I refused to let them have her number, I was going to call her. I didn't want her thinking for even a second that the stranger on the line was calling to say her son was KIA. If she heard my voice, she would at least immediately know I'm alive, no matter how bad things were," said Szott.

On the phone, he assured her he was okay. With tears in her voice, she asked, "Well, you get to come home now, right?" But then he told her a small, white lie—no, he wouldn't be leaving Iraq. Even though he was injured, they were keeping him on.

Treating his left leg, where the bullet had penetrated, was a very long surgery. The bullet came within a quarter inch of his femoral artery. The surgeon was insistent that SPC Szott go to Germany for additional surgeries with SPC Ray.

After two days, word came that the doctor was pushing to send SPC Szott and SGT Ray to Germany for better treatment. But in Szott's mind, there was no way he was going to leave his unit and his band of brothers.

"I came back to the unit because we were just a team of 16, and we'd lost three of our guys and SGT Ray was sent to Germany.

That meant we'd lost 25 percent of our unit overnight. I wanted everyone to know that things were going to be okay. So, I stayed and acted as normal as possible," says Szott.

Determined to escape the hospital, he called up SPC Fugate and a few of the other guys, who made up a reason to drive down to the air base to "break them out". With a clean uniform in hand, he changed clothes in a porta-potty, and departed the hospital with his rescue party. A few days later, he removed the stitches himself with a pocketknife and toenail clippers.

When they made it back to their unit, SSG Darden told them that for 12 hours, the troopers had thought everybody in the truck was KIA.

"Tommy said it was a big deal for us to come back. They'd heard on the brigade command net that someone was alive and at the hospital, but that was it. With us there, they finally knew for a fact that not everybody was gone," said Szott.

The troopers took photos together. SPC Szott had been worried he'd never see them again, and they had thought he was dead. Though they'd all had been in many firefights up until this point, no one had been grievously injured. They'd even joked about the insurgents being bad marksmen. After the long night, however, no one joked about that again.

COPING WITH THE LOSS OF BROTHERS

"The first days and weeks after the ambush were the hardest to deal with," shared Fugate. "We had a memorial ceremony at 4-42 FA headquarters since Scorpion was artillery men. Then there was a memorial service at 4ID HQ with G Troop. It was hard not just going out and being complete schmucks to the rest of the people in Iraq, just because a few of them did what they did that day."

When asked what his biggest challenge was during deployment, Fugate answered it was the loss of their brothers. He'd never lost anyone before. He'd known SPC Arriaga well. The specialist was, "A buck 10 dripping wet with his rucksack on" and nicknamed Little Bully. He came from Ganado, Texas and was one of the youngest guys in the troop. SGT Thompson had just joined our troop a week or so before the ambush. I didn't get to know him very well, but I do remember he was a big South Carolina Gamecocks fan," said Fugate.

The troop rallied around Scorpion Platoon, which strengthened the group: "We'd always give the scouts a hard time, because we're a platoon of forward observers, but at the same time we knew they always had our back," said Fugate. "They were there for us, which helped especially when we were stuck back at the Frat House for a week, trying to get our minds right again before going back out."

Helmrich recalled, "After the night when my three friends were killed, the days and weeks were hard. We expected to hear them on the radio, sit down next to us at the chow hall, or jump in our truck. The worst part was having downtime, because then your brain would start thinking. Up until that night, we were invincible. Now there was a clear kink in our armor."

"It was defeating, because we were doing so good," said Saffeels. "You'd hear about soldiers losing their lives, but they were never *your* unit, *your* friends."

Lay remembered the anger coming afterwards, some of it misplaced. The route they'd taken was one they took often—why had they taken that risk?

He explained, "I kept asking why did we let this happen? Because back then, at my experience and maturity level, I hadn't realized that there's no "letting this happen." This was *going* to happen, and we'd been playing the odds the whole time."

It was also frustrating to him how little they'd been able to assist them from the FOB; shooting into the ambush risked hitting one of their own guys.

"I remember talking to Wright the night before because he needed some extra rounds. Those little things always play back in your head," said Lay. "I was closer to Wright than anybody else. Losing him has stuck with me the longest. As an adult, I've heard others talk about guilt syndrome, and at 19 all the what ifs did eat at me. Was there something I could have done? Was there something I should have talked to him about?"

Back in the U.S., SGT Igor Boyko was informed of the ambush and loss of their teammates by CPT Williams' wife.

"We'd left them just a few days ago," said Boyko. "They were our guys. We couldn't do anything about it. It was a really tough time."

Before deployment, SPC Wright had given SGT Boyko a Gerber multi-tool as a gift. "I also remember he was the guy who liked to sharpen knives. He was always sharpening his own or someone else's."

"Those we led and lost—it's a heavy weight to carry. Every soldier in every unit I commanded was, and still is, my child. I love all of my soldiers," said Bailey. "I'm still so angry with myself because it was my responsibility to protect them…When CPT Williams came over the radio, I could hear in his voice what had happened. It was like opening your front door and there's a police officer outside telling you the person you love most just died."

HONORING THE FALLEN

1SG Justis had been with G Troop less than two months when he had to perform roll call at the memorial. It was held at 4-42FA BN's base, FOB Arrow, in Ad Dawr. Since the three men were field artillery soldiers and forward observers, it was fitting they be honored among their battalion family.

"Major General Odierno and Colonel Hickey attended the service, and it meant a lot that they showed their support and spent time with us. Their hearts were with us that day, and we knew they had our backs," said Helmrich.

The ceremony opened with a prayer from the brigade chaplain, followed by comments from the 4-42 FA Commander and CPT Bailey. Military tradition requires a roll call be conducted in honor of the fallen.

G Troop's troopers lined up in formation behind 1SG Justis. Upon receiving the order to begin, he executed an about face, confronting the troopers. He called each of their names, and in response the identified trooper would respond with, "Here, first sergeant."

Three times 1SG Justis called out Richard Arriaga's rank and name, with no response. Three times, he said Anthony Thompson's rank and name, with no response. Three times he spoke James Wright's rank and name, and only silence followed.

Finishing the roll call, 1SG turned to CPT Bailey stating that SGT Thompson, SPC Wright and PFC Arriaga were unaccounted for. In the final minutes of the memorial, the Honor Guard played TAPS and fired three rifle volleys into the blue sky.

"Standing in formation at the memorial, I broke out in tears. I looked around, everybody else was crying. That was comforting to me. It let me know I wasn't weak. I wasn't the only one so sad to see them go," said Ellis.

Actual picture of the Memorial Ceremony at 4-42 FA

Memorial of G Troop Warriors

9. The Mad Mortar Man and Secret Squirrels

SEPTEMBER – OCTOBER 2003

"There's no honor in killing anybody. As a soldier, I'll throw lead with the best of them, but if it can be avoided and the enemy captured, then that's the better thing to do in this type of war."

—SSG Tommy Darden

G Troop was intent on finding the mastermind behind the September 18 ambush, and its complexity required measures be put in place to avoid a recurrence. COL Hickey believed the attack was the high-water mark for the enemy in that area, and with the swift response by G Troop and 1-22 IN BN following the ambush, they were on the run. To continue the momentum and provide G Troop much needed support, COL Hickey assigned the BRT additional resources. 1-22 IN BN provided the BRT two M1 Tanks, two Bradley Fighting Vehicles (BFVs), and one infantry squad. It was clear that G Troop needed more protection, and in COL Hickey's opinion, the soft bodied Humvees weren't cutting it; he acquired six armored Humvees for the troopers.

Seeking justice for their brothers would not be a lone task as G Troop drew closer to catching the Mad Mortar Man and found themselves augmenting ARSOF operations more frequently.

For three weeks, SFC Flores would keep SPC Szott grounded at FOB Buffalo. He spent most days on the roof, directing harassment and interdiction fires. Three days into his "rest," he had to take a PT test for his promotion board to Sergeant. If he didn't run, he wouldn't be promoted. And, he was still recovering from the wounds he sustained not more than a week ago.

SPC Szott was determined to get promoted, whether he had a bullet hole and shrapnel in his legs or not. With stiches still in his legs, SPC Szott ran the two miles in 14 minutes and 30 seconds.

Brigade Command Sergeant Major (CSM) Lawrence Wilson presented the specialist to the promotion board with a simple statement and single question: "You were shot in the leg, hit by shrapnel in the other, and a week later ran a PT test in 14:30. Correct?"

"Yes, Sergeant Major!" CSM Wilson slowly turned to each of the First Sergeants on the promotion board and asked if they had any other questions for such a "warrior". They all shook their heads, "No, Sergeant Major" in unison. CSM Wilson spoke, "Congratulations, Sergeant Szott."

THE TROOP RECEIVES ADDITIONAL RESOURCES

"After September 18, we were out more often and for longer periods, which I didn't think was possible at that point," said Saffeels.

With the added resources, G Troop now resembled a small task force that included tanks, BFVs, armored gun trucks, and nightly attack aviation or USAF support. They'd rocked the river valley the weeks following the September ambush and put further pressure on the enemy while minimizing troop risk.

One of SSG Darden's main deterrents for fighting was placing a tank unit a few meters behind his troopers when they went to a suspect's home.

"I'd knock on the door and the person would answer—and there'd be a 120-millimeter barrel staring him in the face," said SSG Darden. "If I could intimidate somebody into handing over their weapons or providing information, I could avoid another ambush and keep our guys safe."

Though grateful for the armored Humvees COL Hickey had acquired, after taking one out for a nightly patrol, CPT Bailey considered them practically useless, and hoped to never ride in one again. The doors were heavy and slow to open. Their field of view was severely restricted by small, bullet proof windows. Due to the increased weight of the vehicle, the crew often found themselves stuck in mud and sand. The soft-shell Humvees clearly had their downsides, but he felt less like a sitting target in them.

The troopers tried them on patrol as well, but after a week, all six armored Humvees were abandoned on the vehicle line. CPT Bailey spoke with the platoon leaders and they shared his concerns. He told them using the new trucks was optional, but that decision changed when COL Hickey visited FOB Buffalo.

"COL Hickey told me he hadn't fought to get us the armored Humvees so they could look pretty sitting on the vehicle line," recalled CPT Bailey. "After that, we would use the tanks and armored Humvees for interdiction combat patrols but continued using the light skinned Humvees for recon patrols and missions with ARSOF."

An unlikely resource the troop acquired was AK, a mixed breed dog that resembled a Black Mouth Cur.

"AK needs her moment in the sun," Sparks said. "She was our camp dog and lived with us at the Frat House, and we all loved her. When you bring home a stray and take care of them, they're gonna take care of you. We were her people."

During the day, AK would sleep through the worst of the heat, and at night she'd gear up with the troopers heading out on patrol. Game face on, AK ran behind the trucks, eventually peeling off into nearby orchards looking for anything suspicious. Those on roof guard knew that if she started barking, it was worth looking into.

"One night, AK lost it out in the orchard. We got a team together to check it out. There was a small shack, just a ten by ten, single room, mud brick building without a door. We snuck up to either side, as stealthy as scouts should be, then quickly rounded the corner—and someone almost pulled the trigger…it was a damn horse that had gotten loose, just standing there unconcerned, eating grass. Well, AK was right, that horse wasn't supposed to be there," said Sparks.

After a long night of running the property near FOB Buffalo, AK would turn in with the troopers. Grabbing breakfast, PFC Sparks always made sure to get an extra piece of bacon or two and sit outside with AK to watch the sun rise.

THE MAD MORTAR MAN

For months, mortars were launched at HQ, FOB Raider, and FOB Buffalo. The first attack SPC Corcoles experienced was late in the spring as mortars splashed into the river, just outside FOB Buffalo.

It didn't take long for the troopers to determine where they were being launched from as the angle improved and they drew closer to the compound's walls. A few shots fired from the roof stopped the attacks—but only for a day. The next night they continued, and soon the troopers had dubbed the attacker (or attackers) the Mad Mortar Man or Mortar Mike.

"It was now our side mission to get that guy because he wasn't just hitting us, he was also hitting 4ID HQ," elaborated SPC Corcoles. "At first, we thought it was multiple teams since they fired from several locations. But, after a few months, we found out it was a single team with a mortar in the back of a beat-up Toyota pickup. It was our first confirmed sighting of Mortar Mike, and the night of the first major attack on our troop with an RPG."

SFC Washburn and his crew had been chasing the Mad Mortar Man through the Lollipop and were almost close enough to fire on them when they were attacked. The troop surmised that another team was set aside in case this happened, and they were the ones who'd launched the RPG at SFC Washburn's Humvee. The ambush made their side mission far more personal.

During their patrols, the troopers would ask civilians about the Toyota and the men in it. But time passed with no intel, and the Mad Mortar Man continued showing up across the river to launch a few mortar rounds before dashing off.

"All of us were aggravated. Every day we were told to find the mortar man, find the mortar man," recalled Ellis.

"Our missions required adjustments, fine tuning our responses, making changes based on what didn't work," said PFC Lay. "They also required a lot of flexibility because at any given time, we were going to have to drop what we're doing and do a dead sprint across whatever terrain, wadis, open streets, canyons, whatever, and get to a location as fast as possible with zero warning."

For CPT Bailey, "running to the sound of the guns" required

a more deliberate, cautious procedure. Along with G Troop's platoon leaders, he assessed the mortar attacks and previous ambush to refine their response. Soon they had a far more controlled technique that involved the troopers surrounding the point of origin to prevent the Mad Mortar Man's escape while the observation posts on 4ID HQ's wall and FOB Buffalo employed indirect fires. The troopers, supported by attack aviation, would then close the noose around the target in the hopes of capturing or killing the enemy.

The NCOs used Mad Mortar Man chases as an opportunity to train the troopers. SGT Swilley set up a fake mortar attack as he trained PFC Lay on the FBCB2 map and situational awareness system. Once the mortar launched, SGT Swilley jumped in the Humvee behind PFC Lay, who was in the vehicle commander seat, and told him to guide them to the site based on the grid coordinates. PFC Lay had to then talk the driver through the terrain and get them to the site as quickly as possible.

Meanwhile, in the backseat, SGT Swilley piled on the pressure, constantly asking the private where they were, what was next, and telling him to hurry up. Once they arrived at the launch site, SGT Swilley would discuss PFC Lay's response to the situation.

According to Lay, "Both Sergeants Southwood and Swilley liked to see what you were going to do when put on the spot. In an emergency—real or fake for training purposes—they would sit back and see how those around them reacted. After action, they'd go over what we did and make suggestions on how we could do it better. Instead of telling us we'd done something wrong, they'd show us other ways to accomplish the task. It really got your brain turning."

They did their best to adjust to the mortar attacks, but it always seemed to be an impossible scenario with the troopers setting off from over a kilometer away in hopes of isolating the point of origin or at least getting a glimpse of the truck before the enemy escaped.

Eventually, intel came in with the location of the man who was calling in the Mad Mortar Man's strikes. He lived close to the river, at the end of a long road that was often lined with spotters who would alert him of military presence.

The troop worked through several plans before deciding on the raid they would execute.

In the middle of the night, PFC Lay recalls standing outside the man's house and slowly opening the back door.

"I opened it about two inches and, wearing night vision goggles, peered inside. No one was visible. The door shifted open a little more, and I heard this low scraping sound," Lay said. It was a stick that had leaned against the door to serve as an alarm. As it slid to the floor, the scouts charged into the home.

Even with the makeshift alarm, their visit was unexpected. The man and his family were fast asleep. In searching the house, G Troop uncovered a set of Russian Field Artillery binoculars, which the Iraqi had used to call for fire on their base. Though the mortar attacks would continue, the troop had caught a valuable individual and removed key enemy equipment from the battlefield.

SECRET SQUIRREL MISSIONS

Working with ARSOF was an adrenaline rush. Most of their missions were unexpected and in the middle of the night when the troopers were sleeping, relaxing, or preparing to go out for a patrol.

"We called them Secret Squirrel missions because they were usually last minute," said Ellis. "You never knew what was going to happen. They were high-speed guys who knew a lot more than we did. I always thought of it as getting to play cool guy with special forces."

The troopers would stage up, put their radios on the ARSOF

frequency and wait to be contacted. The moment they got a location, G Troop rolled out. They'd follow behind the special forces souped-up Humvees, pushing their own trucks as fast as they could go. Once they reached their target, G Troop isolated the area to ensure no one got in or out while ARSOF cleared the building. The men they went after were always high level and influential.

"Brigade would task the troop with supporting ARSOF missions because we were flexible and mobile," said Helmrich. "We kept evolving our techniques in clearing hazard areas, hillsides, and houses, and this adaptability grew our skill set. Key to that was having a good crew. The guys in the trucks are watching windows while you're at a door ready to clear. Well, if the guy in the truck stops paying attention, something could happen. Everyone has to be on high alert and reliable."

At first, ARSOF would give the troopers a rundown of the mission and a photo of the target. Eventually, they started engaging G Troop earlier in the planning.

"When they needed help with something, G Troop got tasked to do it. After a while, they started coming over to FOB Buffalo and would hang out, they'd have briefings with CPT Bailey about an upcoming raid or area of interest and want us to take a look at it. We started giving them hands on training with the LRAS so they could see what kind of advanced force multiplier the LRAS brought to the fight," said Sharpless.

Bailey recalled, "The troop had been working with ARSOF since May, but as the hunt for Saddam intensified, so did the requirements to provide support. COL Hickey spent much time developing a positive working relationship with ARSOF leaders working in Sala ad Din province. Weekly situational updates and information exchanges over time enabled the brigade and the ARSOF unit in Tikrit to develop greater understanding of Saddam's inner circle—those who could lead US forces to Saddam.

"As the most flexible unit under COL Hickey's command, he informed the ARSOF commander that G Troop would support any and all missions as requested."

"We ended up doing somewhere around 30 or 40 missions with ARSOF units. ARSOF leadership was very inclusive. They worked us into their rehearsals, and it was beneficial for the guys to see the most elite unit in the Army do the same things they were doing exceptionally well," said Sweigart.

G TROOP'S XO ASSUMES TEMPORARY COMMAND

R&R leave became available in October, and COL Hickey's guidance for 1BCT was to allow leaders and soldiers who'd been in direct contact to be the first to take leave. CPT Bailey was scheduled to take leave in mid-November. While back in the U.S., he would deliver the posthumous awards to the wives of SGT Thompson, SPC Wright, and PFC Arriaga.

"Ahead of R&R, I spent a week with my newly promoted XO, CPT Sweigart, because he'd be taking command of the troop while I was gone," explained Bailey. "We did what the Army calls 'right seat, left seat', which is basically how we bring soldiers up to speed on what they'll be doing when they come into a new role. I had Brian sit in the back of my Humvee and watch what I did. After a few days we switched seats, and he took on command decisions. He was a quick study, and I knew the troop was in good hands."

"I was nervous, but confident at the same time," shared Sweigart. "I had a lot of experience with the troop, and I had the support of our NCOs, First Sergeant, and platoon leaders. But I was concerned there'd be an event, something unexpected, and

I'd have to make a call that could result in one of my men getting injured, or worse."

Not long after CPT Bailey left for the U.S., the troopers were catching up on vehicle and equipment maintenance when the radio call came in from 1BCT HQ that a U.S. Blackhawk helicopter was shot down 20 km northeast of Tikrit. G Troop was to get to the site immediately and secure the aircraft and any survivors.

The troop was well prepared for time sensitive missions with established standard operating procedures—such as their gear remaining stored in the Humvees—and months' of traveling across the terrain. Within five minutes they were out the door, reaching the crash site 20 minutes later.

It appeared the Blackhawk had been shot down by an RPG and the aircraft was half buried in the dirt, its tail rotor sticking up among the wreckage and fires burning in multiple spots. The sight was a shock for PFC Helmrich: these were the soldiers in the skies who supported G troop, and they usually weren't easy targets.

"The frequency of downed helicopters was extremely low, and our helicopter pilots were highly skilled," said Sparks. "Someone got a lucky shot off, but it was a big deal because it was the first one that had gone down in our area."

The crew was already recovered by the theater recovery team, and what was left of the helicopter would be carried out on a flatbed truck once it arrived. Until then, the troopers were to provide security and ensure nothing was stolen.

Though a relatively simple assignment, the troopers did face scattered fire from an apartment complex built atop a cliff. The shots came from across the Tigris, which was a good distance away, but the attackers had elevation on their side. However, their fire was ineffective and the troop continued the mission and secured the aircraft until recovery.

"The downed helicopter mission was stressful at the start with the speed at which we had to reach the site. I was happy with how quickly the troop responded and secured the aircraft, which allowed other units to salvage it safely. In a complex situation like that, speed and efficient support are critical," said Sweigart.

CPT Sweigart's second unexpected event occurred late one night in response to a potential Saddam Hussein sighting. The BRT had set up a flash TCP at the Lollipop and they were under attack. Automatic fire tore through the street and SPC Albert Johnson returned fire first, with other platoon members following.

CPT Sweigart radioed in that they'd made contact and needed support. A quick response notified him that 1-22 IN would send two sections over, and COL Hickey, who was at 1BCT HQ and monitoring the radio net, had called in gunships for close air support.

The enemy broke contact, escaping into a house nearby, but it was too late. The heavily armed gunships had already flown in and identified their location. Watching the house from their LRAS3 systems, the scouts saw faces peeking out through the windows—some of them were children.

Over the radio, COL Hickey told CPT Sweigart he was clear to fire and could engage with attack aviation. The captain acknowledged COL Hickey's confirmation but held off. He had the colonel's support and authorization to make the final decision. However, there was no fire coming from the enemy, 1-22 IN would be there at any moment, and there were children.

Hesitation was unacceptable in battle, and often purposeful aggressiveness was what saved trooper's lives and got their missions done. CPT Sweigart needed to make a decision quickly: wait for the infantry units or swiftly end the engagement at the risk of the children's lives.

He chose to wait.

When 1-22 IN arrived, they cleared the house, rounding up two children around 12 years of age and several men holding weapons consistent with the fire G Troop had received. The children would be taken care of for the night and returned to family members the following day. The men would be detained and questioned.

Not long after, such decisions would be even harder to make. Insurgents realized American troops would take such a course of action and began planting improvised explosive devices in houses and buildings. Once the soldiers entered, the bombs would explode, collapsing the building around the soldiers.

THE DEVASTATING EXTENT OF LOSS

Throughout his life, CPT Bailey had felt prepared for the milestones and challenges he faced. From football games in high school to Marine Corps bootcamp, Ranger School, and a previous deployment to Egypt, he'd faced all of them confidently. He'd grown up listening to his grandfather and great uncles recall their experiences in World War II, most of which were in the Pacific Theater. He visualized their stories, placed himself in them to understand their experiences. CPT Bailey had done the same for OIF1 as he'd watched 3ID and the Marines fight their way north.

Visiting the families of his lost troopers would be very different.

"For the first time that I can remember, I wasn't prepared," said Bailey. "I knew troopers would die, it's the cost of war most people understand. But I hadn't realized that this cost extends beyond the loss of the trooper. Families are impacted...devastated."

When the brigade's chaplain had visited with CPT Bailey shortly after the ambush, he'd cried for the first time in years.

"I cried for the troopers' families. I had never met their wives, but I knew their husbands, they were fearless men, damn good troopers, and I knew they all either had or were expecting children, and now those men were gone. The cost of war would be paid for by their wives and children," said Bailey.

This realization was incomparably hard but visiting with the trooper's wives would be much harder.

Back in Texas, SGT Thompson's wife introduced him to their two beautiful children. He handed her the posthumous award without knowing what to say.

When he visited SPC Wright's pregnant wife, who remained positive throughout their meeting, CPT Bailey struggled with the same issue. What could he say to help her, how could he explain how he and his troopers felt, what could he say that would matter at all?

PFC Arriaga's wife was unable to see anyone from the troop, and CPT Bailey respected her feelings.

"I was sad and ashamed that I couldn't express my grievance for their loss more effectively. We're more prepared today, I think. But back then, I was lost and unprepared for the emotional tsunami I would feel the moment I saw them and when I learned I wouldn't be able to pay my respects to Private Arriaga's wife," said Bailey.

R&R gave CPT Bailey time with his wife, Kelly, and two sons who were one and three years old. It was an exciting reunion he'd looked forward to for weeks, but it was also metered. As the wife of G Troop's commander, Kelly had her own expectations and challenges to meet, serving in the Family Readiness Group (FRG), which kept spouses connected during their husband or wife's deployment. Because CPT Bailey had taken command after the troop deployed, Kelly hadn't met the troopers, only their wives.

While CPT Sweigart's wife, Jennifer, led the FRG at the time and 1SG Justis' wife, Brigit, brought her own significant experience and contributions to the group, as the commander's wife, Kelly had visited both SGT Thompson and SPC Wright's wives with Jennifer and Brigit the night the wives were informed of their husbands' deaths. She'd also prepared and mailed PFC Arriaga's wife her husband's posthumous awards.

"They were all so young and all mothers, the sorrow hit Kelly hard. She was taking care of her two sons alone and coming into a close-knit group like the FRG wasn't easy," shared Bailey. "To this day, Kelly says she can still hear the sobbing of Sergeant Thompson's wife after she was given the news."

JUSTICE FOR THE FALLEN

It was a month to the day when SSG Darden and his section of Black Sheep platoon found the mastermind behind the September 18 ambush. Though G Troop had raided the man's home four times prior, they'd failed to find him. The man's mother and brother who lived there repeatedly swore that no such man even existed.

On October 18, Captain Bailey told SSG Darden to go back to the house and search one last time. SSG Darden and his troopers began their eight-hour search by going to nearby homes to confirm what they knew and gather any new intelligence. As always, the mother and brother insisted they'd never heard of the man. SSG Darden had his troopers search the home while he and SGT Detrick Harris expanded the hunt outside.

"We found Iraqi military uniforms buried in the yard," said Darden, who then told his men to double down on their efforts—there would be more than uniforms found if they searched well enough.

Further out on the property, the staff sergeant found a wide, shallow bowl dug out of the earth, with a stone well in the center—a common enough find in Iraq, but what stood out to SSG Darden were the bushes that lined the hole.

"I said to SGT Harris that there were weapons hidden in those bushes, guaranteed. I told him to pull them out, and under them he found RPGs and other weapons," recalled Darden. "I went on to look into the well and noticed there were stairs made of rebar in the rock walls. Further down, in the water, I saw him…I'll never forget that moment."

SSG Darden called down to him, but the man refused to move. The troopers got him out and took the prisoner back to FOB Buffalo, placing him in a temporary holding cell.

"Once we got him locked up, I noticed that he didn't have shoes," said Darden. "I went into the FOB and grabbed my extra pair of Asics for him. A few of the guys didn't want me to do it. This was the man behind the ambush that had killed our guys. But I reminded them we were there to catch him, not to judge. We treat people like we want to be treated."

10. The Unforgiving Desert

NOVEMBER 2003

"It was wet, cold, and there wasn't much communication or support. It was a change of pace for us. I won't say it was a change of scenery because that place sucked. It was neat. It was fun. You can quote me on that."

—Private First Class Cole Lay

By November, the insurgents east of Tikrit had fled or lay dormant, while in the northwest, near Baiji, activity picked up. Known for its massive oil refinery and numerous pipelines, Baiji was a cornerstone of Saddam's Sunni Triangle. It was quickly captured in April 2003 by Coalition Forces, but by that fall, the town and surrounding area was a hotspot for riots and guerilla attacks.

To investigate reports coming from the area, the BRT would leave their familiar territory and set out for the Western Desert. This vast wasteland spread north of the Thar Thar Reservoir and west of Baiji, increasing in elevation as it neared the Syrian mountains, which meant cold nights and thinner air for the troopers.

They would be searching for Hidoshi, Saddam's financier, again. Unfamiliar territory, but a familiar target. Back in the summer, G Troop went in search of this HVT not far from FOB Buffalo.

Near the house, metal pipes rose out of a concrete slab that stretched for several meters. What the underground structure held was anyone's guess—uranium, weapons, ammunition, or Hidoshi himself. SGTs Szott and Sharpless, with a few of their guys, headed below to clear the space.

The moment the door swung open, an overpowering stench of decay spilled from the darkness. Below, the troopers walked through five rows of chicken coops that rose three meters high. The underground farm had once provided hundreds of chickens with a consistently cooler space, which meant reliable egg production. It was also their tomb when Hidoshi fled the property.

The chickens had died weeks ago, left to rot in puddles of waste and decay. Despite what they had to wade through, the building would be cleared.

"We were walking in six inches of diseased chicken and muck," said Szott. "Some of us were dry heaving, and we were all running to clear it as fast as possible. There was a locked door at the opposite side that we could leave through, so Sharpless, who's a big, tall guy, and I went shoulder to shoulder, kicking the crap out of that door to get the hell out of there. We exited that thing like a gas chamber, gasping for air."

But in November, far from chicken farms and the sweltering heat and humidity of the Tigris river, the troop would venture into the unknown. A vast flat desert at the far west of the brigades' area of operations.

1BCT's intelligence section had received three reports from the Western Desert that G Troop was to confirm or deny—Saddam's financier had relocated to the area; the Fedayeen, a pro-Saddam group, had established a training camp at the northern edge of the Thar Thar Reservoir; and munitions were coming into Iraq from Syria.

"Colonel Hickey wanted to know who and what was out there. The Coalition Forces hadn't had a very big presence in that region, so there wasn't much intel. We needed to know if we should set up a base and bring in more troops, what—if anything—was coming in from Syria and where it was filtering across," explained Helmrich.

Bailey's return from R&R kickstarted the 30-day reconnaissance mission. For much of the operation, they would be far from supporting units, almost 90 kilometers out from Baiji at the furthest point. It would be up to them to sustain themselves and conduct missions with Viper support coming in only when heavy firepower or close air support was needed. Traveling alongside the BRT would be two Bradleys and the joint terminal attack controllers (JTAC) who would manage air support operations.

"I was extremely excited," recalled Bailey. "The reason I wanted to command the troop was for missions like this. I didn't want to remain in one area, I wanted to get out and discover."

Ahead of their departure, CPT Bailey had spoken to ARSOF commander in Tikrit, who'd advised him to be careful because combatants tended to materialize from out of nowhere. His unit had been engaged in that area earlier in the year and an Australian Special Operations Unit had been under heavy attack during the same period. While on first look it appeared to be open desert, the commander warned of 50-foot-deep cisterns, impossible to see at times, and villages that couldn't be found on any map.

G Troop was heading into the unknown and during a particularly challenging time of year. Not only was the desert the most unforgiving terrain they'd dealt with, but the weather was just as extreme. The rainy season began in the fall and the valleys in the Western Desert were prone to flash floods. Temperatures could dip to 42° F at night, a drastic change from only a few weeks ago when the troopers had been out in boiling temperatures.

G Troop set up their base camp on the 3-66 AR FOB in Baiji. While there, they prepped equipment and conducted final coordination with Viper. The airfield would remain their closest refueling point. The troop would establish two patrol bases in the desert and conduct their first reconnaissance mission at the northern tip of the Thar Thar Reservoir.

G Troop departed the FOB on a cold, windy night, and the troopers were relieved that 1SG Justis had suggested they re-attach their Humvee doors. It was pitch black out, except for the occasional headlights of vehicles driving toward Baiji. Only a few hours into the drive, Bailey received his first report: one of the Bradleys had rolled off a narrow bridge. Oncoming traffic with bright lights had flooded the driver's night vision and, in response, he'd veered hard to the right. Two infantry soldiers were injured, and MEDEVAC was required. They'd traveled too far to reach the FOB via radio, but Viper was within range to contact MEDEVAC for the troopers and provide security. Their mission had just started, and they were already down a Bradley and two soldiers.

A plateau close to an access road leading back to Baiji served as G Troop's main patrol base. From it, they could see over 20 km in all directions, though there wasn't much *to* see. A great expanse of flat land spread out before them, broken up by moderate hills and low-lying vegetation.

The ARSOF commander was right, however. As they patrolled

the desert, G Troop came across plenty of the unexpected. There were numbers in the sand, massive shapes formed by rocks, most likely serving as ground reference points for Iraqi aviation. Sixty-foot-deep wells weren't visible until the moment the troopers abruptly came upon them. Numerous villages—nothing but small collections of mud brick homes—rose from the flat land. None of them were reflected on the troop's maps.

Between great spans of arid land, Bedouins materialized along with their camels, goats, and sheep, traveling to some distant location, or encamped with tents and blankets or makeshift huts. The troopers would speak with the friendly nomads and buy stacks of flat bread, just removed from hand-built mud stoves.

"The Bedouins were so far removed from society that they didn't know there was a war or that Saddam was no longer the president. They didn't know who we were or that their country was overtaken," said Justis.

At one point, the troop set up a perimeter to rest and plan for an upcoming mission. It was a good, defensible location, with 15-kilometer views of empty desert. It wasn't long before a trooper on perimeter security reported a lone man walking. CPT Bailey dispatched a two-vehicle section to make contact with the stranger. He was barefoot, with no weapon, no water, and no food, yet when questioned, he told the troopers he knew where he was going and didn't require help. Another crew drove in the direction the man had come from, to ensure he wasn't reconnaissance for the enemy. They found nothing. Attack aviation flew in, yet they didn't see a thing—not even a small village or group of Bedouins.

The BRT's first mission in the Western Desert was at the northern tip of the reservoir, a potential Fedayeen camp. They'd received images of a train station and structures that appeared to be barracks and a training facility. After observing the area, the troopers only noted Bedouins who would eventually move on from the location.

Finding out whether munitions or other supplies were being trafficked in from Syria would take longer than determining there was no enemy camp. It required G Troop to patrol the vast area and survey, then soft search, any villages they found. The troopers were away from their patrol base for days at a time and rarely returned to the FOB at Baiji. A satellite radio served as their only lifeline, but it used a shared frequency that MAJ GEN Odierno used as division commander. This left CPT Bailey waiting through the general's briefs and updates for the 30 seconds he'd get to push his own messages or reports through.

With communications degraded, they couldn't rely on immediate support from Baiji or 1BCT should something happen. CPT Bailey kept the platoons from dispersing too far from one another and carefully considered when they would destroy munitions caches.

"I had to balance risk with remaining independent and performing zone reconnaissance in an area of unknown enemy activity. If we flipped a Humvee, or somebody got sick or was injured, how could we quickly manage the incident and take care of them? While I was more comfortable when I had clear communications or aviation on site, once I got a good feel for the area, I was okay allowing the troopers to spread out and cover larger areas," explained Bailey.

The troopers traveled from village to village, surveying the area at night and then soft searching houses that had shown unusual activity.

"We weren't kicking in doors or flex cuffing everybody. I wasn't getting the indicators of hostilities, and, based on what my interpreter told me, the people were simply scared. Most of them thought the war was over and Saddam had won because they hadn't seen U.S. planes flying over. In one village, several of the men were so frightened when we arrived that they urinated on themselves," said Bailey.

In response, CPT Bailey had his interpreter, a middle-aged Iraqi man who fled Iraq in the 80s and moved to Chicago, Illinois, but volunteered to serve, speak with the village's Sheik, who could then speak to the locals and put their minds at ease. The interpreter's message and line of questioning was standard: they were looking for RPGs, landmines, rockets, or equipment being used to facilitate attacks on the soldiers in Baiji; they would be searching homes looking for those assets.

"The villagers and Bedouins we came across were friendly, happy people, and we reciprocated that friendliness. I remember providing overwatch for a village's grain facility for a few days to help some of the townspeople out," said Bailey. "I was proud of the troop because they never rough handled anyone. They focused on having conversations and explaining to those who understood English why we were there."

Before the troopers searched the home, they'd request to see how many magazines of ammunition the man owned and ask them what was going on in their village and the surrounding area.

"Most of the locals let us look inside their houses without issue, they knew we were looking for insurgents and munitions. At the time, Iraqi people were only allowed to have one AK-47, and we would check for that. While we didn't want them to have 10 AKs, there was more concern if they had large quantities of ammunition," explained Helmrich.

Along with stockpiled ammunition and guns, what also drew the troop's attention were out of place items that villagers typically couldn't afford or have access to, like expensive vehicles or military generators.

Twice the troopers detained men driving surprisingly nice vehicles for such an alienated area. Both ended up being ammunitions dealers. The BMW owner had hidden away multiple caches of weapons, including a 14.5-millimeter machine gun, inside his home. Within a barn, the Dodge Lancer's owner had hidden rockets and ammunitions caches beneath piles of hay. The men were taken to Baiji for the intelligence community to conduct tactical questioning and G Troop destroyed all the munitions.

"We found a lot of ammunition in the area, especially at the northern tip of the reservoir. You could stack a pile of sealed ammo containers across the length of two Humvees and they would be five feet high," said Bailey.

Observing villages or suspicious individuals didn't always lead to a find or capture. Most nights, the troopers watched in the rain and waited in the cold for a brief, critical moment that may never come.

"After three hours of sleep, you'd head out on a 12-hour mission, tired and hungry, your clothes chafing. You can't stand the smell of yourself, and you haven't had a warm meal in days. We'd spend hours sitting in our trucks or hiding in a barn that's full of cow manure, looking out a window and peeing over in a corner. It's the ugly, gritty truth, and we did it for hours on end," says Lay.

It was that diligence and patience that led to much of what they found, and Lay gives credit to the unit's NCOs: "They gave us the opportunity to actually affect things. So, hats off to the NCOs for keeping a bunch of attention deficit teens focused. Grab any 20-year-old these days and try to keep them focused on anything for an hour. I'm pretty sure our NCOs could walk on water after that 30-day mission."

Bailey recognized the influence his sergeants had and watched as his troopers came together even more in that unforgiving place. He learned from his NCOs as well. Five days into their operation, SSG Wommack came up to his command Humvee and suggested a better option to manage troop movements: instead of giving 10-digit grids to the platoons based off a map, they could use graphics and simply report to him where they were.

"It was an excellent idea," says Bailey. "I should have done it initially, but I was too focused on maneuvering the troops and keeping everybody tight since I didn't have much knowledge of the area. I didn't want a platoon getting in contact with the other troopers too far away to respond quickly."

Amidst the unbearable weather, raids, long days, and even longer nights, brief, positive moments strengthened the troop's connection to one another and the good in the world that could easily be forgotten.

One night after a short rainfall, CPT Bailey woke to something crawling and scratching at his sleeping bag. Thinking it was a desert rodent, the captain swatted it away. A few minutes later, it returned, scratching at the waterproof bivy cover of his sleeping bag. CPT Bailey unzipped his sleeping bag and grabbed his red lens flashlight, lighting up a wet, shivering kitten.

CPT Bailey pulled the tabby into his sleeping bag, where it slept, just above his head, the rest of the night.

The following morning, CPT Bailey asked the troop whose kitten he was holding. A few troopers laughed and finally Lapp responded. The kitten, aptly named Cat, had been riding with him for several days, sitting between the radio and windshield, as they patrolled the desert. They'd kept him fed with meat from their MREs and ensured he had plenty of water.

"I let them keep it," said Bailey. "I figured it gave them something different to focus on once in a while. Taking care of an animal would help keep their mindset more considerate and positive."

Desmond Bailey

ERADICATING AN AMBUSH IN THE DARK

It was late at night when a scout section, traveling about three kilometers ahead of the troop's main element, was warned by Viper of an ambush in the making. They reported three individuals directly on their path with an RPG clearly visible.

SGT Szott, part of the forward team, verified the enemy's location and weapon signature. Through the LRAS3, they identified a man armed with a Dragunov sniper rifle, who was most likely providing security for the men who would attack with RPGs. Then SGT Szott reported to CPT Bailey, confirming the armed man and that he was too far away for direct engagement.

"Viper asked if they could engage, but I asked them to confirm the RPG and provide me with descriptions of the activity. It appeared that the men were posturing to ambush the lead element of our troop," said Bailey, who gave Viper clearance to engage.

On high alert, G Troop headed to the site at a slow crawl. After they took out the insurgents, Viper had left to refuel, and it was too dangerous for the troopers to rush in without backup.

"It took us about 30 to 40 minutes to get there," recalled Ellis. "By the time we did, the bodies had vanished. There were two vehicles and blood everywhere. After going through the site, we found ammunition, the RPG, the sniper rifle, a shoe, and a hand."

Looking at their map, CPT Bailey confirmed there were no villages nearby, which meant the men had deliberately driven out there to ambush the troopers. This setup—three men with an RPG and AK-47 occupying a position along a prominent dirt road—was a textbook ambush that the Fedayeen had used plenty of times in and around Tikrit during the summer and early fall.

The next morning, G Troop drove to the closest village. The people there had no knowledge of the night's incident, but they had heard Viper's canon fire. CPT Bailey dispatched Scorpion platoon to the next village a few kilometers away. There they found a large crowd of about 30 individuals preparing three bodies for burial. During the half hour G Troop had taken to reach the ambush site, the men's family members had taken the bodies.

"What I took away from the event was that my ARSOF brother was absolutely correct to tell me that the enemy could show up anywhere. In the middle of nowhere, over 30 military-age males had gathered for a funeral. It was unbelievable, quite frankly, because we weren't seeing these people en masse as we traveled through all the villages. It was hard to believe that the locals could consolidate so quickly while we're sitting out there with long range surveillance equipment and had the Air Force and attack aviation flying overhead," said Bailey.

Despite the distance between villages, word traveled fast in the Western Desert. Before long when the trooper's arrived at a village, its people would be outside with their weapons laid out for inspection. Sometimes, they would wave white flags. Attacks around Baiji began to subside. It appeared the insurgents were catching on — G Troop would find them.

"They seemed to finally realize our capabilities and stopped coming out at night. They knew we were looking at them from miles away through our LRAS3 thermals. They couldn't hide and that, plus the captures we made, put the fear of God in them — and that's such a huge portion of the fight. If they're too afraid to come out and fight, you're halfway to winning. You've demoralized and suppressed their will to attack," said Lay.

Toward the end of November, G Troop had cleared the northern part of their zone. They would head back to 3-66 AR FOB for a refit and Thanksgiving Day before heading south.

"I remember getting woken up on Thanksgiving Day, and being

told 'happy Thanksgiving, go burn sh*t,'" recalled Sparks. "There was a 55-gallon drum cut in half under the outhouse that had to be pulled out. There were about two or three of these outhouses together, and you had to pull the buckets out, dump them all into one, pour in some diesel fuel, light it on fire, and burn it until it wouldn't burn anymore."

HUNTING THE FINANCIER

Following a Thanksgiving break for two days, Blacksheep Platoon welcomed LT Zeke Austin as their newest member. LT Austin had recently served as a platoon leader in 299 EN. His skills in general engineering and demolitions would be a great asset to the troop. He replaced CPT Valero who had maxed his time as a platoon leader and returned to his battalion, 1-66 AR in Samarra, to serve as a primary staff officer. With a bit of a rest and some new leadership in place, the troop departed Baiji to complete the zone reconnaissance mission. Over the past 14 days the troop had cleared over 100 villages, destroyed thousands of munitions, and collected information from the populace that allowed CPT Bailey to hone in on two specific areas—the northern tip of the Thar Thar reservoir, and an area not far from the city of Bayji—two places where HVTs may be hiding.

Indicators pointed to Saddam's financier Hidoshi hiding west of Baiji. It was easy finding somebody as wealthy as him in the middle of a desert, yet despite this fact and several raids, the troopers had yet to capture him. Aviation support had located several concrete homes, which stood out among the typical mud huts, with expensive vehicles parked outside. G Troop systematically cleared each one and found the financier's house with his four wives present. Outside, an 18-wheeler held multiple air conditioning units, the same types sold to the United States Army for their FOBs.

Bailey recalls that COL Hickey had ventured out to join G Troop for this particular search. "While searching Hidoshi's residence, we found a case of expensive bourbon. COL Hickey and I were standing in the room looking at that case of bourbon and talking jokingly. I said a shot of that would be really nice, and COL Hickey looked me dead in the eyes and told me to take it outside and destroy all the bottles immediately. So, that's what we did. It was a sad day."

Toward the end of their 30-day mission, Black Sheep was tasked with returning confiscated vehicles and equipment to a local village. They had belonged to captured insurgents, and it was decided that the local community would benefit the most from having them.

On the way back to the FOB, PFC Lay rode in the lead vehicle with Platoon Leader CPT Jose Valero driving across the roadless desert. Parts of the Western Desert act as a spillway for oil fields, with oil soaked deep down into the sand, making it sticky and impossible to traverse — especially during periods of rain. Traveling required careful planning and figuring out how to get around the dangerous areas and then double back to reach the other side.

The troop had only briefly discussed the route they'd take, and it wasn't long before the muddy areas — made worse by that day's rainfall — did become a problem. The second Humvee behind PFC Lay's truck got stuck, as did the next Humvee, and the next. Following up behind the Humvees, one of the two Bradleys accompanying G Troop was brought to a standstill by the tacky mud.

At first, CPT Valero thought they could reverse slowly back

to the stuck Humvee and use a tow cable to daisy chain them out. The plan fell through when the crew realized their Humvee was trapped, just like the others. The remaining Bradley rolled around to pull out CPT Valero's Humvee — only to become stuck.

With all their vehicles at a standstill, CPT Valero called for support from Baiji, requesting an M88 Recovery Vehicle, also known as a Hercules (Heavy Equipment Recovery Combat Utility Lifting Extraction System). One was dispatched, but on its way to the troop the transmission blew.

Meanwhile, the sun was setting, and the troopers were prepared for a long night pulling close security and waiting for the second M88 to arrive.

"We were taught at the very beginning of the mission that we gotta be self-sufficient because we weren't going to have help out that far," said Lay. "So, we did everything we could to get ourselves out of the situation."

That included sending a dismount team three miles on foot to the nearest village. A farmer, in his late 50s, offered to help. He drove out on his tractor and helped shovel out mud around the lead Humvee. He linked his tractor to it, but it wasn't enough to even budge the truck.

Finally, the second M88 arrived and hooked up to the front truck with the others daisy chained behind. Their fifth try finally worked.

"It was an event and there were some unhappy people at the time. Sweigart had some choices words for the route we'd taken. It shows that any mission, no matter how miniscule, could turn out to be a catastrophe if you don't treat it with the absolute respect it needs," said Lay.

RUNNING HEADLONG INTO THE HOME STRETCH

Back in Tikrit, the culmination of G Troop's efforts began to take shape. Back in August, they had identified a well-built home near the city with a new BMW 7 series parked outside. Based on intelligence, it was most likely one of Saddam's inner circle members who lived there. The BRT had conducted multiple raids on the house, gathering pictures of the man, who was identified by 1BCT's intelligence section as al-Muslit, a member of Saddam's inner circle and bodyguard.

Though several of al-Muslit's wives remained in the home, the man himself had fled to Baghdad, where ARSOF units continued the hunt. In the early hours of December 13, the ARSOF unit commander in Baghdad contacted the ARSOF commander in Tikrit. They'd finally captured al-Muslit and figured COL Hickey and his BRT would be interested in having the HVT hand delivered that morning.

Meanwhile, out in the Western Desert, G Troop had just reached the 3-66 AR FOB. After almost 30 days in the desert, the troopers were in desperate need of showers and a warm meal. They also needed to perform maintenance on their equipment and trucks.

PFC Lay's Humvee had a large hole in the exhaust manifold, so traveling quietly was impossible. Several of the other Humvees weren't in much better shape. Luckily, this down time would give them a chance to fix what they could and get some much-needed rest.

"It's funny how those days off never happened," Lay said.

Desmond Bailey

Trooper atop the Guntruck in the western desert

Shi*t Burning Detail

11. Operation Red Dawn

DECEMBER 13-14, 2003

"Smile for the camera's pretty boy"

—unnamed ARSOF Soldier

From July 16, 1979, to April 9, 2003, Saddam Hussein was president of Iraq, and for many years prior, he had wielded the position's power. During his rule, he committed and commanded war crimes, crimes against humanity, and genocide.

After Coalition Forces invaded in 2003, Saddam disappeared from public view. He was labeled High Value Target Number One (HVT1) and became the focus of one of the largest manhunts in history. From July to December, ARSOF units carried out numerous raids to find the dictator, along with hundreds of other operations against suspected targets. For ARSOF, these were missions in addition to the raids they performed with G Troop throughout the Salah Ad Din Province.

On December 13, months of intelligence collection and aggressive operations within the province and elsewhere paid off.

Together, 1BCT and ARSOF had identified Saddam's inner circle, and now they had one of its most valuable members, Mohammed Ibrahim Omar al-Muslit, hand delivered to them by an ARSOF team based in Baghdad. After several hours of interrogation, Saddam's relative and bodyguard agreed to lead them to the deposed dictator's hideout.

As G Troop neared the 3-66 AR FOB at Baiji for a brief and well-deserved break, CPT Sweigart received a call from 1BCT HQ that included a direct message from COL Hickey to get the troop to Tikrit, immediately.

CPT Sweigart shared the news with CPT Bailey as soon as he arrived, dusty and tired. The urgency made it clear: they were going on a raid for Saddam. CPT Sweigart, 1SG Justis, the mechanics, and a few troopers would remain at 3-66 AR FOB to prepare their equipment for the return to Tikrit and rest. The remaining 32 troopers consolidated as many mission-capable vehicles as they could and headed south to FOB Raider.

"We'd just made it back to Baiji to regroup, do laundry, and actually eat a hot meal. Immediately we got the order to pack our stuff within the hour. Well, we hadn't even *unpacked* yet, and now we're going on another Saddam raid. We were told this one had good intel, and I was thinking 'Yeah, it's always good intel, though.' We weren't happy at all," recalled Fugate.

PFC Helmrich told SPC Monroe that they were going after another ghost, and Monroe agreed. They'd been on many raids for the deposed dictator already.

"We didn't expect Saddam to be there because, after multiple raids with no luck, your brain starts saying it's just a waste of our time," shared Helmrich.

When they arrived at the brigade compound, the troopers

parked their 10 Humvees in a large, open area to finalize prep work while CPT Bailey headed in to speak with 1BCT's Intelligence Officer. He was informed that a Task Force raid in Baghdad the night before had detained somebody important and 1BCT was going to conduct a raid with ARSOF for Saddam. COL Hickey was at ARSOF's base in Tikrit and would return to FOB Raider soon.

"They were pulling in a lot of assets quickly," said Bailey. "At that point I figured they had a legitimate line on Saddam."

"I'm not going on another useless raid again."

Sitting in the truck, confirming FBCB2 connectivity and GPS accuracy, SGT Szott wasn't sure who'd spoken. It was true that they'd found a lot of dry holes so far, and most likely this would be another. But there was always that slight chance this was it, and the days of missing Saddam by just a few minutes or hours would be over.

According to the ARSOF guys, they'd probably missed him by just five or ten minutes on an earlier raid. The objective—a nicer home made of concrete instead of mud bricks—was located near Ad Dawr with a small herd of horses grazing nearby. Horses in Iraq were a rare enough find, but these were well-bred, and everyone knew that Saddam had a passion for horses. In fact, the Iraqi National Herd of Arabian horses was owned by the country of Iraq under Saddam. The herd numbered over 100 and were priceless; their bloodlines dated back thousands of years, interwoven with the region's Bedouin heritage and the desert horses of Mesopotamia and the Sumerians. Many of the horses had been stolen or killed at the outset of the war, but others had been protected and taken by Saddam's men. COL Hickey had referenced the horses and certain markings that distinguished them—they were a strong indicator for a hideout, whether it belonged to Saddam or other HVTs.

One of the horses was located by the troop and reported to CPT Bailey. Standing next to him as he received the report was COL Hickey, who cracked a slight smile...SGT Szott had noticed markings on the horses at that day's objective and had reported in the "captain's bars near their asses" to an unimpressed CPT Bailey. The captain would light him up later that night, but it was still a funny comeback.

"We're getting close, Dez, we're getting close."

However, when the ARSOF teams charged into the house, they'd found an empty table with steam rising from bowls of food and cups of tea. Their intel was right—Saddam had *just* been there—but as always, they were moments too late.

They'd raided the house multiple times with no luck, and SGT Szott wondered if they'd again be heading to that objective or Ad Dawr itself.

"I don't know what's going on," Szott said, "but I'm not missing this one."

On COL Hickey's return to HQ, it was time to discuss the night's plan of attack: Operation Red Dawn. Alongside CPT Bailey, 1BCT's operations officer, Major Brian Reed, and members of the brigade's intelligence team, the COL laid out the plans.

Their mission statement read:

```
1BCT Mission: At 131900DEC03, 1BCT (-) in conjunction
with SOF, attacks to kill/capture HVT #1 in order to
defeat enemy forces in the area of operations.
```

Operation Red Dawn would be executed with elements of

1BCT and ARSOF, covering three objectives: two farms were their focus with a third potential location worth investigating. In total, there would be approximately 600 soldiers consisting of cavalry, artillery, aviation, and engineers forming an outer cordon. G Troop would provide the inner cordon on Objectives Wolverine 1 and Wolverine 2 while ARSOF would enter and clear the buildings on each objective. 4-42 FA was tasked with securing the outer cordon in Ad Dawr, using multiple traffic control points in and out of the city to prevent enemy reinforcements and capture any HVTs that may escape the inner cordon. The brigade engineer battalion, 299 EN, would have their riverine forces form a west bank screen on the Tigris, waiting for anyone who dared to swim away from either objective. In reserve to support the troops were A/1-10 CAV, an armored Calvary Troop from 4ID's Division Calvary Squadron, and to the east A/1-4 AVN would provide AH-64 support to the west of the Tigris.

COL Hickey was confident about the raid, and CPT Bailey felt just as positive. Their intel was solid. Not only was al-Muslit a relative of Saddam and part of the inner circle, he'd also been acting as a personal messenger for the dictator throughout the insurgency. The location of the objectives was promising, too, located close to the oft-raided home and specially bred-horses.

After the meeting, Bailey went back out to the BRT's vehicle line. To link up with ARSOF on time, he only had a few, precious minutes to inform G Troop on the mission. He could already picture the glum expressions he'd get from the troopers, and he couldn't blame them. After 30 days living out of trucks in the desert, they really had needed the three-day break in Baiji.

He'd expected to find them in their Humvees, equipped and ready to ride out at the drop of a dime. Instead, music blared from a Scorpion crew's Humvee while the rest of the troop hung around, smoking, and joking.

"Turn that crap off! What in God's name are you doing," CPT Bailey yelled over the loud music.

Silence descended and he focused his attention on the guilty crew. "Specialist Fugate, your equipment had better be ready."

"It is, sir," the gunner responded.

"We got good intel this time, I promise."

"Yes sir, my bad, sir."

Below the gunner seat, PFC Branch snickered as their captain strode away. "He's not happy."

SPC Fugate held back a laugh. "It's the first time we've really pissed him off. It would've been cool driving out the gates with the music going."

"Yeah, too bad," said Branch.

"Saddam or not, I'm ready to kick ass," the gunner said in all seriousness. Smokin' and jokin' time were officially over.

Over the radio, CPT Bailey said, "It's go time."

TAKING DOWN A DICTATOR

Within the walls of the granary compound, the ARSOF team commander, whipped out a piece of butcher block paper and set it on the ground. CPT Bailey studied the black marker sketches that showed the small town of Ad Dawr, the few farms south of it, running parallel to the Tigris, Objectives Wolverine 1 and Wolverine 2, and key times for action, including their 1900 link up and a "2000-ish" hit time.

"The informant was silent too long, the raid is most likely invalid," warned the ARSOF troop commander. Over 24 hours had passed since al-Muslit's capture and Saddam was unlikely to stay in a location if he'd not heard from a member of his inner circle for so long.

Regardless, the operation would continue in hopes that Saddam would remain static even if communication with al-Muslit was delayed. One platoon from G Troop and an ARSOF element would go to the first objective, Wolverine 1. A similar group would head to Wolverine 2. Both objectives were farms and associated outbuildings, with the banks of the Tigris River, not far away. Wolverine 1 sat at the northern tip of Ad Dawr. Nearby, Wolverine 2 was adjacent to a dirt road with sunflower and wheat fields to its east. Growing between Wolverine 2 and the Tigris River were dense orchards of citrus fruit and date palms. A third possible target close to Wolverine 2 was noted but wouldn't be their focus.

The plan was reviewed quickly, and G Troop didn't need further details. The BRT would do what they always did extremely well as inner cordon on an ARSOF mission. Heading to the objectives, they would spread out while maintaining visual contact with each vehicle. As the ARSOF teams neared the objectives, G Troop would close-in and then isolate the objectives, preventing anyone from entering or leaving and providing reinforcing fires if needed.

CPT Bailey would position his Humvee between Wolverine 1 and Wolverine 2 to coordinate the assisting conventional forces. At his side would be two additional Humvees and eight troopers ready to reinforce either objective.

The outer cordon was far larger than the inner cordon; COL Hickey had a sense that this mission was significant, and its magnitude could quickly grow. With high ground to their east and north, the Tigris on the west, and Ad Dawr to the south, the task force was in a dangerous location. They were easy targets for any enemies above them, and there were few opportunities for exit. They could be overwhelmed by pure numbers.

The units on standby were heavily armed to form a strong defense. A/1-10 CAV was stationed on an old landing strip about 10 kilometers to the north with Bradleys, M1 Tanks, Kiowa Gunships, and mortars. In the west, near 299 EN's screen line, the AH-64 Apache attack helicopters were airborne and ready to provide surveillance and direct fire support across the Tigris River.

After the pre-brief, the ARSOF team commander asked CPT Bailey to confirm their captor's identity. Inside the granary, they stopped beside a Humvee. Inside were two men: an interpreter and a disheveled Iraqi in traditional dress with a cover over his head. The commander asked the interpreter to remove the bag. Frightened eyes, red rimmed with dark circles, met Bailey's gaze.

"This the guy?"

"Yeah," Bailey said, "that's the fella that lives in the really nice house next to the river."

"You sure?"

"I know that's him," CPT Bailey said. "We've been hunting him for six months."

Nearby, one of the ARSOF guys was talking to the team leaders, SGT Szott and SGT Branch about the Belgian Malinois that sat at his side. "Above all else," he said, "do not shoot this dog. His name is Rudy, and if he runs over and starts chewing on you, just scream like a little girl, and I'll come get him off. Just don't shoot my friggin' dog. Everybody clear?"

The ARSOF team commander slammed the Humvee door shut, then clapped his hands together. "Then let's roll out."

G Troop, interlaced with ARSOF and accompanied by COL Hickey and his vehicle crew and CSM Wilson and his crew, rolled through the traffic circle, heading south. PFC Ellis drove his Humvee at full speed to stay behind the ARSOF vehicles. Special forces had far superior equipment; their up-armored trucks were faster, quieter, and in far better condition than G Troop's Humvees. For too long they'd had to scrape by with what they had, fix what they could, and roll without the rest.

The ARSOF team commander's vehicle had the informant in it, a member of Saddam's inner circle. *This time really could be different*, PFC Ellis thought as he pushed past 55 mph. Suddenly, their infra-red headlights disappeared. He didn't slow down. Though they were traveling in blackout, he could see well enough with his night vision goggles.

About a kilometer from their first objective, the lights of Ad Dawr vanished, enveloping the area in pitch black. Messages passed over the Platoon and Troop Net—was it planned or a typical power outage? It didn't matter, in fact it would only benefit them. They continued on.

The unit entered northern Ad Dawr. As 4-42 FA closed the outer cordon behind them, the soldiers split off into the pitch-dark night, heading toward their assigned objectives.

OBJECTIVE WOLVERINE 1

SSG Darden, PFC Ellis, and PVT Mosier were forced to stop on Highway 24 just outside a village of about 80 mud huts. The Humvee's headlights had disappeared earlier because the brush guard had partly fallen off, and now it was stuck. Cursing, PFC Ellis jumped out of the truck and rigged the brush guard up, with the staff sergeant snickering from the vehicle commander's seat.

At 2000 hours, they pulled up to the northwest corner of Wolverine 1, a quiet, two-story home as dark inside as it was out. PFC Ellis and SSG Darden dismounted, weapons at the ready. Their gunner kept his M19 trained on the house. Should anyone rush out blindly, they were ready to open fire.

Nothing stirred, and ARSOF gave the signal they were entering the building. In the distance, PFC Ellis could just make out popping gunfire, possibly from the river if 299 EN had made contact, but it didn't sound like much resistance. Further away, ARSOF aviation, or "Little Birds," roamed the skies. None of the distant sounds were enough to wake the hut's inhabitants.

Behind Wolverine 1, COL Hickey and his crew waited with the ARSOF commander. Along with the gun truck manned by SGT Saffeels, SPC John Almen, and SPC Ribus, they'd pulled away from the convoy earlier to secure the backside of the building. PFC Lay, who was driving for LT Austin with their gunner SPC Cantou, was pulling local security at the intersection of Highway 24 and the dirt road leading to a few farms that included Wolverine 2 and the potential third objective the informant had vaguely pointed out.

No gun shots or screams came from the house.

"Must've caught them asleep," PFC Ellis said as one of the ARSOF soldiers stepped outside. He beckoned PFC Ellis and SSG Darden over, asking them to watch the detainees, whom they'd gathered on the roof. One of them was Saddam's cook, and the house belonged to the cook's brother and his small family. The ARSOF soldiers took the cook with them and moved on to the next objective

SSG Darden radioed LT Austin to let him know the objective was cleared, no gun shots, no runners, and no Saddam Hussein.

OBJECTIVE WOLVERINE 2

As the captain's driver, PFC Helmrich had the benefit of hearing all the critical communications during the BRT's missions. For this type of mission, CPT Bailey used two radios, one tuned to their Troop Net to speak with supporting conventional forces and G Troop's platoon and section leads, and the other for communicating with the ARSOF team commander. A muted explosion signaled ARSOF had entered the first objective, and a second later LT Austin confirmed the action over the Troop Net.

It wasn't long before the objective was reported cleared, and several personnel detained.

Wolverine 2 would be next. To reach the objective, PFC Helmrich had followed LT Tapp's crew and ARSOF as they drove down a lone dirt road that disappeared into an orchard and eventual darkness. CPT Bailey had him stop a few meters from the objective to maintain a clear view of the high ground—where the enemy could emerge at any moment—as well as the farm buildings. From their location, PFC Helmrich could make out three structures and brief flashes of chem lights within them as ARSOF silently cleared the buildings.

Beside him, CPT Bailey completed conditions checks with attack aviation. With ARSOF air assets already providing security overhead, they were simply lying in wait should their firepower be needed.

Over the radio, the ARSOF team commander confirmed that the objectives were abandoned.

"This is BS," CPT Bailey said to no one in particular. "We got the best intelligence, he's here, somewhere."

The Humvees surrounding Wolverine 2 pulled out, heading further down the road. There was still the unnamed objective that had been treated as a last thought by the informant. G Troop was to isolate the area on all four corners. Over the Troop Net, LT Tapp asked for one more truck to complete the cordon.

"We'll fill in," CPT Bailey said.

As they passed the two farmhouses and mud hut that made up the objective, PFC Helmrich caught a glimpse of an orange and white taxi. Now *that* was a hopeful sign—they'd searched for and chased similar taxis for weeks now after getting reports that Saddam was purportedly driving one.

CPT Bailey had him park at the edge of the orchard, 50 meters from the objective. The six-foot tall thrash fencing that spanned much of the orchard prevented a clear view of the structures. PFC Helmrich could only make out the hut's flat roof and upper portion of a tin lean-to resting against it.

"We're going in," the ARSOF team commander said over the radio.

A burst of communication came over the Troop Net from LT Tapp: "We got a 'squirter' heading northeast, Iversen's guys'll intercept him."

ARSOF cleared the first farmhouse, reported that the one-room building was empty.

SPC John Iversen spoke up on the Troop Net: "Recon 6, we got the squirter. Says he's Saddam's driver."

"Hold on to him," CPT Bailey responded.

On the troop net, the ARSOF team commander spoke up, "We'll get some guys out there and look at him when we're done."

Suddenly multiple pops like pistol fire went off close to the truck. CPL Monroe traversed the turret, prepared to fire into the trees.

CPT Bailey's tight voice rose over the sound of cracking limbs, "Hold your fire."

Most likely a few guys from ARSOF were in the orchard looking for potential hideouts; no tracers flared in the dark and there was no further sound of ammunitions. It was too risky to shoot blindly into the trees.

"Hearing shots fired within the orchard," CPT Bailey said into his mic. "Have you made contact?"

The ARSOF team commander responded, "No, just clearing the orchard. Used a 9-banger. Sorry 'bout that."

PFC Helmrich let out his breath. Further away he could just make out laser lights from ARSOF weapons jumping from spot to spot around the thrash fence and mud hut.

A few minutes later, the ARSOF team commander was back on the radio. "Looks like a dry hole."

CPT Bailey cursed. After a tense pause, he responded, "This is the best intelligence we've got. Can we check again?"

The silence was too long, and PFC Helmrich was sure the commander would turn the idea down. On past raids, once ARSOF determined the objective was a dry hole, they'd left immediately.

Finally, the ARSOF team commander broke the silence. "Yeah, we're working through it again."

From the gunner's seat, SPC Fugate could see the farmhouses and mud hut, though much of the mud hut was surrounded by a tall fence. The ARSOF soldiers moved from building to building, their infra-red lights shifting and swinging like blaster fire and lightsabers in the Star Wars movies he'd watched as a kid. Somewhere in the orchard, small explosions like rifle or pistol fire were followed by the sound of crashing brush.

ARSOF cleared the buildings in a few minutes, but instead of leaving or communicating out on the Troop Net that they'd found an HVT, they brought over three figures in Iraqi clothing—most likely detainees and their translator—and led them into the fenced-in area. He wasn't sure if either of the detainees were from

Wolverine 1 or 2 or if they'd been brought along as informants. Either way, he bet they were terrified. If Saddam was found, they'd be known throughout Iraq, even across the world, as the ones who'd turned him in. They would be everyone's enemy.

The ARSOF soldier and his dog, Rudy, searched the area. Rudy was following some scent, halting, backing up to retrace his exact steps. SPC Fugate wondered how much money and time went into training those dogs.

Silence, but for the distant, monotonous thump of helicopters, fell around them.

JACKPOT

After persuasion from ARSOF soldiers, Al-Muslit finally caved, pointing to a dusty prayer mat. The mat was removed, uncovering two cotton webbing handles connected to a block of Styrofoam. An ARSOF soldier pulled out the block and exposed a 2x2-foot opening. The prayer mat was a clever idea—no trooper would have considered touching, let alone moving one, out of respect for Iraqi customs.

Once ARSOF removed the lid, they filled the narrow hole with infra-red light and muzzles. The first thing they saw were two hands, pressed on a dirt floor. The once all-powerful Iraqi President was on his hands and knees in a space too shallow to fully stand in and only about five feet in length and width.

They yelled at him to put his hands up and come out and asked who he was, keeping their weapons trained on the prisoner.

Extending his hands, Saddam stated, "I am the President of Iraq, and I'm willing to negotiate."

"President Bush sends his regards," replied an ARSOF soldier as his men placed the dictator in flex cuffs.

Inside the hole they found a Glock 18C fully automatic pistol, a green box filled with stacks of U.S. dollars, a rug, and pair of brown flip flops. It was a sad, cramped space that the dictator had hid within during his last hours of freedom. A light gave off a weak glow against dirt walls, and an electric fan connected to a ventilation system circulated fresh air through a metal pipe. The light and fan were powered by a communication wire strung down the pipe — it had also served as the dictator's sole way to communicate with the outside world. Like the prayer mat laid over the entrance, the pipe was hidden in plain sight with the communication wire strung with sausages. This was a common enough find throughout Iraq, with civilians using such wires for just about anything, from tying up old fences to hanging their clothes out to dry.

At approximately 2026, the dry double clicks and crackle of deep break squelch broke the silence in Bailey's truck. "Recon 6, possible contact with HVT 1. Out."

In the distance, PFC Helmrich could hear yelling, but only for a moment. Silence followed. A few minutes slowly ticked by.

The radio double clicked. "Jackpot! Jackpot! Jackpot! Confirming. Out."

From the gunner's seat, CPL Munroe asked, "Did they just say jackpot?"

"Focus on manning the gun," CPT Bailey replied with a calmness PFC Helmrich didn't feel. The dictator that everyone wanted to capture, the ultimate jackpot, was in the hands of ARSOF just a few meters away.

"Confirmed, we got him," the ARSOF team commander said. "Transporting him off the objective."

SPC Fugate's hands automatically tightened on his M19 the moment brief shouts cut through the silence. Below, there was chatter on the Platoon Net, but he couldn't make out what was being said.

A Humvee shot off into the wheat field, driving in hasty circles to flatten the crops. Overhead, a Little Bird swung in, landing on the cleared area. Two ARSOF soldiers walked out of the fenced area, dragging a stumbling figure that uselessly tried to get away. His hands were flex cuffed behind his back and a sandbag covered his head.

The soldiers shoved the person into the helicopter, and within seconds it lifted off, angling northeast for Tikrit.

The ARSOF team commander radioed CPT Bailey. "We're finishing up a few things before heading out."

"It *was* him, right?"

"Yep."

CPT Bailey grinned.

"We'll be heading out," he replied. "You and the boys smile for the cameras."

"I'll tell 'em. Thanks for letting us play."

"Thanks for playing."

The remaining ARSOF elements headed out, slowing down for a moment to yell at LT Tapp's crew, "*Smile for the cameras, pretty boy,*" before speeding off.

CPT Bailey could hear their laughter even from several meters away. He grabbed the troop radio and said sharply, "Everybody shut up. We ain't talkin about nothin' yet and we ain't celebrating. Pay attention to your surroundings. We could be ambushed."

Not long after ARSOF departed, G Troop had tightened up their defense and established points of domination.

"Listen," COL Hickey said, patting CPT Bailey on the back, "I know you guys are tired, but you're going to have to secure this place, and I don't know how long that's going to be. 4-42 FA will maintain their cordon around Ad Dawr. I'll leave Alpha 1-10 CAV for reinforcement and see if I can get a few sorties from attack aviation to stay on site. You guys button up and be prepared to defend."

"Yes, sir." CPT Bailey spoke without hesitation, though exhaustion was creeping in as his excitement wore off. After nine long months, they'd accomplished their mission, and now all he wanted was to be back home with his wife and boys.

"By the way, you ever seen a million bucks?" COL Hickey pointed to a green box sitting on the ground just outside the hole where Saddam was hiding. Inside were several piles of hundred-dollar bills.

By 2100, only G Troop was left to secure the objectives, which split their troop up between Objective Wolverine 1 on the high ground and Objective Wolverine 2 and Saddam's hideout on the low ground. Being tired was nothing new for the young men, they'd gone from mission to mission without pause and had many sleepless nights and days. However, the long month in the desert culminating in an exhilarating win had forced them to the very brink of exhaustion. All that kept them going now was fear of retaliation.

Much like Saddam's sons had put up a substantial fight against U.S. forces, there was a chance for significant retribution now. G Troop was a small shoal of fish in a tub. There was only one drivable road in and out of their location. They were surrounded by the Tigris on the west, high ground to the north and east, and the town of Ad Dawr to the south. While the people of Ad Dawr wouldn't have significant firepower, CPT Bailey was concerned about the power of the masses. If hundreds of Iraqis descended on them, G Troop would need help.

This dominating presence was ready. COL Hickey had left Alpha 1-10 CAV, which would more than make up for any resistance G Troop's .50 CALs and MK19s couldn't handle. Simply put, as an armored calvary troop, Alpha 1-10 CAV was best suited for obliterating the enemy and everything around them, and they'd been looking for a fight the past nine months.

"I knew that if I did have to call them in, Alpha 1-10 CAV would take out everything. So how would I get my boys out of the way? I was looking at the map, developing a scheme of maneuver, making control graphics in case the worst happened," said Bailey.

Once he'd set up the plan for response and evacuation, CPT Bailey texted it over the FBCB2 to the Alpha Troop commander. The plan was for Alpha 1-10 CAV to travel four kilometers from their current location, which would set them on the high ground, not only above the basin that G Troop was in, but also above the outer cordon set up by 4-42 FA. They would attack by fire position north and suppress any attacks. Most importantly, CPT Bailey noted that the tanks would need to lower their barrels to avoid firing on 4-42 FA's checkpoints in Ad Dawr.

"I told the commander that if things went to hell, my guys were withdrawing to the river. There was an orchard, open land, and then the Tigris—we'd be in that open area. Everything over the crest of the hill was fair game except for the open land and river," explained Bailey. "From there, we could—with or without our Humvees—head north and link up with them or link up with the 299 EN boat patrols on the river and egress if needed."

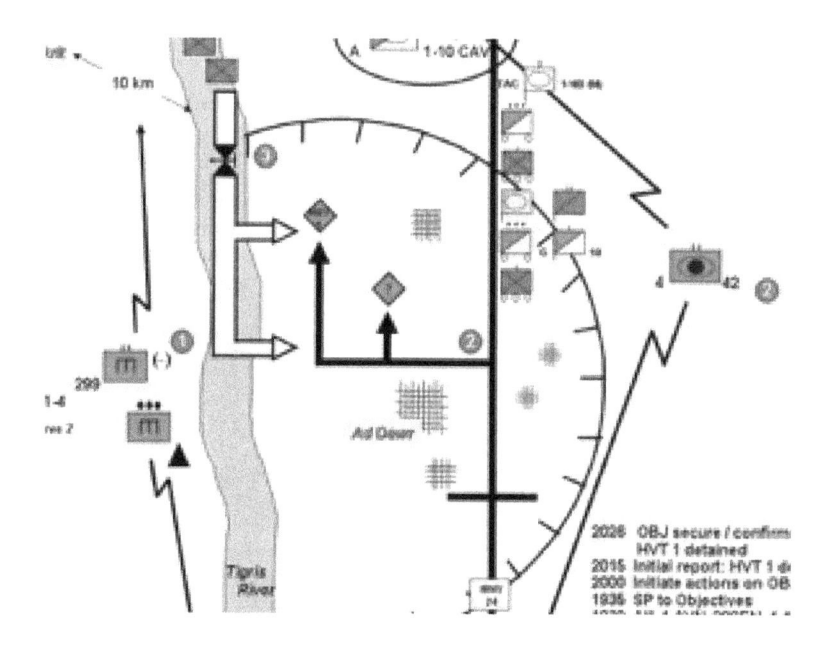

Operation Red Dawn Mission Plan

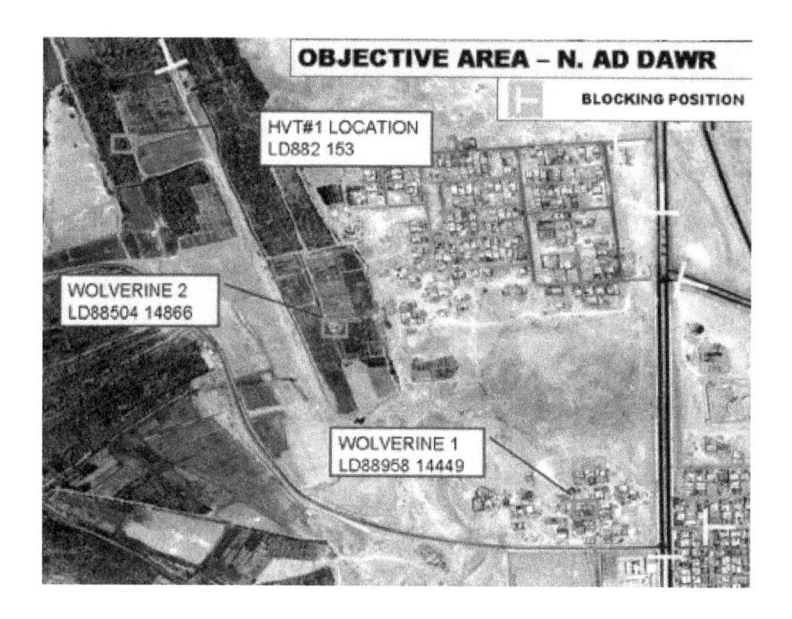

Aerial view of the three objectives and Saddam Hussein's location (HVT#1).

Aerial view of the objective where Saddam was captured

Photo of how Saddam's hiding place was obscured and entrance plug

Recon 701

Photo of how Saddam's hiding place was obscured and entrance plug

Money found in Saddam's possession

12. When teenagers and 20-somethings make history

DECEMBER 2003

"I rarely think about the significance of what we did and what it entailed. It's surreal to think about, though. We were just 20-somethings going through this stuff, but we made history."

—Sergeant Daniel Saffeels

G Troop had come a long way since they'd left Fort Hood nine months prior. They'd pushed through Baghdad and into the unknown, accomplishing a staggering number and range of missions throughout Salah Ad Din Province. Challenging the ever-evolving threats head on, the troop had grown remarkably fast into a first-rate unit. Their resilience—a result of continual training, determined leadership, and care for one another—served them well. Multiple HVTs, including al-Muslit, were found either directly by G Troop or by other Army units based on intelligence the BRT had uncovered. On December 13, 2003, this small group of young troopers reached the ultimate end game: capturing Saddam Hussein.

A DIFFERENT TYPE OF SECRET SQUIRREL

Though Saddam was captured, the night wasn't over for G Troop.

"We were more than exhausted that night. Some of the men dozed for minutes at a time while others kept watch on the objectives. At 3:30 a.m., Captain Sweigart radioed in, waking me from a short nap," said Bailey.

A site exploitation team would arrive soon, and the troopers needed to clear a landing zone for two CH-47 Chinooks. SGT Szott joined SSG Womack—who was formally trained in establishing and illuminating a landing zone to guide in aircraft for landing—to an old soccer field, just beyond the orchards. While SSG Womack removed several yards of barbed wire, SGT Szott laid down two Chinook J-landing patterns within the confines of the soccer field.

Through his night vision goggles, CPT Bailey watched the Chinooks slowly approach the objective, just as the troopers started laying down two 26-foot chem-lights to illuminate the landing area. It would be a tight fit, but would have to work.

The Chinooks landed in complete darkness with over two dozen individuals in various uniforms and civilian clothes exited, some carrying large boxes of equipment. SGT Szott and SSG Womack loaded two vehicles and quickly moved them to the objective.

"I ended up pulling entrance security that morning," said Lay. "I'm so tired, thirsty, hungry, and I can't remember when I'd last slept. These two freshly showered guys come up to me, asking where my commander is. They've got sunglasses on, gel in their hair, clean black uniforms, spotless black vests, polished black boots. They're holding short barrel rifles. Obviously, they were some type of secret squirrel from a three-letter agency or civilian group and hadn't been in Iraq over a day."

CPT Bailey's truck blocked the lone road leading to Saddam's hideout. From his vantage point, the very efficient and very clean strangers who'd descended with boxes of equipment were an entertaining side show. They would spend the entire morning there, searching the site for any evidence that could be used to further efforts against the insurgency and prosecute Saddam. From hair follicles to documents, clothing to fingerprints, everything would be recorded, packed, and taken away.

Not long after the site exploitation team's arrival, a man wearing a white button-up shirt, black Members Only jacket, blue jeans, and penny loafers. Several forms of identification hung around his neck and a short barrel rifle was strapped across his chest.

After a short introduction, the man asked, "Who's in charge here?"

"That would be me," replied CPT Bailey. "My troop's currently securing both objectives." He then gave a brief situation report on the location and number of his men, vehicles, and detainees.

"Okay, so here's the deal," the man said, "Nobody gets in, nobody gets out."

CPT Bailey nodded and spit out a wad of tobacco — one of the few things keeping him awake. "Understood."

"When's the last time you had stateside Copenhagen?"

"Eleven months, four days."

The man dug out a cardboard can of Copenhagen from his pocket, handed it over.

CPT Bailey grinned. "You're the man! Thanks."

The man gave him a slight smile and nod before disappearing into a gathering of men outside Saddam's hideout.

Unsure how much longer they'd be left to secure the area, CPT Bailey had the platoon leaders confirm how much water the troop had—it wasn't much. They also didn't have any food and hadn't eaten since yesterday morning, over 24 hours ago. He radioed 1SG Justis to coordinate with 4-42 FA and get them some MREs and water.

Hours passed; an overbearing heat settled around them. In the passenger's seat, CPT Bailey closed his eyes to the glaring sunlight, exhausted.

Beside him, someone cleared their throat. He didn't move.

A moment later, a hand pressed on his shoulder. "Hey, buddy, stay with me just a little while longer...you with me?"

The captain opened his eyes, straightening up in his seat. Standing beside him was an average-looking man, his clothes and features dusty.

"Yes, sir. Sorry for being out of it," CPT Bailey said.

"No worries, man. I need a ride to the first objective."

"Yes, sir," CPT Bailey said.

The man jumped on the hood of Bailey's Humvee.

"You wanna get in the back, man? It's not safe on the hood."

"Nah, I'll be fine," he said stretching out his legs. "Just take off."

Shrugging, CPT Bailey told Helmrich to drive them to Objective Wolverine 1. After dropping him off, they drove back to Saddam's hideout, but came to a stop on the dirt road as the orange and white taxi that had been parked at a shed nearby pulled up next to them. Inside, sat a pale American civilian.

Rolling down the taxi window, the man asked, "What's the best way south, the best way to get out of Ad Dawr?"

"Are you serious? Do you need an escort?" CPT Bailey asked.

"No escort, just directions."

THE SADDAM MEDIA FRENZY

When the sun rose on December 15, G Troop was still awake and still guarding Saddam's hideout.

"We were exhausted," recalled Szott. "At that point, you're looking at rocks in riverbeds and they're moving around in weird ways because you're hallucinating from being up so long. You get used to it, though, we'd had plenty of missions that went two or three days. If you can make it to sunrise, you can be up for another day. And we did get some short naps in, laying on Humvee hoods or sitting straight up, whatever we could do."

SPC Fugate and his crew had crawled into the hideout and taken pictures as soon as it was light enough. Someone had peed in the hole, and he felt bad watching the troopers who climbed down into the small space the remainder of the morning.

MAJ GEN Odierno had come through, stopping by his Humvee. "So Ray Ray—that's what we called him back then—stopped and asked us how we were doing. At that point I figured the war was over, at least it should have been over," says Fugate.

Well into the morning, CPT Bailey received a call from COL Hickey telling him 4-42 FA would replace G Troop, and they could return to their command post. CPT Bailey's first stop was at FOB Raider where COL Hickey and Major Reed informed him that President George Bush and Ambassador Paul Bremer had formally announced to the world that Saddam was captured. Media from the U.S. and across the world would be in Iraq, expecting a tour of the objective and as much information as they could get. Inevitably, reporters would make their way to lower ranking troopers. It was imperative leadership determine what information was safe for public knowledge and agree to a specific narrative for the world to read and hear.

This was the first time CPT Bailey had ever heard of a media narrative or messaging. "I remember wondering what the big deal was. We should just tell the people what the heck happened," recalls Bailey. "But COL Hickey had far more experience, and he knew that we had to be careful about what was revealed to the media."

There was much they couldn't divulge at the time, such as the name of the source who'd given away Saddam's final hiding spot and the organizations that made up the site exploitation team. To avoid any slip of restricted information, they agreed to avoid mentioning certain aspects of the mission and the agencies involved. This included avoiding any mention of the ARSOF soldiers, as well as their role in Iraq. ARSOF was a highly confidential unit, and its operatives lived a secluded, secret life for three reasons: to protect themselves, their families, and their mission.

After laying out the aspects of the mission they would share with the public, the remaining concern was that the media would want to know who specifically had pulled Saddam out of the hole; they would want to talk to the trooper and ask them how it felt, what Saddam had looked like or said to them. CPT Bailey, COL Hickey, and Major Reed wanted to recognize ARSOF for what they'd accomplished. They'd worked with G Troop and other units in 1BCT for months, and Bailey's troopers had learned a great deal from the skilled troopers. They deserved a significant amount of the credit that 600 soldiers from 1BCT would share across the world. However, with no special operations media guidance, COL Hickey eventually decided they would state that "a *Special Forces* soldier pulled Saddam Hussein out of the hole."

After going three days non-stop, CPT Bailey was in dire need of a shower and clean uniform before entertaining the media. Getting a freshly starched uniform was going to be a significant task. Hurrying to the troop's FOB, he pulled out a uniform that he'd stashed under his bed mat for emergencies. He'd slept on it whenever he was at FOB Buffalo as a way to press it—a helpful trick he'd learned in the Marines.

"It was flat, but there were a few creases I didn't like, so I took the uniform downstairs and Sergeant Faucette pulled out a blow torch and piece of steel to use as an iron. I pressed out the creases and was ready for prime time," Bailey recalls, laughing. "By that afternoon, I found a moment to call Kelly. I told her I loved her and to watch the news. I gave Helmrich and Monroe the option to stay at troop HQ and rest or go with me, and they chose the latter. They were determined to always go wherever I was heading."

Twenty-six media agencies descended upon the brigade and Saddam's small hideout.

COL Hickey and Major Reed hosted the agencies and Bailey escorted the reporters around the objective, pointing out where his troopers were positioned and what their role had been. At the spider hole where the special forces soldier had pulled the dictator out, he described what the troopers had been doing and where he'd been, and what it had felt like to hear "Jackpot" over the radio.

By the end of it, Bailey was ready to get back to work.

On December 15, the troopers started calling home to tell their families they'd been a part of the historic mission. SPC Fugate called his aunt that day, which was his 21st birthday, to tell her they'd caught Saddam Hussein on *her* birthday—a surprising gift for them both.

Many of those moments were shared by family members with newspapers and television stations when word spread about the units and 600 soldiers that were involved. SGT Saffeels and PFC Helmrich were mentioned in multiple articles and news segments in their home state of Iowa. SGT Saffeels had called his mother to recount the dream-like experience. She recalled that he'd sounded tired, almost discouraged, on past calls but when he called her on December 15, he was ecstatic and had told her that everything he'd gone through was worth it to catch Saddam.

Their biggest moment came when they were featured on Good Morning America. The troopers welcomed the nation with a "Good Morning from Tikrit, Iraq" as the unit that captured Saddam Hussein. Group photos in and around the hideout were taken and interviews held.

During one interview, SPC Ryan Brescher was surprised by the Good Morning America team with a phone call from his wife and newborn daughter.

"They had a camera in his face, and Brescher broke down in tears," recalled Lay. "He was nine months into deployment and hadn't seen his daughter yet. We were about 20 feet behind him, not knowing what's going on, all we know is that he's crying. So, we're heckling him and calling him a wimp. Of course, all that was caught on camera."

"Even now to say that I was a part of that…it's overwhelming in a way," said Ellis. "Leading the way deep into Iraq and then capturing Saddam made me a part of history."

Looking back, few of the troopers are surprised by where they found Saddam. After a failed assassination attempt on the prime minster of Iraq in 1959, Saddam had hidden in Ad Dawr as well and then escaped by swimming across the Tigris to exile in Syria. One evening near Ad Dawr, G Troop had trailed an orange and white taxi that had a large man in the backseat with a large beard. Its lights were all blacked out, and they were driving fast on a dark road at a high rate of speed. SGT Szott gave his gunner authorization to fire, but seconds later reverse it as the call came over the radio to stand down. They'd lost the cab soon after. The beautiful

Arabian racing horses G Troop had come across weeks ago were nearby, too.

"It was surreal, looking back at how close we'd come so many times and where Saddam ended up getting captured," shares Corcoles, who'd been part of the outer cordon with 4-42 FA during Operation Red Dawn. "I'd been in the area so many times with G Troop and 4-42 FA. The locals there were nice, and we engaged with everybody we could. The kids would always come up to us and tell us that they'd seen Saddam. We'd give them candy. Some of the people there knew. But you can only do so much because you know of the risk, and you only have so much information at the time."

For Saffeels, it was an incredible experience getting to call his family and tell them what he'd been a part of, which followed up with several media interviews. Even his parents got a call from a CNN news crew — already on the way to their house in Iowa — requesting an interview. Despite the extraordinary night and excitement that followed, Saffeels shares what matters most about G Troop's triumph: "I felt that we hadn't lost our guys in vain. There's a purpose for everything, and they were part of what we accomplished."

"After the capture, I thought it was done," says Sparks. "We'd be heading home soon — maybe not by Christmas, but definitely by New Year's. Of course, that didn't happen."

Picture of Saddam Hussein following his capture

MG Ray Odierno briefing reporters from all over the world about the capture of Saddam.

Recon 701

Multiple Troopers posing for a photo at the Saddam hole

COL Jim Hickey, CO of 1BCT and MG Ray Odierno, CG of 4ID

13. The Mission Continues

DECEMBER 2003 – MARCH 2004

"Things started to feel repetitive—we'd go out on patrols, try to keep the peace. At the same time, it started getting more dangerous across the country."

—**Private First Class Brandon Ellis**

While their sense of accomplishment remains two decades later, the elation G Troop felt following Saddam's capture was short lived. The exhausted troop received just two days of rest before setting out to capture additional high value targets alongside ARSOF while maintaining daily patrols and the counter-mortar fight.

The BRT received new tasks as well. They would expand their reconnaissance north and east of Baiji and find the insurgents responsible for an increasing number of long-range rocket launches steadily impacting near 4ID HQ. This provided many opportunities for the newest platoon leaders, LTs Allen Renazco and Zeke Austin, to lead critical missions with limited support from the spread-out troop.

Though the mission continued, the end of deployment was in sight. All 4ID soldiers would be back in the U.S. by March, replaced by 1st Infantry Division (1ID).

BATTLING EXHAUSTION, COMPLACENCY, AND INCREASED RISK

"Everybody was riding a huge high, we were all stoked," said Lay. "We'd had front row seats to the end finale, or so we thought at the time. The excitement wore off quickly, though. I'm sure that was another challenge for leadership: how do you refocus a group of guys from that level of elation? We still had a job to do, we had to get back to the nitty gritty, sitting in a cow barn for 12 hours looking for a specific vehicle. How do you get a group of guys back to that level?"

They still had many jobs to do, and they were all exhausted. "It's mission complete then, right? We were tired and ready to get the hell out of there," said Saffeels. "But it wasn't over. It was still mission upon mission, every day. We started wondering why we were still there, what more was there to do other than hand the country over to the Iraqis and head home?"

Refocusing his young troopers weighed heavy on CPT Bailey's mind, "I wondered how I could keep the troop focused on the old and new mission requirements. With the fanfare over, news of redeployment, and overall troop exhaustion, I was concerned we'd become complacent. I think I *may* have increased the stress levels of my platoon leaders and sergeants with daily brow beatings over the radio, but I didn't want their edge dulled. I was going to make the cost of stupid mistakes utter hell and keep them working hard in order to keep them alive," said Bailey.

Homemade bombs were becoming a bigger issue, and though

no one in G Troop drove into an IED, the risk was made pointedly clear when SGT Bernard Walla radioed CPT Bailey one morning to tell him they'd found a potential IED where the captain had been establishing his observation post at night to overwatch the troopers while they patrolled.

"The enemy had taken an air defense artillery shell and threaded a wire through it. They'd sat it in the exact spot I'd parked my truck several times because it was a great vantage point. They were testing us to see if we'd even notice it. That bothered me, and put me in a different state of awareness," said Bailey.

WELCOME TO THE TROOP ... SEVEN MONTHS IN

LT Allan Renazco arrived in Iraq with with 3-66 Armor on April 1, 2003, just two weeks out of Ranger School. Like Bailey, he'd first enlisted in the Army and then shifted course to become an officer. For six months LT Renazco and 12 NCOs helped recruit, train, and deploy 200 members of the Iraqi Civil Defense Corps. It was a task he'd never imagined being assigned.

"On the first day, I had 28 men to train. I'd prepared a speech, and as my interpreter read it, the Iraqis started walking out. The reality was I'd written a speech that would inspire Americans, not Iraqis. I had to learn fast what they cared about and how to motivate them," said Renazco. "Did I see myself doing that before I got there? No way. But I knew I had to figure it out, and I did. With that first group, I was honest and told them if they wanted me out of there, they had to learn how to defend themselves and their people."

In early December, LT Renazco's commander told him he was being re-assigned to G Troop and would be taking over 3rd Platoon. On December 14, mid-way through transitioning the Iraqi

Civil Defense Force to another lieutenant, he was told to get his things ready. The morning of December 15, he was Scorpion's newest lieutenant.

"These guys had just captured Saddam Hussein, and they were rock stars. There was such a buzz going around the whole country. It was a whole other level of surreal because I realized that I was those guys' leader," said Renazco. "When I arrived, staff members at Brigade HQ kept congratulating me for capturing Saddam, and I kept telling them I wasn't there. It wasn't long before one of my troopers told me that I was part of the 'we' now."

And there's a good chance that he was. In November, LT Renazco had been part of a unit that reconned the objective and surrounding homes where Saddam was found. They'd uncovered legal documents and other items that the lieutenant had handed over to 4-42 FA's Intelligence unit.

Having worked in 3-66 Armor's Tactical Operations Center, the lieutenant recognized the uniqueness of G Troop's command structure. In 3-66 AR, the processing of orders and coordination of missions had felt slow and clunky to LT Renazco.

"G Troop was different," explained Renazco. "We were directly under Colonel Hickey, and he was also in charge of the whole brigade. If he had a hunch, we'd go and validate it. There was a lot of upside to responding quickly and not knowing far in advance what we'd be doing. It kept us from slowing down and kept pressure on the enemy."

Resources remained minimal, and there was no command Humvee for the lieutenant. Making the best of the situation, instead of taking a truck from an existing crew, he moved from truck to truck for each patrol and mission. Getting to know the trooper's personalities and perspectives on an operation was invaluable for the steep learning curve he climbed.

Shifting from an artillery unit to a brigade reconnaissance troop was a crash course for LT Renazco who had no experience with scout units, technology like the LRAS3, or the extent of resources at their command. With Bradleys, tanks, and helicopters supporting the troop, he had battalion-level assets at his disposal but lacked experience in the extensive coordination they required.

"I probably didn't plan for them as efficiently as I could because I didn't have experience doing that," shared Renazco. "I talked to Flo, my sergeant, and spoke with the troopers, who manned the assets, about their capabilities before drawing up a plan in the dirt."

SFC Flores and LT Renazco were close in age and had both enlisted around the same time. Though LT Renazco had moved on to become an officer, they both had a similar mindset, and SFC Flores was a reliable and straightforward NCO.

"I always asked for Flo's assessment, and I trusted what he told me. It was incredibly humbling, and I knew as the platoon leader, I needed to look, listen, and learn from my non-commissioned officers. So, I was learning and I valued his perspective," said Renazco.

Taking on a platoon so far into their deployment had its fair share of challenges. The troopers were exhausted from the constant high tempo operations. This led to mistakes, like failing to follow mission orders. CPT Bailey's response over the radio would be loud, frustrated, and direct. This was unsurprising to those who knew how calm and collected he was when the risks and stakes were high, but it was a shock to G Troop's newer troopers.

Being worn out left everyone tense and stressed. At times animosity or irritation was palpable between leadership or the younger privates and specialists.

"There's also the reality of this type of war," added Renazco. "It's 99 percent boredom and one percent sheer terror. You're on missions for hours, waiting and watching for something that might happen. You got to do it in the rain, in the dark, in the cold, and in the heat. It's easy to drift off. You have to keep your mind sharp in whatever way you can."

HIGH PLAINS DRIFTER

"This is crazy. That's Ray Ray's house," SSG Darden said, standing on the edge of a stony outcropping.

"Yep, and that's the chow hall," CPT Bailey replied, just as surprised.

Beside him, SPC Helmrich reached out from the driver's side of their Humvee, pointing south. "There's the Frat House."

"The river looks nice," said SSG Darden, "too bad it's full of shit."

Near the chow hall, the main palace that MAJ GEN Odierno quartered in rose up, a massive structure compared to its surroundings. Set on a ridge that dropped sharply into the sparkling Tigris, the palace towered over the palm trees and farmland, which spread eastward several kilometers, petering out as the desert slowly rose, transforming into rocky hills that met the Jabal Hamrin Ridge.

After traveling 26 km, they now stood on one of its highest points, watching the morning sun glint off the bright white chow hall roof. The FOB was such an easy target.

"I'll radio Colonel Hickey. He's right, they're aiming for General Odierno," CPT Bailey said.

For several months, 4ID artillery units had captured incoming artillery on their radar. These weren't the more common attacks from the Mad Mortarman, who had yet to be caught. The acquisitions were coming out of the northeastern desert, most likely not far from where CPT Bailey and his patrol stood.

At first, CPT Bailey had thought little of the reports. The radar could pick up shots from weaponry as small as a pistol and no one had heard any explosions from larger artillery nearby. The acquisitions were coming from outside G Troop's area of operations. Nevertheless, ahead of going out west, G Troop had investigated. Driving wherever their Humvees could reach, the troopers had searched the Jabal Hamrin Ridge for signs of rocket launchers. After several fruitless days, they'd headed back to base.

Not long after G Troop returned from Operation Red Dawn, however, the artillery brigade reported several more acquisitions from the northeast. This time a G Troop trooper manning an observation post on the 4ID HQ perimeter wall *had* heard an explosion in the Tigris River. The smell of rocket fuel had followed.

A few days later, an SS30 rocket slammed into the northeast corner of 4ID HQ. Measuring 3.9m in length and 127mm in diameter, the 68kg rocket could easily have destroyed the FOB's chow hall. They'd lucked out this time—no one was injured.

COL Hickey told CPT Bailey to take G Troop back to the Jabal Hamrin Ridge and figure out what was going on and where the rockets would come from next. Looking back at the artillery unit's reports on point of origin and how the locations and arcs had changed would give CPT Bailey some idea of where to expect the next launch site. It would still be a large area to recon, and he doubted they had much time before another launch. They'd have to increase and expand their patrols and recon missions.

CPT Bailey assigned 18 troopers on one-day and two-day missions to the northeastern desert to look for suspicious vehicles. The troopers would take two and three hour shifts to keep watch over small villages or expanses of desert and lonely roads while the others slept or caught up on letters home.

Most days were uninteresting, and time passed slowly. Sometimes, they would run into pop up ambushes, with machine guns firing at them from the roadside. They'd rush through the kill zone, and by the time they'd turned the trucks around to battle back in, the attackers had usually fled.

One day, SSG Wommack and LT Renazco came across a group of Iraqis having a barbecue. After the men left, the troopers surveyed the scene. Earlier, they'd found an area with scorch marks blackening the ground, and COL Hickey believed it was where rockets had been launched from. Those marks looked eerily similar to the ones left behind by the barbecue pits, though, and so they couldn't confirm one way or the other.

Their search took them further and further out from the troop's original AO. LT Renazco was assigned a mission called High Plains Drifter, after the 1973 Clint Eastwood movie, of which CPT Bailey was a fan. They were to recon the village of Al-Shirqat, which was a few kilometers north of Baiji, and gather any information they could. Though 3-66 AR was responsible for the area, they'd gathered very little intelligence on the small village.

"They never went on patrol in that area because their battalion deemed it too dangerous. We didn't think that way, though. We operated with a simple mindset: we were there to maintain pressure on the enemy and find the bad guys," recalled Renazco.

Later, as the other platoons from G Troop patrolled the east side of the Tigris where they believed the rocket attacks were originating, a report burst across the troop radio: an AH-64 pilot had seen an approximately 6-foot-long rocket shoot past him. In the reflection of his helicopter's canopy, it had resembled a "telephone pole with its ass on fire." He reported to CPT Bailey that he had the guilty parties in sight; their expensive white car was speeding down the desert highway, and he only needed the command to fire. CPT Bailey told the pilot to shoot along the sides of the vehicle—the men needed to be alive for questioning. Once CPT Bailey, and several other troopers arrived at the scene, they quickly realized how fortunate that was.

"It was several government leaders of Salah Ah Din province and a bodyguard," Bailey admitted. "The pilot may have been chasing the perpetrators and then briefly lost sight and confused them with the group of government leaders, maybe it was a coincidence altogether...maybe not."

The search continued. As the troopers traveled from village to small town, SGT Szott who spoke enough Arabic to be helpful, showed the civilians a rocket he'd sketched on a 3x5 card. The simple drawing paid off. Locals pointed the troopers to where they'd seen rockets launched, and CPT Bailey shot azimuths and triangulating points of origin based on where the civilians gestured.

After several days of civilian questioning and pointing, CPT Bailey did a bit of "trooper math" and pointed out an area on their map. The Scorpion patrol headed out. Enroute, they found an abandoned rocket launcher, which was a man-made patchwork of materials, including an irrigation pipe cut in half to form a sled with metal legs and a plate welded to the bottom. The enemy would ignite the rockets with an electrical charge that was connected to a battery-operated washing machine timer. In the distance, the silhouette of 4ID HQ rose dark against the auburn sky.

Though they didn't catch the men behind the rocket launches, the attacks finally stopped.

"You don't always catch the bad guy," Bailey said. "But a part of war is exhausting the enemy—their fire power, their willpower, their money, their resources. Did the rocket launches stop because they ran out of ammunition? Or was it because they only had the one launcher that we found? Maybe they gave up out of fear since we were so close to finding them. Whatever the reason, the attacks stopped, and this consistent whittling away at the enemy was critical to finding Saddam, stopping the ambushes and, ultimately, keeping all the American and Iraqi men and women safe."

THE FOGGY NIGHT

For the remainder of their deployment, G Troop continued working alongside ARSOF, but now they had less requirements to support the unit, whose focus had shifted to Baghdad and Mosul. Instead of heading out on raids with multiple teams, the troopers would work with only a few ARSOF soldiers. At times, the troopers would even take on smaller ARSOF missions alone.

"We were the easy button for the brigade when they needed something handled. Then we became the easy button for the ARSOF guys. At first, they gave us little jobs here and there. We did them right. Next thing you know, we're handling whole objectives, and that's a big deal," said Szott. "Everybody in the unit should be proud of that because we did so much with very little resources."

As close as they were to re-deploying, PFC Lay figured this was one of, if not *the* final, mission G Troop would take on with the ARSOF team they'd captured Saddam alongside. The special forces soldiers were cycling out, and his unit would soon be working with a new batch of ARSOF soldiers.

As usual, the team they'd accompanied that night had stayed silent on who they were searching for at the two objectives. But, with the ARSOF troop commander present, PFC Lay wondered if it weren't al-Duri they were after, the number 3 HVT. Before the Coalition Forces invaded, Izzat Ibrahim al-Duri had been the deputy chairman of the Revolutionary Command Council and another of Saddam's right-hand men. Now he was considered a leading figure behind much of the resistance.

"It figures we'd be driving blind tonight of all nights," Lay said to LT Austin, adjusting his failing night vision goggles.

A thick fog blanketed the dry ground and sat heavy in the winter air. Even if his goggles worked properly, it would be hard to see where they were going.

"Still not working?"

"No, like everything else," Lay responded. Their Humvees and equipment had been falling apart for weeks, and there were no replacement parts. While the mechanics were working miracles with the trucks, his night vision goggles would stay broken.

PFC Lay swung open the door and looked down. "I can see the road." The speedometer read five miles per hour. He called up to the gunner, "Cantu, tell me if I'm about to hit something."

"Will do."

The fog had settled in as they headed to the second objective, and with all their top of the line, space age equipment, the ARSOF team had sped off. On the Troop Net, they heard LT Renazco and SSG Darden's crews had kept up with their ARSOF teams, meanwhile PFC Lay couldn't see the front of his truck, and the Humvee behind him was keeping nose to butt trying to keep them in view.

LT Austin was switching between the radio and looking at their FBCB2, trying to guide SGT Middlebrook's truck back to where they were. There was a delay on the machine, so each time he told the sergeant where to stop or turn off, the truck had already passed the spot.

Radio silence broke on the Troop Net, "Target's on the run."

LT Austin sighed, giving up on trying to navigate the other crew.

"This'll be funny in ten years," Lay said, braking the already slow moving vehicle.

"Assuming we make it back to base," Austin replied.

Their radio clicked on again, "Caught him, let's get ready to go."

CPT Bailey, who'd accompanied them with his own section to provide reinforcements, radioed for his troopers to check in just as the commander's Humvee took shape in the grey mist.

Looks like we'll make it back this time, Lay thought. Beside him, LT Austin was telling the captain they were giving SGT Middlebrooks directions without much luck. By CPT Bailey's tone, it was obvious there'd be hell to pay when they did make it back, though.

Despite his frustration, CPT Bailey didn't slam the radio down this time after his Platoon Leaders checked in. They were better and smarter than this.

"Black Sheep 1," he finally said over Black Sheep's Platoon Net, "if your driver's night vision isn't working, give him your goggles or get in the driver's seat."

The ARSOF team commander, stood outside his team's Humvee, waiting nearby. Two of his men had sprinted after the running target, quickly catching him despite the heavy fog and insurgent's track star speed. ARSOF needed to get back to HQ with their prisoner ASAP, but instead were waiting around for certain members of the troop to figure out how to work a compass and link up.

Sparks recalls the moment during the mission when the two ARSOF soldiers running after the enemy paused at SGT Marroquin's truck, saying they needed two of his men.

"So here SGT Brooks and I are, trying to keep up with two super elite guys running with their full kit on like it's nothing. We end up at a house and they tell us to post outside the door, not let anyone in or out," said Sparks. "They go in, and it's quiet for about five seconds, then all hell broke loose because they knew one of the people in that house didn't belong there."

The ARSOF soldiers had first looked at the shoe rack in the front hallway—noticing a pair of freshly muddied shoes. When they entered the main living area, everyone was distressed and nervous, but one of them was sweating and more jittery than the rest.

"He'd barreled into the house and threatened the family. But the special forces guys knew what to look for. Being with them was like being a college athlete joining a pro team for a practice session. They never sat down and formally taught us, but we picked up on things and implemented them," said Sparks.

Overhead, Little Birds circled the area, their sound dampened by the fog. They had more powerful thermal imagery, but still hadn't caught site of the missing patrol. *Where in the world are they?*

SSG Darden radioed in. His crew was on the road with the rest of ARSOF, smoking cigarettes while they waited.

"Y'all go ahead and go," CPT Bailey told the ARSOF team commander. "I'll get the guys rounded up."

"We're only two vehicles, so, no."

The ARSOF team commander didn't seem at all irritated by the situation, but it was taking CPT Bailey all his patience not to pick up the radio and remind them they were the troopers who'd been on the ground at Saddam's capture, they'd been the tip of the spear through the desert, busting through enemy territory and giving the insurgents a well-deserved fear of America's soldiers.

SGT Middlebrooks finally came over the radio. He had no idea where they were.

CPT Bailey cursed under his breath.

"We could shoot up a star cluster," the ARSOF team commander offered. "There's no way they won't see it."

Bailey agreed and told SGT Middlebrooks to keep an eye out.

A few moments later, a ARSOF soldier lit the star cluster. Within seconds, bright, white light split the sky.

There was silence on the Platoon Net. "Black Sheep 3, do you see it?"

"No, sir," the sergeant replied.

"I can't believe this," CPT Bailey said. "Do a 180 and watch again."

A second star cluster shot into the sky.

"I got it, I got it!"

"Great," CPT Bailey replied dryly.

Bailey thanked the ARSOF team commander, who shook his head. "Just don't be too hard on the boys when we get back. It's been a long deployment."

PREPARING FOR THE RETURN HOME

"I remember hearing buzz of our heading home in January, but there was always talk of it. Honestly, I didn't think about home much, other than this unnatural craving I had for an Arby's sandwich that started in July," said Lay. "Something I've carried with me from that time is knowing not to bother with stuff until you know it's going to happen. When the topic came up, I didn't think much about it. I'd be happy when it actually happened."

In February, it finally became real with the troopers assigned preparatory tasks that included orienting the incoming unit to the battlespace. These right-seat, left-seat rides were a chance to familiarize the new troopers with the area and what the BRT had experienced and fought against over their deployment.

As the troop maintained daily operations and filled in the new unit, CPT Sweigart and 1SG Justis added to their responsibilities as well. CPT Sweigart oversaw redeployment administrative tasks, including accounting for and preparing the equipment, while 1SG Justis planned for an early return to the U.S.

"I left a definitive timeline with Darden, Womack, and Flores, covering everything they'd need to go forward and be successful while I was gone. I knew there was a land grab going on at Fort Hood, and in the briefings I'd attended, all 4ID's units were accounted for back at Hood except for G Troop. I wasn't going to let them be an afterthought," said Justis.

Along with a small, advanced party that included troopers from HQ and the BRT's Supply Sergeant, 1SG Justis arrived home at the beginning of March. Much of the base was under hurried reconstruction, and temporary double wide trailers for the troopers sprawled across a large, open field. The first sergeant would ensure his men didn't end up in them. His eyes were set on the newly renovated barracks.

"I found the people at housing and told them to give me the keys to the barracks building. I made sure to get rooms for every one of my troopers in a single building," said Justis. "My wife and kids came up with me to set up every room with drinks and snacks, toiletries, and welcome home cards. My wife was instrumental in coming up with a plan to celebrate these troopers' return. We wanted to make them feel good. That was always my main focus: to take care of them."

"Even though our unit was small, our family support group and 1SG Justis were the freakin' best. In all my years served and all the deployments I went on, no one has come close to what they did to support us. There's nothing comparable to what they did," shared Sharpless.

THE LAST AMBUSH

Back in Iraq, even as G Troop brought on the new unit and packed their equipment and belongings, combat operations continued. During a dismount operation with Scorpion Platoon, Renazco and five of his men were crossing through a backyard, heading to a location where an overwatch element had spotted suspicious activity. Midway across, they were stopped by an elderly woman's cries of "Alibaba! Alibaba!"

"Immediately following the woman running into the house, her husband ran outside with an AK-47 and began firing on the patrol," recalled Renazco. "I yelled at him that we were U.S. Forces, but it didn't matter. He shot at me. I heard that bullet go right past my head. In the very same moment he fired, Szott returned fire, nearly separating the shooter's arm. I'll always remember that night. Szott saved my life."

SGT Szott on initial contact suppressed the attacker with three rounds. Screaming "on me" he raced to stack-up on the door. The attacker was lying on the ground moaning in pain with a large amount of blood around him. With the rest of his team on the door, they kicked in the steel down and cleared the house. A few weapons but no additional contraband. Several of the troopers not clearing the home or securing the perimeter provided first aid to the attacker and escorted him to the hospital in Tikrit.

It was during their final week in Iraq that the BRT faced their last ambush. The troop had relocated to the brigade HQ, FOB Raider, and CPT Bailey had spent time that morning on the familiar rooftop veranda from his planning days, soaking in the dusty view while he drank a coke, knowing it was the last time he'd have such a view. He kept busy the rest of the day updating situation reports, answering questions for the new ARSOF team on the ground, and discussing redeployment preparations with CPT Sweigart. That night, he headed out on patrol with CPT Mark Payne, a good friend, an operations officer for BDE HQ staff. COL Hickey had initiated a program for his brigade staff where select staff members would occasionally join CPT Bailey when he commanded evening patrols to better understand the area. Looking at maps and screens to plan missions and write reports was useful but connecting that with what it looked like on the ground was immensely better.

CPT Bailey had just shown him the grain feed facility where they'd met with ARSOF and COL Hickey ahead of capturing Saddam when the pop of small arms fire broke through the sounds of evening traffic.

SPC Helmrich drove them north toward the sound as air support radioed in that they were on the way. A quarter mile up the road, a car parked in the road turned its headlights to their brightest setting. The captain's Humvee swerved from time to time as SPC Helmrich, whose night vision goggles worsened the flare of headlights, tried to keep the truck from driving off the levee road. If they hit the wrong spot at the worst time, the Humvee would roll. Bailey radioed the truck behind him to stay on guard.

"They're trying to bait us into an ambush," explained Bailey. "I told Mark to get his rifle and point it out the door while I looked for a way to get off the road and hit a trail. Then they started firing at us."

CPT Bailey, CPL Munroe, CPT Bailey's gunner, and CPT Payne returned fire. As Attack Aviation swooped in, a man dressed in a black jumpsuit cut off from the ambush, running. Bailey shot at him, but missed, and the aviators were unable to find him.

Like most of the ambushes they'd faced, this one was small but no less dangerous. When G Troop returned to base much later that night, Bailey turned in his report at HQ. COL Hickey had already retired to his quarters, but CPT Ian Weikel was there to accept it.

"Weikel told me that as soon as I'd radioed 'contact' and they heard shots fired over the radio, Hickey put his head down and said, 'Lord, please don't let any of those men die out there tonight'," Bailey recalled.

After CPT Weikel received the report, COL Hickey appeared in the brigade command post. "I told him what had occurred, and he said he was thankful no one was injured, and then he saw a burn mark on my neck". Recalls Bailey. "The burn mark came from hot expended brass as I fired my rifle left-handed; the brass landed in my neck gator, causing a burn mark."

"Is that an injury from enemy fire?" Hickey asked.

"No, sir. Fired my weapon left-handed, neck was burned from brass captured in my neck gator."

"Well then...no Purple Heart for you..."

RETURNING HOME

The drive from Tikrit to Kuwait was long, but less rushed than when they'd first set out into Iraq.

"It was still a mission," said Ellis. "You couldn't be relaxed just because you're going home. You had to be on guard and resilient."

LT Renazco and Scorpion Platoon were entrusted with a convoy of 28 vehicles, many of which weren't combat ready.

Renazco recalled, "Oh man, it was like herding cats. I had captains in the convoy who were giving me crap because I was a lieutenant. I told them to shut up, that I was running the show. The drive had its own set of challenges, and it was very unique to the times."

This uniqueness translated to many things, including a Cannonball Run between LT Renazco and a Marine convoy as they neared the Kuwait border.

"We were heading south, neck and neck. And we knew that whoever got in front was the one who'd set the pace. He didn't want to give up and I didn't want to give up. Finally, I remember looking over and he's behind us, his convoy spread out. The Army and my platoon won the race and set the pace. I never did see him again," said Renazco.

CPT Sweigart and the remainder of G Troop escorted Brigade Headquarters back to Kuwait, and it was an uneventful, three-day return trip.

"It was a good feeling once we hit that final stretch of highway, getting out of there and heading into Kuwait," said Sweigart.

As they neared the border, there was a final stop for the troopers where they left behind all their ammunition. From there, they went from open desert and a narrow highway to a large, Los Angeles-type freeway: Iraq was finally behind them.

"Cars were everywhere on that freeway. I tried to stop traffic to allow our convoy through, but no one would stop. I got out of the truck and raised my weapon up, aiming it at a driver coming toward us. And then I realized I didn't have any ammo. The Kuwaiti guy drove past me, laughing. Life was gonna be different with no ammo," said Renazco.

"It was really different coming back into the real army again. People had soft hats on, clean clothes, actual uniforms. We were in green vests and tan uniforms, completely mismatched. I remembered leaving behind tents, dirt, snakes, and spiders when we left Kuwait. Now there were Pizza Huts and McDonalds," said Lay.

G Troop remained in Kuwait for a week, and as long as they were there, the return home wasn't laid in stone.

"We were down at the wash rack with 2nd Armored Cavalry Regiment (ACR) when the uprising in Sadr City kicked off. At that moment, I thought G Troop would get called back up," says Sweigart. Instead, 2nd ACR was called north to reinforce and ended up staying several months.

The unknowns didn't stop there. "It was Lord of the Flies," said Renazco. "No one knew what was going on, but everyone's working around the clock. If you get a break, you find a bunk somewhere to sleep. You're waiting to hear your name called to go back home. It was like purgatory."

The troop's primary task was to clean their trucks in preparation for their being shipped back to the U.S. To pass inspection, every ounce of dirt was to be washed away. The troop spent hours at the wash rack, endlessly rotating people in and out so they could rest for a few hours.

"It was an insurmountable task. We could burn the truck to ash, and there'd still be dirt everywhere. At one point they said we didn't pass inspection because there was dirt inside the frame of the truck. So Cantou took an axe to it, cutting open the bottom so we could spray water in there. It was ridiculous. We were so tired, but we didn't want to sleep—we just wanted to get on a plane," recalled Lay.

In the end, the trucks remained in Kuwait, which made little sense to the troopers, but served as a reminder of how the larger army network worked compared to their unit. For troopers like Lay, it was an example of inefficiency and irrelevant assignments based on too many opinions at the higher level.

"Despite that sort of system," said Lay, "despite how the big machine works, our troop found a way to make things work at a small level. The sheer amount of work that our leadership did on that level and what we accomplished will always amaze me."

Recon 701

Finally, over the course of several days, members of G Troop were called to redeploy. PFC Lay and members of Black Sheep flew back on MAJ GEN Odierno's plane, a double decker Boeing 747.

As the plane took off, Lay recalls a moment of panic—no one in his family knew he was coming back. He hadn't made any phone calls to tell them. When they landed in Prague to refuel, he volunteered to stay back on the plane to guard their gear and rifles while the troopers went to have a beer in the airport.

"It was hard to be in the mood to celebrate when you thought that, after a year of being at war, no one would be around to welcome you back," said Lay.

He had no reason to worry, of course. The FRG had his family's contact information, and they knew he was heading home.

"Here's the thing, the biggest thing I remember after we landed in Texas: I stepped off the plane and took a deep breath of fresh air," said Lay. "You'll never realize how fresh the air is here until you've spent time in a country that has no sanitary system and you've become used to it. That breath of fresh air, well, it was shocking. It blew my mind."

14. Life After Deployment

MARCH 2004 – PRESENT

"We had very good people and great leadership that created a cohesive, trusting unit. It's almost impossible to replicate, and that's why it was hard to leave. For me, it wasn't the thrill of combat, it was the community. I felt like I was running around with 30 of my best buddies."
—**Captain Brian Sweigart**

The youngest troopers were teenagers, the oldest a few men in their early thirties. They had gone to war and returned home, reuniting with family and friends. They had faced danger and death every day and each night, lost three brothers, and taken down a dictator. Now, it was time to reintegrate into normal military and civilian society.

How *do* you reset yourself to that previous life? How do you replace the rush of adrenaline in a firefight, or the camaraderie born of great effort, pride, and loss? How do you shoulder the memories of fallen comrades or moments of terror in a world where only a very few can understand that ceaseless weight?

MAJ GEN Odierno's Iron Horse University was a helpful

beginning for members of G Troop. Meetings with psychiatrists, doctors, and small groups as well as courses in topics like finances and reintegration with family—especially children—provided some help and identified issues before they became serious problems. However, reintegrating is a lifelong journey for many.

THE RETURN TO NORMALCY

The troopers returned to the U.S. in groups over the course of five days.

When PFC Lay arrived in the Fort Hood gymnasium with dozens of other troopers, he was tackled by his mother and sisters, who had arrived earlier with his brother and father. The troopers were given a week off, and PFC Lay headed straight for the nearest Arby's with his family.

"I ate two sandwiches and finally got that craving out of the way. I remembered my priorities," Lay recalls. "I also nearly crashed the car. I wasn't driving, we weren't allowed to, but there was a traffic counter box on the side of the road, with a hose going across the road. I tried to grab the steering wheel from my mother because I thought it was going to blow us up."

The family's next stop was a shopping center north of Dallas to replace his only pair of shoes: the worn and disgusting combat boots that had seen far too much action. As he was placing the new shoes in the trunk of his parent's car, a vehicle backfired. PFC Lay grabbed his sister, almost heaving her into the trunk before he realized what he was doing.

"We were wired different," Lay said simply. "I made it home and unwound. It was the end of that downhill run, I could relax. But this is what everybody struggles with: how do you stop that downhill run?"

PFC Spark's parents lived further away, over 700 miles in north Alabama. Melissa, SGT Swilley's wife, called the private's parents at 2:00 a.m. to let them know their son was in Ireland and would arrive at Fort Hood later that day.

At the Fort Hood gymnasium, PFC Sparks looked for his family, but saw no familiar faces in the crowd. He grabbed his duffel bag and walked outside to wait, watching troopers and their families pass by, hugging and laughing.

"I'll always remember how cold and lonely it was to sit there and watch others without having my own family beside me," said Sparks.

When his parents arrived, PFC Sparks' mother had his father stop the car at the gymnasium entrance. She jumped out, running inside and then hurried back out looking for him. As soon as she saw her son, she called out his name, tackling him.

That day, PFC Sparks decided he would never let anyone feel that same sense of loneliness.

"Since that deployment, I celebrate "Shrimpsgiving" on Thanksgiving. I visit my family for Veterans Day, which is also my dad's birthday, instead of Thanksgiving. Then, for Shrimpsgiving, I grab troopers who don't have anywhere to go and bring them over to my house. We eat crab legs, shrimp, scallops, a whole pile of food. When we're done, I pack them to-go plates—it's a fire sale, everything must go. They may not have somewhere to go for Thanksgiving, but at least they can come hang out with one another and have a good meal," said Sparks.

After the brief week off, the troopers returned to Fort Hood on a month-long, half day schedule. Each morning they'd be in formation for physical training by 6:30 a.m., then be ready for the workday at 9:00 a.m. 1SG Justis would hand over the day's tasks to the platoon sergeants.

"We functioned so efficiently and with such purpose that we'd have everything done by lunchtime. We ended up on the half day schedule for three months because we were producing results," said Sparks.

The troopers kept busy during their free time. PFC Lay and others would play Halo tournaments on Xbox, those who had family nearby would head home, and some, including PFC Sparks, would take short trips to nearby cities.

"I'd go to Dallas, Austin, College Station, Houston, Galveston. I remember SPC Mosier ended up getting an upright punching bag. You're supposed to put sand in it, but he filled it with water. That's all well and good until that water starts shifting and dancing all over the room at seven in the morning while he's singing Britney Spears at the top of his lungs," said Sparks.

SPC Fugate would head out to Austin with civilian friends. Driving down highways at night, especially those with few lights from Killeen to Georgetown, had its own set of challenges.

"I was following my friends in my car, and I'd told them to go a little bit ahead of me because I don't like to follow close. I was actually seeing tracers going across the road. I knew it was in my mind, but it's impossible to explain to people why you just drove across the road because of a box or why you threw someone across the bed because outside somebody's dragging a cardboard box on the sidewalk, and it doesn't sound quite right," said Fugate.

Both PFCs Sparks and Lay recall the instant panic felt upon waking and not having their rifles next to them. Not having your weapon with you at all times was a cardinal sin during deployment. If you didn't have it, something horrible had happened. Years after OIF1, PFC Sparks has woken in a cold sweat having dreamed he was going from trooper to trooper asking if they'd seen his rifle.

This adjustment period is a struggle that every soldier faces to different degrees over varying lengths of time.

"When I first came back, there were things that bothered me, like people honking horns. I'd see something on the road and turn my car around because I thought it was a bomb. I've kind of lived past that stuff, though it always stays in your mind," explained Almen. "I got out of the Army after OIF1, and here I am 16 years later. I used to wonder if I should've stayed in, but I'm glad I got out when I did. I'm also glad I did what I did. I wouldn't change anything for the world. I'd go back and do it the same way, 100 times over. But I'm glad it ended when it did."

PFC Sparks was glad to be back in civilian clothes, drinking cold beers and hanging out with friends. But he missed having a greater purpose, something more than the typical day job.

"Of course," Sparks added, "it was also a complete adrenaline junkie thing. At some point, it's hardwired into you. You start getting antsy for absolutely no reason, and there's nothing that can help."

While deployed, there were times when the troopers would go two or three days without making enemy contact. PFC Helmrich recalls the guys wishing that someone would shoot at them.

"When you make contact, you get through it with high emotions and your adrenaline is up. You might live on adrenaline for a few days. Then you're waiting on the next attack. People say there's no higher high than being in combat. I haven't found it yet in the civilian world either," said Helmrich.

Civilians associate war with killing and destruction, but for the men and women who were there, what strikes them hardest and never leaves is the brotherhood that's formed—a connection stronger than friendship and far different from family. Through the challenges, fear, anger, and joy, they are beside one another and putting the safety and well-being of everyone in their unit above their own.

"There's a magic to being surrounded by a bunch of like-minded individuals when you have control of your life in a way that you don't get in the civilian world," says CPT Sweigart. "Once you've been downrange in a combat zone, whether you are special ops, infantry, or even transporters or fuelers, you have a confidence about the world because you know that not everything out there is going to kill you. It takes a lot to kill a human being. Nowhere else in life do people get the chance to face that challenge and come out of it surrounded by their tribe. It's a very empowering feeling, and you lose that when you transition out."

In 2016, SGT Szott and CPT Sweigart co-founded a physical security firm that focuses on retooling veterans so their military skills can be utilized in civilian defense. "I survived my PTSD, and I've learned so much from my own journey. I'm honored to be here serving again with my community of my fellow veterans," said Szott.

"The ever-rising suicide rates of veterans still climbs today. I still get phone calls nearly 20 years later of friends and brothers giving up their fight, letting the enemy win.

"I fully understand now what a doctor shared with me at the beginning of my career with the Central Intelligence Agency: we're all a little broken, a little blown up, a little shot up, a little scarred and damaged—but we're not alone, look to your left and look to your right," shared Szott.

When Szott first left the military, he felt that everything had come undone around him. There was so much left to accomplish, but he couldn't figure out what it was. It was as if he were doing nothing at all, and he missed the profoundness of what he'd once done on a daily basis. He was 23 years old attempting to finish college. With two years of combat tours, he didn't find much in common with his fellow students or professors.

"Going into military contracting helped me so much, I was able to recondition my mind and create an environment similar to what I'd left. I no longer felt underutilized," said Szott. "Our company is doing something right, and I hope others begin to copy us. The feedback we get from our veterans is that they feel useful again, connected and making a living-wage. PTSD is not like scar tissue that thickens to protect you, it's more like a cup that can only handle so much volume. After combat, we are all walking around with very full cups, so things that are normal stressors (money, job, spouse, children) become too much to handle. So, it becomes a delicate process of emptying that cup without "throwing it away."

COPING WITH POST-COMBAT LIFE

"In war, terrible realities exist all around you. I was 30 and leading a bunch of troopers in their early 20s at best. We were doing the best we could. We were there for the right reasons, and we did things the right way. I wasn't always okay with what I did out there, but I had to do it," shared Renazco, as he recounts the evening an NCO saw the dead bodies of a family sprawled in a courtyard.

"I told him to take the night off and forget about it, he'd talk to the chaplain in the morning. That was my line, and I regret not having conversations with the troopers, not validating their feelings. But at that point it's about survivability. If you think too much about things, you start to make mistakes."

Renazco valued Iron Horse University and the attempt to address what he describes as a mortal injury that occurs in war, the stigma of negative feelings, like cowardice and weakness, kept the benefits of such courses at bay.

"It's hard to open up about your fear and be vulnerable around these guys that you've been pounding your chest and being falsely brave with," explained Renazco. "You can't easily say that you were afraid to shoot. It's most likely not going to happen, but it's what needs to happen."

Many years after OIF1, Renazco began seeing a therapist and over time has recognized the importance of getting emotions out while balancing the focus required for every mission.

Corcoles took all the courses offered and believes that they—as well as his shift to the National Guard after transitioning out of active duty—helped him better reintegrate. There were many soldiers that shirked off the classes, even though they were mandatory. Those who didn't pay attention had a hard time later on.

"From day one, the military trains you to stay in your lane, be at the right place at the right time, and do as you're told. You'll never be wrong. The Army gives you structure and that keeps a lot of people sane. So, they're in their lane for three, ten, or twenty years and then get out and become a civilian—well, now everybody's coming in and out of their lane with no turn signals," explained Corcoles.

On the second night of his return, LT Renazco received a late phone call at his sister's house. His troopers had been drinking together, and the NCO who had seen the civilian bodies in the courtyard was drunk and frantic about going on a mission and saving a baby.

The lieutenant had his sister drive him to Fort Hood where he walked into a shocking sight. Unable to control him and afraid for his safety, the young men had tied the crying trooper to a couch. LT Renazco had him untied, and they drove him to the nearest hospital.

As nurses tied him down once again, the NCO recognized LT Renazco and told him over and over that they had to go on a mission to get the baby.

"I just went into it with him," said Renazco. "I agreed and said I did need him to go on that mission tomorrow, but he had to calm down first. It actually worked, and the nurse was able to sedate him."

Renazco remembers wondering if these events were going to be the norm and happen to all of them.

The following day, the doctor said they were going to put the trooper on a 51-50 and keep him in the hospital for three days, which LT Renazco wasn't going to have.

"I was lippy with him, even though he was a colonel. I told him he wasn't going to keep a man who'd just returned home tied up in a hospital. He asked me if I was familiar with PTSD, which I was to some degree. But I still insisted my NCO be let out. Finally, the doctor agreed, but said the trooper was on my watch," Renazco said, and then adds that he didn't feel any of the troopers from G Troop were seen as the good guys at the hospital. The staff and even the doctor he spoke with had looked at them as though they'd just returned from Vietnam, a bunch of falsely accused baby killers. It was an alienating and lonely experience.

"OIF1 was a great experience for me, but it's taken its toll on some of the guys. There's some great things we did, and there's some things I would love to go back and change," said Helmrich. "Philip Cantu took his life in 2006. I wish I'd stayed in contact with him more when we returned, but I was gone for a year on my next deployment. Even with how close knit our family was, you're still going to have the consequences of going overseas. It's part of life, and you can't go back and change it after it's done."

Survivor's guilt is nothing new or strange to troopers who have deployed overseas and seen atrocities occur, watched their friends get injured or killed, and returned home without comrades beside them.

Not long after returning from Iraq, Fugate recalls sitting alone in his barracks room after having too much to drink. "I was beating myself up about how I'd gone left instead of right the night we got ambushed. Luckily, two of the guys came to my room and asked why I wasn't at a party downstairs. They asked why I was crying, and I told them. They took away my alcohol and dragged me to the party, making me hang out with everyone. That was a normal thing we'd do for each other, and I was mostly okay afterwards. I won't say I was great, but I was okay."

Szott recalls the advice he was given by the Criminal Investigation Division (CID) soldier who'd interviewed him after the ambush that took SPC Wright, PFC Arriaga, and SGT Thompson. The CID soldier had been a Marine in Desert Storm and the Marine Corp tattoos on Wright's body had resurfaced SGT Szott's own terrible memories of loss.

With tears in his own eyes, "He told me that the pain I felt then was never going to leave me; it would only get easier to deal with. It was the best advice I've received, and its advice I've shared with anyone that will listen. The reality of the statement is very conditioning for the mind. The anxiety of when the feelings will end or when you'll stop thinking about what happened is gone because you've accepted reality—it's done—that this will stick with you forever. Now you can start being able to live with it and move on like all other injuries," said Szott.

THE END OF G TROOP

Not long after their return, the BRT was replaced by the RSTA (reconnaissance, surveillance, target, acquisition) squadron. G Troop, 1-10 CAV was now A/7-10 CAV.

"I don't know this for certain, but I'm told that they picked seven because it drew its lineage from G Troop, and G is the seventh letter in the alphabet. We had a strong core that was original to G Troop, so even though this group was Alpha Troop 7-10, we chose Ghost for our callsign," said Sparks.

Some of G Troop's original troopers joined the armored cavalry squadron while others moved to different units, continuing their service in the U.S. or overseas. Some were deployed again to the Middle East. Those who returned to civilian life became police officers, social workers, security contractors, construction workers, bail bondsmen, and entrepreneurs (to name a few).

"We connected with the new guys coming in, but it was a different time. We were older, most of us had been deployed. I got married, I had kids, a lot of my time went to that instead of the unit. Instead of spending day and night together, hanging out every weekend, we went our own way," said Ellis.

Going to war had given the troopers a new perspective on what mattered in life. Time with family and loved ones was to be cherished above all else. Many of the troopers, now in their thirties and forties, are fathers, grandfathers, uncles, and husbands.

Though much has changed in their lives and the world since 2004, those who took part in the interviews for this book all agree: in the military or civilian world, they've never experienced the brotherhood or recaptured the sense of belonging that they had in G Troop.

SUNSHINE BEAR

"If you've seen the movie *Band of Brothers*, you have a kind of a glimpse into the brotherhood of G Troop. That's the best way I can explain it. Certain moments in time occur and cause people to be closer together in different ways. That's why I think we were closer to the leaders who were there when Saddam was captured than the leaders we initially deployed with," summed up Almen. "We all grew closer together. We were friends in the beginning, and we were brothers when it was over."

Twice the troopers of G Troop have met for reunions, and everyone who's attended at least one says once they're together, it's as though no time has passed. Almen recalls training to be a scout with SPC Leboeuf who was a "Joe Nobody, a little freckle faced kid from down the street." Now Leboeuf is a Sergeant First Class.

"It's hard to believe when you look at them now, 15 years later, and they've got two or three kids," said Almen. "Helmrich, who I met when he was just 18, has a whole gaggle of kids now. Good grief, we've all gotten old."

Only living 55 miles apart for a while, SGTs Boyko and Southwood would visit each other regularly. In 2021, Bailey and Darden took a cross-country motorcycle trip, swinging through Texas for lunch with Sweigart. Many of the troopers keep up to date with everyone on social media, and most of the guys remain a text or phone call away.

This lasting bond is now crossing generations.

"When we were deployed, if we knew that some guys were having a hard time, we'd try to cheer them up when the mail came in. We'd go out of our way to find them and very excitedly tell them they got a letter, ask them to quickly open it and tell us what it said. We liked hearing from each other's families and seeing pictures," remembered Corcoles.

Sometimes, the guys would read letters out loud. In the summer of 2003, SPC Wright shared a letter from his wife with news he'd long been waiting for: she was pregnant.

Weeks later, SPC Wright would be gone, and he would never meet his son, Jamison.

"I've told Wright's wife and son about the letter, it was so funny," said Corcoles. "Wright yelled out that he'd finally gotten his wife knocked up. While he was reading the letter, he kept interrupting himself saying, "yes!" over and over. This was what he was all about, all he wanted was to be a father.

G Troop, of course, had their own nickname for the tall, pale, blonde-haired, and blue-eyed trooper: Sunshine.

SPC Wright and his wife had a special story about why she called him "sunshine"—but the platoon had their reason too. "We told him he was so white and so blonde that looking at him was like staring into the sun!" said Corcoles. Adding to the nickname was when SPC Wright's wife sent him a fluffy toy rabbit that when squeezed played the song You Are My Sunshine.

After returning to the U.S., SPC Andrade joined Corcoles on a long drive from California to Texas with a four-foot-tall Sunshine Care Bear in their back seat. They delivered it to SPC Wright's infant son and spent time sharing memories with his wife.

Desmond Bailey

*Members of the troop posing with a car that featured
SGT Wright's image on the hood*

15. The Secret Sauce

"Capturing Saddam Hussein earned us a place in history, but what really matters is how we got there."

—Colonel (Ret) Desmond Bailey

Can the mentality of G Troop be recaptured? Can the tip of the spear be re-forged and sharpened to that perfect, precise point again and again?

The odds were against them, and nothing came easily. Despite the rushed, haphazard start, despite facing a type of warfare no one had prepared for while covering a battalion-sized area of operations, despite being outnumbered two to one in an ambush that killed three of their brothers, G Troop never faltered. They adapted and improved.

"G Troop shifted and evolved over time. We started out with a very traditional reconnaissance mission before the deployment. And then, right before the deployment, we shifted and put all our effort into understanding urban operations, raids, and anything that we thought we might come across. That kind of mission shift happened probably three or four times at a macro level within the troop, but people didn't bat an eye," said Sweigart.

G Troop was undoubtedly distinctive. They were a small reconnaissance troop which directly reported to the brigade commander. It was a highly maneuverable unit given leading-edge technology and a wealth of assets to bolster their efforts. This kept them agile and flexible. But there was something beyond the reporting structure and size of the unit that led to their achievements.

"There was something unique about them. Somehow these troopers went from being the troublemakers at Fort Hood while in garrison to an efficient, precise, and deadly force in combat. For years I tried to recreate G Troop, to build a unit with that level of esprit de corps and skill. I never could," said Bailey.

WHAT MADE G TROOP EXCEPTIONAL?

1. The leaders didn't tell. They listened…

LT Renazco relied on SFC Flores' experience and advice; CPT Bailey invited the ideas of his privates and specialists and valued the opinions his NCOs and lieutenants provided. G Troop leadership—especially those new to reconnaissance—recognized that one can't know everything and that diversity of thought only benefits the team. Platoon Sergeants and the First Sergeant, with much reconnaissance experience, were willing to coach the officers and help them develop into effective leaders.

…and they taught.

Both SGTs Southwood and Swilley would sit and watch how the troopers reacted in an emergency, whether real or planned and false. Lay likens these experiences to a crucible—but they provided value. After action, the NCOs would acknowledge what the troopers had done well and then make suggestions or foster discussion with the troopers to determine better actions.

"They wouldn't tell us that we needed to do this or that. Instead, they'd engage us and get your brain turning on it," said Lay.

Sometimes lessons must be learned the hard way, but a patient teacher can make a strong point.

"On my first mission as a driver, Sergeant Swilley let me drive the Humvee how I wanted," recalled Sparks. "My gunner, Anders was irritated the whole time because I'm hitting potholes and taking turns way too fast for his comfort. Swilley was quiet about that, and when we got back to base, he told me he'd be surprised if I hadn't torn up everything under the suspension. He had me take each wheel off, take the split ring apart, take the run flat out of it, check the tire, and put it all back together.

"Afterwards, he told me not to be a dumbass and to take care of my equipment. I had to be more particular with it and take care of it because one day I may need to really drive it that way, and it needed to be in good shape in case the worst happened."

SGT Egli, who had led the mechanics for the first half of deployment, spent a little more time on issues to determine the root of the problem instead of simply replacing a part and moving on.

"He'd explain the problem to us and how he fixed it in a simple way so anybody could understand," said Lapp. "I remember some of the scouts complaining about wasting their time having to blow out their truck's air filters. SGT Egli asked if they'd ever tried running with a sock in their mouth — because if they didn't blow out their air filters, that's what it would be like for the engine. That explanation made a difference, and no one questioned why they were doing that task again.

"I can comfortably say I wouldn't have been able to do the things I did in Iraq if SGT Egli hadn't been there. He was full of knowledge, and he shared it well."

2. Leadership cared, and they showed it…

Leadership was very aware of the moments when a trooper needed guidance, a task to focus on, a teacher, or a listener. Such decisions had meaningful—and critical—purpose, even if it wasn't as apparent. Knowing that his troopers could become complacent after hours and days of patrolling, Darden would keep their interest piqued by gamifying the task. Every few hours, he'd stop the patrol at a grove of trees or similar location and have his troopers search for weapons and munitions. This kept them moving, energized, and determined. It also led to a lot of unexpected caches.

"CPT Bailey and 1SG Justis loved everybody in the unit like a son. We knew that care and love was there. Respect and love go a very, very long way. If either of them or SSG Darden called me tomorrow and asked something of me, I'd be there in a second. When you have people who care about you and that you trust, that's when you're willing to go work in the office until midnight and that's when you're willing to go out on a mission no matter how dangerous," said Sparks.

For Helmrich, the recipe for a good leader is simple, but no less profound: have a good base of knowledge and care about your troopers and their wellbeing. Then, if you're lucky, they'll nickname you SAM (short angry man) just like they did SGT Crosby, who wouldn't let anyone mess with his guys.

…this made team trust and commitment the norm…

Darden says it best: "A troop's success boils down to the level of trust that another human places on you. Bailey and Sweigart placed their trust in me. They didn't hold me back, and they let me do what I thought should be done. That trust filtered down to my guys. I told them they knew what to do and to make it happen—they liked that."

Although, notably, Helmrich mentions CPT Bailey could be a "little high strung," the troopers knew that if they were heading out on a mission, their captain would be with them. If CPT Bailey couldn't accompany a platoon on a mission or be in close proximity because of another mission requirement, he would scope the platoon's objective area out during the day.

This type of leadership isn't a completely unique trait, as Helmrich said, "I think commanders would do that if we went back to that type of warfare. Now, officers are getting back to where we were before Iraq—sending platoons out on missions and they're guiding from afar."

Bailey recalls 1SG Justis "arriving" just in time to facilitate casualty collection or advise him on courses of action when troops were in contact and multiple organizations were involved; as well as SFC Flores always being on patrol when new NCOs were leading their first patrol, not to micromanage, but to teach coach and mentor.

Many of the troopers acknowledged that a trooper will fight harder for the leader who's out there, fighting with them.

...and it made the impossible achievable.

The troop never slowed down, and with multiple, ongoing missions of high importance, the troopers could have easily become overwhelmed. However, leadership kept them focused on the present and the steps they needed to take each day to achieve the bigger goal.

"They broke things down into bite size jobs so there were never any moments where we wondered how we'd manage it all. Leadership acknowledged the big picture but told us to focus on what we were doing that day or night. If everyone did their job right and did it well, then we could move forward to the next mission. Eventually these would chain together, and we'd achieve the impossible," said Lay.

3. *Time together strengthened bonds and created a culture of care…*

It's common for units that see combat to form an instinctual bond. The bond of brotherhood started for G Troop far before they deployed, however. The troopers were young, and most were single, living in the barracks with one another, spending weekends together. In Kuwait, they slept inches away from each other, crammed together in large tents that were still too small. On patrol and overwatch, they spent hours with one another, day after day, month after month.

"We were close knit and did everything together. We lived together, we worked together, we hung out every night and weekend," explained Helmrich. "We were also a very small unit—in typical troops you have 100 to 150 troopers, but with our unit there was just around 70. If we were running around with 25 guys on the weekend, that's already a third of the unit."

"We would talk about sports, families, politics—everything. In Kuwait, we couldn't breathe without being in someone else's personal space," shared Ellis. "When I deployed the second time with 7-10 CAV Squadron, we had plenty of space in Kuwait and at our base in Taji. We only had one roommate, so it was never crowded. I think that stopped the camaraderie from strengthening."

Being so close paid off in war. The troop trusted one another, and this helped them manage endless challenges. "We didn't train for guerilla warfare, and I think we overcame that issue because we knew each other so well and trusted each other," says Helmrich, who also compares G Troop to a family.

"If a guy calls me and needs anything, help moving or figuring out finances...anything, I'll head out the very next day. We bought into the family concept, and we lived it. We decided early on that when we deployed, we'd take this—we called it "the suck"—together, and we're gonna figure it out," Helmrich said.

...and this made them resilient.

"We would sit down and talk when we had downtime or were on patrol, it was a time for decompression," said Corcoles. "We'd ask each other how we were doing, if we'd heard from kids or family lately, or just talk about what was on our mind. The guys we knew were having an especially hard time, when mail came in for them, we'd go out of our way to find them and see what they'd gotten, get excited with them."

Despite the stress and challenges, G Troop's camaraderie kept them going. "Everybody had their disputes or opinions, like a big family, but we could put that aside when needed and get the mission done. I think that's what made G Troop good. When it counted, everyone came together," said Ellis.

"G Troop is one of the few organizations I've been part of where people legitimately problem solved. There was rarely anyone saying we couldn't do something," shared Sweigart. "Instead, we'd dig into it and come up with reasonable responses to everything thrown in front of us."

4. The troopers and leadership balanced the line.

There is a time to joke around and decompress, and there's a time to be serious, focused on the task at hand. There's a time for a leader to engage and be a part of the team, and there's a time for them to be hard, decisive. The troopers of G Troop understood this balance and walked the line without faltering.

SFC Michaud often had the troopers over to his home, for holidays if they had no family, or for parties on the weekends. Lapp recalls several of the troopers getting inked at SFC Michaud's house when a professional tattoo artist and friend of the sergeant's swung through town.

"Rick was like a father figure for a lot of us, especially single troopers living in the barracks," explained Boyko. "I asked around other units to see if their platoon sergeants invited them over for Thanksgiving or for dinner, and they'd all tell me no, that it was unheard of—because there was a clear line."

Yet, in blurring that line, SFC Michaud—and other NCOs in G Troop—showed the younger troopers how much they cared.

"We noticed that," Boyko continued, "and it made us want to do our best for them."

"Even with CPT Bailey, you could, within reason, smoke and joke with him," said Sparks. "As long as everything was good, as long as everything was done, he'd laugh, crack jokes with you. You could tell the gears were always turning, though. He was constantly analyzing the what-ifs. When the time came, he could make a decision. A lot of people get scared, paralyzed, when that time comes, but he never did. If the decision was wrong, he knew we'd adjust on the fly."

5. *Everyone fostered a learning, supportive culture.*

The corporate world will reference Plan-Do-Check-Act or the Deming Cycle–processes and philosophies that stand for one critical concept: *continuous improvement*. It creates industry-leading, efficient, safe, and sustainable companies—no matter the sector, whether it's manufacturing, construction, or war, continuous improvement builds vital skills and saves lives.

Good-natured rivalry from the start set the troopers up for success. "Everyone wanted to be the best at everything," Helmrich explained. "We challenged each other from Patrol Base chores to weapons drills — everything was a competition, and this drove us to be better. I think this atmosphere was one of the best things we had."

"It was a healthy dose of competition balanced with cooperation. Everybody tried to be better every day. It wasn't competitive in the sense of the cutthroat business world where people only care about making themselves look good. We improved together," shared Sparks, detailing a time back in their barracks when the guys played a drinking game as they quizzed one another from their Scout Handbook.

"We could have been playing video games or watching TV, but instead we were sitting there pinging each other with questions and improving our knowledge," said Sparks.

Typical training continued during deployment, as did the less expected "emergency tests" that the NCOs would put the troopers through to gauge their responses.

"Even if we did something 10,000 times at Fort Hood, once we were in Iraq, we'd do it 200 more times before going out to do it for real," said Almen.

"We all had our lows and highs. If one of us was low, others would pick up the slack. We'd motivate that person and help them out. We all looked after each other, and if there was a point to improve, we'd jump on it," said Ellis.

"We put in the hard work to prepare," said Sparks, "then we deployed. We executed, adjusted, re-executed, and adapted. All these pieces are critical to produce results — if there's a break in the chain, you won't succeed."

6. Strong teams will always have intangible aspects — G Troop leveraged them.

While age, marital status, training, and unit structure were tangible factors that played into G Troop's evolution and success, much of what's mentioned in the preceding pages ties back to individual personalities and leadership styles. What can be distilled from that?

There's no easy answer, of course. To Lay, creating that secret sauce is never a simple matter, but leadership is key:

"Throughout military history you see a certain group of people who fall together because they're in the right place with a mixture of people who have the right drive to accomplish things. We saw it with Easy Company, a unit in WWII, and there are others further back than that. You can't hunt down the ingredients you need and force them together — it just happens. I think if anybody could have written down the secret sauce to that recipe, it would have happened a long time ago.

"I think the true mark of any leader is to recognize when you have the right ingredients. What you do with them at that point is really what defines the unit. How many hundreds of times have we had cohesive units that could make the secret sauce but lacked the leadership or opportunity to do so?

"I think we had the right ingredients and we had people like Captain Bailey, Captain Sweigart, 1SG Justis, and several good NCOs in the chain of command who made use of them properly. I won't be vain and say I thought we were anything special at the time. Looking back, though, I realize we really did accomplish something incredible.

"We had what it took, and it was what it was. In the end, you can't make intangibles quantifiable. Sometimes you just enjoy the recipe after you get done cooking it and then spend the rest of your life trying to recapture it."

Many others in G Troop recognized that their leadership realized the unit's potential and made use of it.

To Darden, "What made G Troop successful is hard to pinpoint—like a lightning strike. I think it was the right group of guys with the right personalities coming together. Everyone had a common goal of keeping each other safe. Bailey saw that, and he knew how to employ us. We needed somebody aggressive at that time because that was how the BRT had to perform. If I know CPT Bailey, I'm pretty sure he was thinking that he had the perfect unit, the perfect tool to make things happen."

It wasn't just CPT Bailey leading the troops, Almen adds, nor was it 1SG Justis or CPT Sweigart. "This was top down, side to side leadership effort—they were all strong leaders," said Almen.

When asked about their leaders and what made them so adept at fostering the troop's skill and camaraderie, responses range from personalities—Darden's absolute drive and redneck sayings; Sweigart's quiet leadership and sly sense of humor; SGT Egli's passion for digging in to find the root of the problem—to specific lessons that left a life-long impression.

"The pandemic's been tough," Fugate said, "But I'm not going to let it put me down. SGT Flores and SGT Branch taught me how to look at things in a positive way. Even when you're doing a crappy job like sweeping the motor pool every Friday. Why are you doing it? Because that's what you do every Friday. Are you going to sit and bitch about it, or do you want to talk about your plans for the weekend while you sweep? Always make the best of things."

RECREATING THE SECRET SAUCE

Having thought often on the mentality of G Troop, Sparks provides a useful and actionable target for leaders:

"You need a nucleus of people who are bought into the program and culture. They need to care about others, have a strong work ethic, believe in personal accountability, and be willing to hold others accountable. The best people in an organization will gravitate to something of value, and that nucleus is the thing of value.

"Everyone must buy into the fact that succeeding alone while the team fails means nothing—success can only be realized together. If there's somebody who's willing to trip someone else up to make themselves look better, then that's toxic, and you need to correct the situation. Bring others in to patch up and grow the nucleus. Don't let those new people carry any bad habits they had coming in. While you can't force someone to change, if they want to change themselves, you're hard pressed to find a better, more solid outcome after the fact."

While he may not know all the ingredients to the secret sauce, Bailey has determined one key element: "I believe mindset is the key secret ingredient. The troopers and their leaders either have it or they don't. They either want to be the best or they don't."

When Bailey was commissioned as an Infantry Officer and assigned to 82d Airborne at Fort Bragg, his battalion commander had served in the Ranger Regiment and ARSOF, his company commander had served in the Ranger Regiment, and one of Bailey's XOs had served in the 82d Airborne during the Panama Invasion.

"Needless to say, those men collectively fostered a culture of 'can do' and 'get after it'. Life as a platoon leader in the 82d was one of constant competition, the need for self-improvement, and just trying to make your unit the best at everything."

"I carried that mindset with me to G troop and most of the

troopers either already had that mindset or took it on. I then carried it forward to other units...and it didn't work so much. Every individual's mindset feeds the unit's mindset. So, it comes down to individuals and what type of person and soldier they want to be. Hopefully leaders can sense the mindset if it's there and not stomp it out for fear of perception or risk of mistakes. G Troop was a bunch of reckless, wild men in garrison, and they developed their own identity as a rough and tumble group of troopers who could accomplish anything. That translated into a fine unit down range. My job as the commander was to keep the mindset going and focus their energy on the mission/task at hand.

"Ultimately," said Bailey, "I believe the "can-do" spirit of G Troop leadership from young enterprising troopers, to NCOs, to officers—their bravery, commitment, and perseverance is what made them great."

Lessons Learned (By Col(R) Desmond V. Bailey)

What has been will be again, what has been done will be done again; there is nothing new under the sun.
—Ecclesiastes 1:9 (NIV)

The scripture above is true, and the reality is that while there is nothing new under the sun, we tend to repeat the same mistakes and learn the same lessons as each generation comes into its own. Many of the lessons learned from the G Troop experience have been passed on. Many soldiers, airmen, seamen, and Marines who have fought the twenty-year War on Terror will read the following lessons as a review of what they indeed learned during the conflict.

However, during a recent visit to an Army base, I was amazed at the number of company grade Soldiers not wearing a combat patch. Those are the primary audience for this section. They are the future warriors who need to understand the context and application of the following lessons learned.

Some lessons are learned through planning, others through training, and some through hardship—on the ground and in the thick of combat—these are the hard and costly lessons learned.

The goal is to pass on lessons learned with an aim towards preventing future generations from learning the costly way.

Whether you are an old warrior, a Cold War warrior, a COIN warrior, or a future warrior—what makes our fighting force so great is the continued integration of lessons learned into current training and in anticipation of what must be learned in the future.

CHAPTER 2

Discipline. Being good in the field, but a problem in garrison is, quite frankly, unsatisfactory. In most circumstances, disciplinary problems can be solved with corrective actions. I was once asked by a former division commander, "What do 18-24-year-olds do?" His answer, "Some make poor choices, some get in trouble, and some lack discipline; but not every offense is a hanging offense."

The general further explained that leaders must allow for mistakes and try to understand why their soldiers made them. If leaders understand their soldiers, they can help them learn from their mistakes while simultaneously harnessing their skills and energy to accomplish the mission and improve discipline. Fortunately for G Troop, the antics that gave them the reputation of being rough and tumble, was transformed into effective combat performance because they had good leaders who knew when to raise the discipline level. The leaders at the time focused on creating a cohesive unit with grit, toughness, and discipline that spurred on the esprit de corps, panache, and can-do attitude that would later allow the troopers to operate in fast-paced combat.

Be ready for anything. Units simply cannot train for every possible task, situation, or environmental condition on the battlefield; but the unit must perform well under any circumstance. The BRT was a relatively new formation, but every leader from Brigade Combat Team to troop level knew to focus on the fundamentals of reconnaissance operations, be experts with their equipment, and know the strengths and limitations of all troopers assigned. Ultimately, the soldiers' train-up prior to deployment to Iraq oriented on the basics: shoot, move, communicate, first aid and sustainment, which combined with an understanding of reconnaissance and security operations, gave them a strong foundation from which to build future success. Mastering these basics allowed G Troop to be ready for anything and succeed while deployed.

Leaders who care lead soldiers to care. Simply put, "love your Soldiers and most will love you." It is a sad fact that some soldiers either do not have families or relationships with their families. However, several troop leaders like Rick Michaud would open their homes to soldiers during the holidays. Imagine being a new private in a unit. Your NCOs bark at you during the day, push you to your limits, and then invites you into their home for a holiday dinner because you have nowhere else to go. How would you feel? For those soldiers in G Troop, it meant everything, and it helped create a bond between leader and soldier.

CHAPTER 3

Be able to integrate other forces. Forces may train at home station within a certain organization, but when deployed, that organization may change. When the 4ID deployment plan changed, and 1BCT had to enter Iraq from the south, the super cargo ships transporting the equipment shifted course through the Suez Canal and arrived in the port of Kuwait out of order. The division was in a rush to get in the fight, and therefore ships were unloaded as they arrived. The units that received their equipment first would be deployed into the fight first. G Troop's equipment arrived on one of the first 4ID ships, and they crossed the berm into Iraq with 1-10 CAV, the division cavalry squadron, and a mechanized infantry battalion from 3BCT. The bottom line...account for what you have, organize forces available, understand the mission, and fight.

A good plan doesn't have to be complicated. Most often a quick and simple plan works. It doesn't have to take months to develop and perform a sound tactical plan. After a few days on the ground in Kuwait, the 1BCT plans team issued an order that took one tenth of the time to develop than the four-month order that was developed prior to deployment, and the brigade crossed the berm and successfully executed the mission. Having a clear understanding of the Corps' campaign plan and understanding what the Marines, 3ID, and the 101st ABN DIV were going to do helped 1BCT quickly adapt. Execution wasn't pretty, but it was effective, and that's what matters.

CHAPTER 4

Understand your environment. The troop did extremely well to maintain a presence in their area of operations through daily combat patrols, speaking with the locals—even becoming regulars at some of the restaurants and shops—and conducting raids in the evening to locate weapons and munitions caches. Many members of the troop were so in tune with the local populace that when the resistance began to build, the troopers could sense a change in the civilians around them. The extensive and continuous reporting from G Troop and other units within the 1BCT area of operations enabled the brigade to sense and adapt to changes by understanding their environment.

Apathy is deadly. Be vigilant. Look for even the smallest signal that shows a change in enemy tactics. It would have been easy for soldiers to let their guard down after President Bush declared major combat operations over in May 2003. A lax attitude could have been driven by the Civil Affairs teams coming in to assess local infrastructure needs or 1BCT leaders having frequent dinners with Iraqi leaders. None of these events spelled war. However, things weren't as they seemed. The frequency of small attacks on combat patrols steadily increased and populations in cities like Tikrit, or small villages outside the city center, became less friendly. Noticing these signals, the troop stayed on guard. They maintained their tactical senses, prepared FOB Buffalo for defense, continued combat patrols in their AO, and most importantly—remained vigilant.

CHAPTER 5

Flexibility is key. The uniqueness of the brigade reconnaissance troop was that it answered directly to the brigade commander. The brigade commander controlled several battalions that controlled subordinate companies; however, the BRT was his alone. He could speak directly to G Troop's commander and send the reconnaissance troop anywhere in the brigade area of operations. He could use them to find the enemy, assist another battalion, or provide security. The troop provided the BCT with flexibility, and, once augmented with Infantry and Armor capability, they became an even more beneficial asset for the brigade.

Leadership changes need not be disruptive. The key to managing change in leadership is to assess the unit and identify what needs to change, and what needs to remain unchanged. Upon assuming command, my job as the commander was to keep the platoons oriented on the missions assigned, ensure they conducted daily operations in a tactically sound manner, and maintain pressure on the enemy in accordance with the brigade commander's guidance. Our non-commissioned officers were strong, the platoon leaders were capable, so my job was relatively easy and only a few changes were in order. 1SG Justis' job was to ensure the troop had the supplies required to accomplish the mission, manage casualty evacuation, and as the senior non-commissioned officer in the troop, train the other non-commissioned officers how to be better leaders. He also improved morale, such as getting a basketball goal, improving meal options, and fixing the showers. When required, he reeled in the troop commander, and was his primary advisor. Fortunately for G troop, the change out of soldiers and leaders during the duration of the deployment was effective; not disruptive.

CHAPTER 6

Adaptability is critical in warfare. The traditional role for a small scout unit in combat is to locate the enemy, report pertinent information, avoid direct fire contact, and identify opportunities to employ other means to affect the enemy, such as indirect fires, attack aviation, or U.S. Air Force capabilities. This was the primary training focus for G Troop prior to notification of deployment to Iraq. Once notified of deployment, G Troop's leaders understood the need to expand training to urban operations, survival techniques, and dismounted patrolling. However, anticipating that 1BCT would face Iraqi armored forces, such as tanks and armored personnel carriers, a greater emphasis was placed on avoiding decisive engagement.

Once major combat operations ended—at least against enemy tank formations—the troop had to adapt to the emerging enemy style of warfare, which became small roadside bomb attacks and RPG and small arms ambushes at close range. In this style of warfare, dismounted patrolling would be the norm and direct fire contact was required to close with and destroy the enemy. To succeed and survive, the troop had to continually train and learn new ways of fighting, including perfecting Battle Drill 6, which describes how we enter and clear room within a building. In the midst of war, this wasn't easy, but our leaders leveraged their own knowledge to train their troopers, and the soldiers themselves supplemented the training with their own experiences from other units. This allowed the troop to continually adapt tactics, techniques, and procedures over time.

Continuous improvement is required. Training on new ways of fighting is important, and so is continual training on perishable skills. Two major ambushes on the troop exposed two critical problems:

First, one patrol that was ambushed immediately moved to a secure position some distance away from the ambush point. However, they had no serious injuries and far more firepower and men than the attackers. Subsequently, the soldiers realized they could be more aggressive on combat patrols when enemy contact was made.

Second, upon inspection of the engagement areas, the enemy had used walls and above ground aqueducts for cover. Looking at the ambush point in daylight revealed .50 CAL MG and M4 bullet impact marks on the walls and the top of the aqueducts. The MK-19 rounds impacted nowhere near the attackers. Marksmanship training—a perishable skill—was required and the troop spent several days each month on marksmanship training and cross-training to maintain proficiency.

Leverage all the skills of your soldiers. The troopers, just like most soldiers in the Army, have a range of skills. For example, some spoke the local language; some had college degrees in engineering, political science, and economics; some were resourceful while others were aggressive, and some were trained in other military skills such as Infantry, Mortars, Armor, and Engineer. To effectively leverage soldiers' skills, leaders at all levels must know their soldiers professionally and personally. Learn their hobbies, their history, and their skills. Ultimately, leaders must learn to harness the collective capability of their unit—and a little research allows leaders to understand all capabilities the soldiers can bring to the fight.

CHAPTER 7

Relentless pursuit of the enemy will trigger a response. The troop's transformation from soldiers conducting escort and security patrols to performing offensive operations, like locating and capturing or killing resistance leaders, didn't lead to the enemy melting away as leadership had first thought. Instead, it triggered violent responses from the enemy. Mortar attacks, ambushes, and roadside bomb attacks increased as the brigade pursued, killed or captured the enemy. Multiple ambushes of increased scale and complexity occurred from July to September 2003, signaling the resistance was increasing and U.S. operations were pressing them to fight harder.

Situational awareness matters. When the Scorpion patrol was ambushed on September 18, the remainder of the troop was on the opposite side of the Tigris River. As the Troop commander and executive officer tried to gain situational understanding, the platoon leader in contact, and the platoon leader manning the observation posts on the walls of the 4ID HQ were instrumental in assisting the troop command with developing situational awareness. As the remainder of the troop linked up with the Scorpion platoon, AH-64 attack helicopters and 1-22 IN deployed to support the ongoing fight. With one trooper missing in action, two AH-64s engaging enemy personnel, troopers entering and clearing houses, and a mechanized company merging into the fight, the situation was ripe for fratricide and confusion. Timely and accurate reporting, clear articulation of where units were on the battlefield, use of digital command and control systems, and troopers and soldiers scanning to identify friend from foe, resulted in no fratricide incidents, and the capture of approximately twenty enemy personnel involved in the ambush.

CHAPTER 8

Plan for combat losses. Combat results in destruction of life and equipment. Processing fallen soldiers, caring for their families, recovering their personal belongings, CASEVAC, recovering equipment—all these aspects of war are a reality that must be planned for. When 1SG Justis arrived, he prepared the unit for this reality. His ideas for "preparing the battlefield" helped the troop respond to the September 18 ambush as quickly and efficiently as we could, given the circumstances. Additionally, 1BCT staff, in particular the chaplain, was of great assistance. The chaplain immediately met with Scorpion platoon and made himself available for others in the unit. He assisted with the memorial ceremony details and provided me with example speeches on the topic—a memorial ceremony must be first class, those who gave the last full measure deserve only the best.

CHAPTER 9

War is a "one team, one fight" affair. Every unit in Iraq wanted to find the key clue that would lead to Saddam's capture. Finding it required exchanging information between those units. Initially, the exchange of information between lower-level conventional forces and ARSOF was limited. However, the 1BCT commander demonstrated a willingness to share knowledge and provide quality support between G Troop and ARSOF. ARSOF demonstrated the same level of trust and willingness to exchange information. This fostered an excellent working relationship and, as the deployment went on, a sense of teamwork and unified action grew—eventually leading to an historical achievement.

Train the Bench. R&R Leave was good for two reasons: 1) It gave leaders and hard charging soldiers a chance to decompress, rest, and recharge, and 2) it required each unit to train others to fill the void created when a leader or trooper departed for R&R. Over two months of R&R, G Troop's capability improved as our leaders and soldiers gained experience by serving in multiple positions.

Train leaders and their soldiers to integrate all available resources and capabilities. By mid- November, most of G Troop's men had conducted combined arms operations with Bradleys, Tanks, AH-64 Attack Helicopters, AC-130 Gunships, 155 Artillery, 120 Mortars, Infantry squads, UAVs, PSYOP teams, ARSOF, and

Iraqi Police. Sergeants integrated and synchronized fires. Lieutenants managed an array of aerial attack platforms, maneuvered forces, managed observation posts, and directed fires from each asset. The ability of leaders and troopers of all ranks to understand the complexity of combined arms warfare made G Troop extremely lethal. After suffering through a few hard lessons learned during early ambushes, G Troop—and 1BCT—gained a decisive advantage when the troop was provided more resources and leveraged them while modifying tactics, techniques, and procedures. After the September 18 ambush, G Troop would not lose another trooper, and the enemy mortar and ambush teams were soon defeated in the area directly across from 4ID HQ and FOB Raider.

Families back home can assist. FRGs are extremely important in garrison and during deployment, and they should be treated like any other combat multiplier. Like soldiers, spouses must be trained on what to expect and actions to take for a range of possible scenarios. They should understand how death notifications are conducted, whom to contact for assistance, and how to organize and assist as a group when the worst occurs.

CHAPTER 10

Maintaining continuous pressure on the enemy breaks them. Continuous pressure in the form of raids, terrain denial fires, intelligence collection, and interdiction operations caused the enemy to stay on the run and exhaust or lose supplies. The September 18 ambush was the high-water mark for the enemy in Tikrit. The complex attack on that day was the most aggressive and audacious attack in Tikrit, but it failed, and many of the perpetrators were captured. They were young men, with little training, and limited means to defeat the troop and the supporting mechanized forces. After that ambush, the enemy went on the run—out to the Western and Eastern deserts, or to other areas where US Forces were not as aggressive.

CHAPTER 11

Be mentally and physically ready. The day the troop conducted operation Red Dawn with ARSOF, it had just returned from a 30-day operation in the Western desert. Soldiers were tired, equipment was in need of repair, and before notification of the mission, they had planned to take a day off patrol to relax. Despite the plan, the soldiers fixed what they could, topped off supplies, and hustled from Baiji to Tikrit, linked up with ARSOF, conducted a raid, and the rest is history. Some ways to be ready: The troop had trained on the basics—shoot, move, communicate, sustain, and medical care. Those were a given. Over time in combat, the pace of operations, the impromptu mission with ARSOF, and the mission of preventing or responding to rocket and mortar attacks changed the troop DNA so to speak. Troopers, understanding they had to "be ready" would fuel their vehicles upon return from patrol; clean all weapons immediately upon return from patrol, sleep in uniform without boots, their kit (vest, ammo, weapon, etc.) next to their beds, and eat and drink water when it was available, whether they needed it or not.

CHAPTER 12

Have a plan for success. Following the capture of Saddam, it became apparent additional actions were in order that were not addressed prior to the mission. The capture was a major event, and the media would soon flock to Tikrit in hopes of conducting interviews and viewing the area where Saddam was found. Thankfully, the brigade commander had a plan that consisted of maintaining a secured site, preparing a specific statement, and controlling media movement to and from the objective. G Troop and other units from the brigade had conducted many raids over the course of nine months to capture Saddam, yet the strategic messaging for the capture was not developed until the actual capture. Building a plan for success at the time could have included the following prior to the capture of Saddam: discussions with ARSOF for what can be said or not said, identification of a relief in place unit for the troop; recognizing that media would appear overnight and have a media brief and media control plan in place; and discussions with the division and corps as to what the political leaders wanted immediately following the capture.

CHAPTER 13

Continue the fight, even when you believe victory is secured. It could have been easy for the troopers to get lost in the fanfare of the Saddam capture and let down their guard. However, troop leaders stayed focused on the fight. Mortar and rocket attacks continued in and around Tikrit throughout December and early January. It was important for leaders to emphasize to their troopers that the war was not over, combat patrols continued, and the enemy continued to fight.

CHAPTER 14

The cost of war is physical, mental, and emotional; it's our duty to support those who gave so much for our country. "Blood and gold" is accurate phrasing–war steals lives and takes dollars. Like all units, G troop bled, and those wounds remain today. Many of our troopers still struggle with the loss of Arriaga, Wright and Thompson. The emotional repercussions are impossible to explain, and there is no single answer or solution to the emotional and mental challenges soldiers battle after war. MAJ GEN Odierno made a significant step forward in supporting our soldiers by launching Iron Horse University, a series of classes taught by professionals to help soldiers reintegrate into society and with their families. This program helped identify PTSD symptoms and treatments prior to redeployment, and upon return stateside several weeks after arrival to help soldiers and families cope with emerging stress.

Families do one of three things in the military — thrive, survive, or die; train FRGs so that they thrive. The emotional and mental cost of war affects soldiers' families as well. Our Family Readiness Group was young and inexperienced, but they never quit, and their efforts remain a positive memory for many of G Troop's soldiers to this day. Training FRGs prior to deployment and ensuring those troopers and family members remaining at home station have the best leadership available, are equipped to handle a range of situations, and competent in their roles and functions is critical for morale and welfare.

ALIBIES

First reports are usually inaccurate. Leaders may receive first reports from different units with different views or perspectives of the same event. Critical to first reports is for leaders to take a tactical pause—discern what was reported, compare received information with pre-planned ideas, and divine follow-up questions to confirm or deny report accuracy. The leaders of G Troop developed this skill over time, but the first few months was difficult because everything was reported. More "information" isn't the best solution for decision making. The right information is required, and it takes planning and time to understand what information is crucial for effective decision making.

Staff officers need to see and feel the terrain. A common complaint from subordinate commanders in the field is that the staff has no appreciation for the context of operations. Planners plan operations but are separated from the execution and outcomes. The 1BCT commander implemented a program for select staff officers to ride with commanders and units in the field. This allowed them to see the terrain, meet the people, see the unit in action, and gain an appreciation for the environment and challenges the units faced on a daily basis. This ultimately produced more effective staff officers. Fear, stress, pain, fatigue…these aspects impact execution of orders. Having a stable of brigade staff officers that have patrolled with the combat units enabled those officers to more effectively plan because they could "feel" the impacts of the operation as they planned.

A final note. Leaders must ensure they pass on lessons learned. Develop training plans and educational moments that allow leaders to teach, and soldiers to learn. The goal is that new leaders and soldiers do not make the same mistakes their predecessors made because…there is nothing new under the sun.

G Troop Roster for OIF I

To the best of our ability, the writing team has attempted to capture the names of all troopers assigned to G Troop during the deployment to Iraq for OIF I. Troopers came into the unit, and departed the unit throughout the deployment. Ranks and platoon assignments are not reflected intentionally. The aim is to simply preserve the names of all troopers assigned—those who deployed with, and fought with the troop during OIF I.

John Almen
Matthew Anders
Roberto Andrade*
Ezekial Austin
Richard Arriaga*
Desmond Bailey
Jason Beberness
Christopher Beran
Caleb Branch
Ryan Brescher
Tyron Buchanan
Igor Boyko

Desmond Bailey

Philip Cantu*
Christopher Carpenter
Jason Carr
Christopher Clingempeel
David Crabil
Christpher Cross
Jeans Cruz
Donnie Dalton
Thomas Darden
Jose Diaz
Kenneth Dishman
Fred Dominguez
Alan Dunn
Winston Edwards
Brandon Ellis
Jesse Enge
Matthew Fauth
Michael Feola
Joe Flores
Nicole Fosset
David Forney
Justin Fugate
Kevin Hays
Kevin Hall
Joseph Hand
Christopher Harding
Detrick Harris
Christopher Hartman
Aaron Helmrich
Bryce Hicks
Carrol Houck
John Iverson

Recon 701

Tim Jacobson
Albert Johnson
Matthew Jones
John Justis
Koel Knight
Jeremy Lapp
Robert Lay
Cyril LeBoeuf
Robert McClusky
Raymond Michaud
Jose Marroquin*
Hector Medina
Roderick Middlebrooks
Brian Mosier
Jesse Molina
Clifton Munroe
William Palizo
Darin Pederson
Roy Poper
Peter Ranchor
Hammond Ragin
Grant Ray
Billy Reaves
Allen Renazco
Thomas Ribas
Julio Rodriguez
Jeremy Ruegge
Daniel Saffels
Christopher Sharpless
Kamdon Shaw
Tyler Shaffer
Robert Southwood

Desmond Bailey

Andrew Smith
Marcus Solis
Adam Sommerville
Joseph Sparks
Travis Stiles
Braxton Swilley
Brian Sweigert
Dale Sylvester
Joshua Szott
Eric Tapp
William Taylor
Brian Tripiciano
Anthony Thompson*
Shane Valley
Jose Valero
Clayton Vaughn
Bernard Walla
Jason Washburn
Christopher Watkins
Joseph Wightman
William Wilkinson
John Williams
James Wright*
Joey Wommack
Joe Wooley

*Deceased

About the Author

Desmond V Bailey is a 26-year veteran who currently serves as a parttime police officer and fulltime systems engineer. During his military career he served as a U.S. Marine Reserve Rifleman, and as an Infantry Officer in the U.S. Army. Desmond began his Army career as a platoon leader in the 82d Airborne Division. He was fortunate enough to command three company level formations, B/1-19 IN, a basic training company, G/10 CAV, a brigade reconnaissance company, and C/1-22 IN, a mechanized infantry company. Desmond's final command was 2nd Battalion, 8th Infantry Regiment, 2nd Brigade, 4th Infantry Division.

During his career, he was deployed multiple times serving in command or staff positions. Multinational Observer and Controller, Egypt, (1998) Operation Iraqi Freedom I (2003-2004), The Surge, Iraq (2007-2008), New Dawn, Iraq, (2011), Spartan Shield, Kuwait, (2013-2014). In 2018, Desmond retired and became a police officer for a department close to his hometown. In 2020, he transitioned to a parttime police officer and became a systems engineer for a non-profit organization. He resides in Alabama with his wife and two grandchildren.